Cooperative Learning and
Second Language Teaching

CAMBRIDGE LANGUAGE EDUCATION
Series Editor: Jack C. Richards

In this series:

Cooperative Learning and Second Language Teaching

Edited by

Steven G. McCafferty
University of Nevada

George M. Jacobs
Broward Community College

Ana Christina DaSilva Iddings
University of Arizona

CAMBRIDGE
UNIVERSITY PRESS

CAMBRIDGE UNIVERSITY PRESS
Cambridge, New York, Melbourne, Madrid, Cape Town, Singapore, São Paulo

Cambridge University Press
32 Avenue of the Americas, New York, NY 10013-2473, USA

www.cambridge.org
Information on this title: www.cambridge.org/9780521844864

© Cambridge University Press 2006

First published 2006

Printed in the United States of America

A catalog record for this publication is available from the British Library.

Library of Congress Cataloging in Publication Data

Cooperative learning and second language teaching / edited by Steven G.
McCafferty, George Jacobs, Ana Christina DaSilva Iddings.
   p.   cm. – (Cambridge language education)
Includes bibliographical references and index.
ISBN-13: 978-0-521-84486-4 (hardback)
ISBN-10: 0-521-84486-X (hardback)
ISBN-13: 978-0-521-60664-6 (pbk.)
ISBN-10: 0-521-60664-0 (pbk.)
1. Language and languages – Study and teaching.   2. Group work in education.   I. McCafferty,
Steven G.   II. Jacobs, George, 1952–   III. DaSilva Iddings, Ana Christina.   IV. Title.   V. Series.
P53.42.C66   2006
18.0071 – dc24   2006042562

ISBN-13   978-0-521-84486-4 hardback
ISBN-10   0-521-84486-X hardback

ISBN-13   978-0-521-60664-6 paperback
ISBN-10   0-521-60664-0 paperback

Contents

Contributors

Steven G. McCafferty, University of Nevada, Las Vegas, USA
George M. Jacobs, Broward Community College, Singapore
Ana Christina DaSilva Iddings, University of Arizona, USA
Pete Jones, Durham District School Board, Ontario, Canada
Anne Taylor, Durham District School Board, Ontario, Canada
Jane Joritz-Nakagawa, Aichi University of Education, Aichi, Japan
Kim Hughes Wilhelm, Southern Illinois University at Carbondale, USA
    University of Macau, China
Ghazi Ghaith, American University of Beirut, Lebanon
Anwar Kawtharani, Amjad School, Beirut, Lebanon
Sheila Wee, Ministry of Education, Singapore

Series editor's preface

The approach known as cooperative learning has long been of interest to practitioners of communicative language teaching since it offers a body of widely tested classroom procedures for implementing group-based activities in the language classroom. Although there is a considerable and growing literature on cooperative learning in mainstream education, there have been few recent accounts of its application to second language teaching. The present book is therefore a welcome account of the background of cooperative learning, its theoretical and research underpinnings, and its applications in a number of different ESL/EFL classroom settings.

The authors make a strong case for applying the principles of cooperative learning to second language classrooms. They show its roots in social psychology, developmental psychology, and cognitive psychology, and they further link it to motivational theory and humanist education. The authors suggest how cooperative learning connects with second language acquisition theory, with the notions of input, interaction, output, and learner autonomy, as well as with sociocultural theories of learning through collaborative and dialogic interaction. Since group-based learning lies at the heart of cooperative learning, considerable attention is given to the nature of and conditions for successful groups. The book then provides a number of teacher narratives that show how cooperative learning can be implemented in different ESL/EFL contexts. These narratives illustrate how teachers prepared students for group-based learning. They also demonstrate the activities and materials the teachers employed to teach various language skills, the difficulties sometimes encountered and how these were resolved, and how cooperative learning took different forms based on the contexts in which it was being implemented. This book concludes with a very useful glossary of commonly used cooperative learning techniques.

This book will therefore provide a useful introduction to the field of cooperative learning for teachers wishing to better understand how its group-based learning principles can be successfully used in second and foreign language teaching.

Jack C. Richards

PART I:
COOPERATIVE LEARNING AND SECOND LANGUAGE CLASSROOMS

Introduction

Purpose of this book

If we had to choose one word to symbolize the changes in second language teaching over the years, it would be *communicative*: the idea that the surest path to engagement in learning a second language lies in students – even beginners – communicating in that language. Indeed, if asked to describe their teaching methodology, many teachers today would say they use communicative language teaching (Richards & Rodgers 2001). Group activities (pairs are included herein) have become one of the key tools in communicative language teachers' toolboxes because groups provide so many opportunities for students to communicate and because groups provide a means of integrating listening, speaking, reading, and writing (Crookall & Thiyaragarajali 1997; Harmer 1998; Jacobs 1997). However, despite the many advantages of group activities, problems also arise – problems that have led some teachers to give up on using group work. These problems include members not participating, groups not getting along, or learners unable to do the task.

Cooperative learning arose in mainstream education as an effort to address such problems and to generally facilitate student-student interaction. As is the case elsewhere in education, definitions vary. Johnson, Johnson, and Holubec, leaders of cooperative learning since the 1970s, offer the following definition: "Cooperative learning is the instructional use of small groups so that students work together to maximize their own and each other's learning" (1993: 9). If we are to maximize the benefits of groups, we need to understand the complexities that are involved in collaborative interactions. In this book, we aim to convey to pre- and in-service language teachers what the chapter authors and we (the editors) have learned collectively from our many years of using cooperative learning with students.

Contents of the book

The first part of this book lays out the theoretical, historical, and research foundations of cooperative learning, and the second part provides illustrations of the application of those elements as part of teachers' professional practice. As such, this volume is meant for teachers who are actively searching for means to implement philosophies that put learners at the center of the learning process. Moreover, it aims to facilitate the many decisions teachers need to make in attempting to maximize the great potential of group activities. Specifically, in the first part of this book, we discuss some of the work in general education that supports the use of cooperative learning, make evident its connections to second language teaching and learning, and provide a framework for making choices about the use of cooperative learning.

The second part of the book, in our opinion, is the most exciting. It consists of six classroom narratives illustrating how second language teachers have implemented cooperative learning in second language classrooms around the world, across primary, secondary, and postsecondary educational levels. Each of these chapters ends with a section entitled *Discussion Points and Tasks*, which is an opportunity for the reader to analyze how each author has implemented cooperative learning in a particular setting, and then to apply the ideas in the chapter to your own teaching situation.

What is cooperative learning?

Although a more extensive treatment of the characteristics of cooperative learning will be provided in Chapters 1–3, the key point is that not all group work constitutes cooperative learning. Instead, cooperative learning represents the product of ongoing investigation based on theory, research, and practice as to how to maximize the benefits of student-student interaction. The introduction of student-student interaction into the classroom initially may make teaching more difficult, because, if teachers just put students in groups and ask them to work together without considering these factors, the chances of fruitful interaction diminish.

Two crucial concepts in almost everyone's definition of cooperative learning relate to the amount of group support and to the degree to which each individual member of the group needs to learn and to exhibit his or her accomplishments. The first of these crucial concepts is *positive interdependence*, the perception among group members that what helps one group member helps all group members, and what hurts one group member hurts all (Deutsch 1949; 1962). Positive interdependence encourages cooperation and a feeling of support.

The second crucial element is *individual accountability*. Slavin (1987: 5) defines individual accountability as being present when "[T]he team's success depends on the individual learning of all team members." To accomplish this, groups encourage all members to participate and to meaningfully demonstrate their knowledge and skills. By doing so, individual members add to the overall knowledge of the group, reveal areas of weakness that group mates can attend to, and develop a common sense of what the goals and subgoals are both for the group and for individual members and how they can be reached. An example of a group activity that does *not* encourage individual accountability would be an assignment for the group to work together to write one composition for the whole group. In this situation, the best writer in the group might do all the writing, while the other members are off task.[1]

Individual accountability does overlap with positive interdependence. However, the two outlooks will not always exist together. For instance, using the example in which primary and/or secondary students work in a group to write one composition, they may feel positively interdependent with one another (for example, if they all want their composition to achieve its communicative purpose). But such an activity might do little to encourage all the group members to feel that they need to participate and learn. On the other hand, if students are sitting in a group and each is to write a composition with no mechanism for providing each other with feedback or other types of assistance, they would be more likely to feel individually accountable but would not feel positively interdependent with their fellow group members.

One more point should be covered in this brief definition of cooperative learning. For some educators, it is synonymous with *collaborative learning* (e.g., Romney 1997). Romney sees *cooperative learning* as the term used in primary and secondary education, with *collaborative learning* used for joint learning efforts among older students. On the other hand, Chung (1991) sees *collaborative learning* as an umbrella term that includes cooperative learning as one part. Other educators worry that some cooperative learning techniques make the learning environment too structured and thus artificial, depend too much on extrinsic motivation, and focus on lower-order

---

[1] At the university level, having one student do all of the writing may lead to productive collaborations because, unlike primary or secondary students, university students may be able to take on the needed sense of individual responsibility without difficulty.

thinking tasks, thus robbing students of initiative and of opportunities to exercise higher-order thinking skills (Matthews et al., retrieved 1/31/99). In an address to the 1994 conference of the International Association for the Study of Cooperation in Education, Kenneth Bruffee stated his belief that cooperative learning was beneficial for students at primary and secondary school levels, but that collaborative learning was the better option for older students. Indeed, Bruffee, who works in the area of writing pedagogy at the university level, is associated with collaborative learning (Bruffee 1993). In a discussion at the same conference, Yael Sharan suggested that there exists a wide range of options in terms of teacher influence of student-student interaction, and that the cooperative learning technique called Group Investigation (Sharan & Sharan 1992) allows students a great deal of control over such matters as selection of topic, group mates, and collaboration procedures. We agree with Sharan's broad interpretation. Thus, in this book the term *cooperative learning* should be understood as including collaborative learning.

Cooperative learning has a strong foundation in research. Many hundreds of studies across a wide range of subject areas and age groups have been conducted (for reviews, see Cohen 1994b; Johnson & Johnson 1989; Johnson et al. 2000; Sharan 1980; Slavin 1995). These studies suggest that when compared to other instructional approaches, cooperative learning activities are associated with gains in achievement, higher-level thinking, self-esteem, and interethnic relations. Students in cooperative learning settings tend to like the subject matter and their school more. Indeed, Johnson (1997) claims that cooperative learning is one of the best-researched approaches in education, and that when the public asks educators what we know that works in education, cooperative learning is one of our surest answers. In an earlier interview (Brandt 1987: 12), Johnson stated:

If there's any one educational technique that has firm empirical support, it's cooperative learning. The research in this area is the oldest research tradition in American social psychology. The first study was done in 1897; we've had ninety years of research, hundreds of studies. There is probably more evidence validating the use of cooperative learning than there is for any other aspect of education.

Although cooperative learning is thought of as being predominantly founded in American social psychology and used on American grounds, the narrative chapters included in the second part of this book take this approach to an international realm. Only two of these chapters take place in the United States, and in both of these courses the students are nonnative speakers of English. We believe that broadening the scope of cooperative learning, by taking into consideration some cultural dimensions in its application, is one of the major contributions of this book.

Cooperative learning derives inspiration from many areas of educational endeavor, some of which might seem to contradict one another. In the first chapter, we discuss its roots in general education. In Chapter 2, we discuss its application to second language teaching and learning, and in Chapter 3, we examine issues that arise in implementing cooperative learning.

Six narratives about teachers using cooperative learning

To find contributions for the second section of this book, we looked for teachers who had a good grasp of what cooperative learning is about, and who had had experience using it in a variety of countries and situations. We wanted – and believe we have found – teachers who offered unique perspectives, yet who, at the same time, were united in a common effort to advance language learning via group activities. We asked these teachers to write about their experiences in a narrative form. This style is different from what is usually encountered in books about language education, but we believe that this style provides important insights into the thinking involved as the authors made decisions about how best to implement cooperative learning in their complex and constantly changing classrooms. The narratives presented in Chapters 4 through 9 are not intended to provide cooperative learning recipes. Rather, the purpose is to provide insight into key concepts of cooperative learning as contextualized and to illustrate the great range of possibilities that exist in using it for language teaching.

Suggestions for using this book

We believe this book is useful to a wide range of language teachers. It serves as a useful companion to an earlier book in this series (Johnson 1995), which dealt with the broader issue of communication in second language classrooms. Those with little experience with cooperative learning will find this book an introduction grounded in the experience of specific classrooms, while those with more experience will find fresh ideas in the experiences of their fellow teachers.

We hope you will put into practice the ideas for implementing cooperative learning that the narratives spark in your mind. As you read, imagine that you and the chapter authors have formed a group to discuss the use of cooperative learning in second language teaching. How do the authors' experiences relate to yours and those of your colleagues? What advice might the authors give about using cooperative learning in your context? We trust that generating and discussing answers to those questions will prove to be an enjoyable, thought-provoking experience.

1 Roots of cooperative learning in general education

George M. Jacobs, Steven G. McCafferty, and
Ana Christina DaSilva Iddings

As we proceed with our discussion about cooperative learning, we must take a moment to present a basic overview about four foundational psychological theories. In so doing, our purpose is to acquaint the reader with aspects of theory and research that may be helpful in understanding the historical development of the cooperative learning approach and its significance to the teaching of a second language.

Social psychology

Alport (1954) worked on the goal of facilitating effective group dynamics. His investigations of how best to help people from different racial groups come to live together more harmoniously led him to derive three conditions that he believed essential for interaction to result in greater harmony and more productive relations: 1) interactors must be of equal status, 2) they must have common goals, and 3) their collaboration should be officially sanctioned.

In the 1970s, Aronson and his colleagues (Aronson, Blaney, Stephan, Sikes & Snapp 1978) applied these three conditions to the classroom and created the well-known cooperative learning technique, Jigsaw. They were working at the time to improve racial relations among students in recently integrated schools in the southwestern United States. In Jigsaw, each member of the group has unique information (helping to promote equal status) that they must share with group mates in order for the group to achieve its common goal. This collaboration, of course, takes place with the teacher's official sanction.

Jigsaw, which is appropriate to any subject area, has been used in second language teaching using print (e.g., Coelho, Winer & Winn-Bell Olsen 1989; Geddes 1981; Johnson 1981) and spoken texts (Harmer 1998). Furthermore, the concept of providing each group member with unique information that must be combined has long been popular in second language teaching. Spot-the-Difference tasks (Morgan Bowen 1982) and Strip Stories (Gibson 1975)

9

are just two examples. In the literature on second language tasks (e.g., Pica, Kanagy & Falodun 1993; Platt & Brooks 1994), the terms *information gap* and *required information exchange* have been used to describe tasks like Jigsaw, in which group members are each given unique information.

While Alport's original three conditions are very useful to consider, it is also important to note that since 1954 there have been developments in our understanding of each. For example, it is highly unlikely that any two students are really of equal status in any real sense; that is, how they are treated by other class members – both by individuals and groups within the class as well as by the teacher – is bound to differ despite being in the same classroom and following the same behavioral guidelines. This same point of view holds with regard to the notion of common goals. Indeed, how goals and subgoals are formed and how they change in relation to working with particular people in particular circumstances has become a primary area of focus within the study of classroom interactions (for example, see Engestrom et al. 1999 and McCafferty et al. 2001). Finally, the role of the teacher as a sanctioner of activities, attitudes, and so on, has changed considerably; teachers have become more "facilitators" than "ship's captains," the prevalent model in the United States in the 1950s.

Subsequently, Johnson and Johnson (1994b) developed many applications of the concept of *interdependence* to education. They believed that too many instructional practices, for instance, teacher-fronted pedagogy and norm-referenced assessment, encouraged students to feel negatively interdependent with their classmates. The Johnsons' goal was to find ways to increase the feeling of positive interdependence within learning groups. A whole approach to cooperative learning, known as Learning Together, has developed from their work.

Developmental psychology

Although throughout history there have been many prominent thinkers and researchers who have diligently studied human cognition as it unfolds in the course of a lifetime, we have chosen to turn our focus to two of the most notable developmental psychologists of the twentieth century: Jean Piaget and Lev S. Vygotsky.

Piaget contends that each person constructs his or her own personal understanding of the world around them through a search for equilibration (i.e., a match between current *schemas* – background information – about the world and how it works, on the one hand, and what is experienced, on the other). Piaget's ideas have been widely interpreted as supporting the creation of classroom environments in which students play active roles as they engage in real or at least realistic tasks (Slavin 1995). Scholars working in the Piagetian tradition emphasize the value of social contexts for arousing productive cognitive conflicts (Doise & Mugny 1984). For instance, Murray (1982) found that two students – neither of whom was able to do a particular task alone – were able to learn to complete the task when working together.

Piaget's epistemological views about psychological development assume that the growth of consciousness progresses through preordained, irreversible levels (i.e., what happens at a later stage of development is enabled by what happened at previous stages). Thus, according to this theory, every child must go through the same structure of cognitive development in a fixed sequence, the stages of which are distinctively graduated.

In this regard, Piaget and Vygotsky greatly differ. Because Piaget considered development to be a precoded aspect of our biology, the attempt to accelerate development through learning with the help of teachers or others is highly restricted: Essentially, learning cannot precede development. For Vygotsky, on the other hand, a child is at once surrounded by sociocultural contexts that exert an immediate influence on development through interaction: In other words, learning leads development. For example, through play children dress up as adults, pretending to speak and act like those they will become. In such circumstances, Vygotsky argued that "a child always behaves beyond his average age, above his daily behavior; in play it is as though he were a head taller than himself" (1978: 102).

Moreover, Vygotsky stressed that *semiotic mediation* (i.e., the use of signs and symbols – principally language – deriving from the sociocultural milieu that help us to understand our world) becomes the primary vehicle for human cognitive growth. He (1981: 163) explained:

Any function in the child's cultural development appears twice, or on two planes. First it appears on the social plane, and then on the psychological plane. First it appears between people as an interpsychological category, and then within the child as an intrapsychological category.

Thus, for Vygotsky, there is a very definite role to be played by actively directed learning, both in the cognitive development of individual human beings and in the history of human culture. Vygotsky called the theoretical construct that enables this process the *zone of proximal development.*

The zone of proximal development (ZPD)

As previously stated, the ZPD is a key concept for Vygotskian theory in that it distinguishes between what a child can do on her or his own cognitively, and what she or he can do in conjunction with an adult or more capable peer (Vygotsky 1978). However, Newman and Holtzman (1993) for instance, believe that Vygotsky had a more dynamic view of the ZPD: The spatial metaphor (i.e., speaking of what is "in" the zone) detracts from its transformational powers. They argue that the ZPD is better thought of as an activity rather than a place, and moreover, that it is capable of transforming the thinking of all participants in interaction. This perspective further accentuates the co-constructed nature of interaction (more on this in Chapter 2) and adds an important dimension to thinking about positive interdependence in relation to cooperative learning.

In a related concept, Wood, Bruner, and Ross (1976) introduced the notion of *scaffolding*, in which an analogy is drawn to the process of building an architectural structure. As the building nears completion, the scaffolding is gradually withdrawn. In the same way, helpers remove the support given to students as the students move closer to being able to do the task independently (although this construct is aligned more with a transmission as opposed to a transformational model of learning, and thus better suited to an instrumentalist view of the ZPD). Many cooperative group activities have emerged from this perspective on human development, for example, peer tutoring (Alfassi 1998; Palincsar, Brown & Martin 1987) and cross-age tutoring (Samway, Whang & Pippitt 1995).

Also, while Vygotsky may have emphasized the role of more expert others in co-constructing ZPDs, more recently attention has turned to how students at a similar level of shared understanding can help one another. For instance, Koschmann (1996) states that the interaction patterns of scholars working to create new knowledge in their field shows how people's ideas can converge to mutually construct knowledge.

The notion that peers can help each other is very much in line with student-centered perspectives on education, and it also fits with what Johnson et al. (2002) say about positive interdependence. This notion can be further elucidated by the concept of a *community of practice*.

Community of practice

The community of practice approach to learning derives from a sociocultural perspective and emphasizes the relationships between human action and the social context in which the action occurs (Lave & Wenger 1991). Within this framework, the potential for learning in educational contexts is broadly seen as a set of social practices as situated within specific classrooms. One of the essential premises of the community of practice approach is the notion of *legitimate peripheral participation*, which holds that learning occurs as newcomers fulfill various peripheral roles alongside more experienced or competent members of the community as they gradually become able to fully participate. This is based on an apprenticeship model. Lave and Wenger (1991: 92) argue that "the social structure of [a community of practice], its power relations, and its conditions for legitimacy define possibilities for learning."

From this point of view, cultural, historical, and institutional forces can afford or constrain the types of practices available to a particular community. Certainly this concept applies to cooperative learning, which aims to create a highly specified sense of community in order to induce learning. However, the particulars – who the students are, how they relate to the teacher and each other, how the teacher interprets cooperative learning, the nature of the school and educational system, and, of course, the culture – all exert influence on how cooperative learning actually takes shape in forming a community of practice (see DaSilva Iddings 2005 for L2 concerns).

Cognitive psychology

Cognitive psychologists, such as Craik and Lockhart (1972), Palincsar and Brown (1984), and Wittrock (1974), have also been looked to in validating the use of cooperative learning. Wittrock emphasizes the value of having students repeat and restructure information and ideas. Webb (1989) and Webb and Farivar (1994) report that in groups of primary school students learning math, greater learning occurred when students asked for assistance from groupmates and received explanations compared to times when requests for assistance were ignored or responded to with answers that did not include explanations. Furthermore, contrary to what some critics of cooperative learning fear, these explanations benefited both the receiver and the giver. Webb and Farivar go on to speculate that students may be more aware of what their peers do not understand because the material is new to them as well, unlike the teacher for whom the material has often become second nature. Moreover, again because of being closer to them in terms of background knowledge, fellow students may also be able to explain material in ways that their peers can understand better.

Craik and Lockhart developed the *depth of processing* concept, which says that the deeper the elaboration of thought, the more likely something will be understood and remembered. In an attempt to bring the work of Craik and Lockhart and Wittrock into the classroom, a number of cooperative learning techniques have been developed by scholars in the cognitive psychology tradition. An example is the dyadic MURDER script (Hythecker,

Dansereau & Rocklin 1988). In MURDER, pairs of students read a text divided into sections. After reading a section silently, the pairs stop, and one summarizes the main points of the section while the other checks the summary. Then they both elaborate on the main ideas, for instance, providing examples, opinions, and connections to prior reading. The pairs continue to go through the sections of the text, rotating the roles of summarizer and monitor, until completing the text, at which point they formulate an overall summary. Furthermore, the Cooperative Controversy technique (Johnson, Johnson & Holubec 2002) promotes students' ability to see different perspectives by asking them to alternate – representing opposing sides in a debate before finally speaking on behalf of their real view and striving to reach consensus with their group mates.

Motivational theories in psychology

In a teacher-fronted classroom, reinforcement for positive learning behaviors usually comes mainly from the teacher. Indeed, in the typical teacher-fronted classroom, students often feel negatively interdependent with one another, competing against each other for reinforcement from the teacher in such forms as praise and grades. In contrast, when students feel positively interdependent with each other, they become an alternative source of positive reinforcement for one another.

Slavin (1995) and his colleagues at Johns Hopkins University have done a great deal of research and curriculum development in cooperative learning from this tradition, generating and testing techniques such as Student Teams-Achievement Divisions (STAD). For STAD, the teacher first presents material, then students work in teams that are heterogeneous with regard to such characteristics as past achievement, gender, and ethnicity to study together in preparation for a quiz. Each student contributes to any rewards the team may get (for example, certificates) based on a comparison of the scores for the team across time; grades, however, are based solely on the scores that each individual student achieves. This approach has also been demonstrated to be useful in relation to second language learners. For example, Gomasatitd (1997) in a modified version of STAD found that its use significantly correlated with improvement in English language proficiency for second-year business administration majors at a Thai university.

While STAD and many other cooperative learning techniques are designed for use with any subject area, researchers at Johns Hopkins designed Cooperative Integrated Reading and Composition (CIRC) specifically for the language arts curriculum in American schools (Slavin 1995).

Recognizing that within a single class there may be a wide range of reading and writing proficiencies, CIRC involves students in two types of groups in addition to whole-class instruction on reading strategies. They meet in same-level reading groups in which the teacher introduces a text for reading; teaches vocabulary and skills, such as prediction; and discusses texts after they have been read. However, the students' main group is a heterogeneous one formed with one member of their reading group and two students from another group. In the main group, students work on activities based on the texts introduced in their reading group. Students check the progress of the members of the other pair in their group and provide peer feedback on group members' writing. As in STAD, a cooperative reward structure is used in which students earn points for their group based on a comparison of their most recent work and their past average. These team points go toward certificates or other rewards. Also, like STAD, while individual performance affects group rewards, each individual's grade is based solely on his or her own work.

In a number of studies of second language learning, CIRC was associated with higher achievement (Calderon, Hertz-Lazarowitz, Ivory & Slavin 1997; Hertz-Lazarowitz, Lernor, Schaedel, Walk & Sarid 1992; Slavin & Yampolsky 1991). Calderon et al. studied the use of CIRC in a transitional bilingual program for Spanish-dominant lower primary school students in the United States. The researchers found significantly higher mean scores on measures of both reading and language for third-grade students who had participated in CIRC for two years and longer when compared to those who had received "traditional reading methods emphasizing round-robin reading and independent workbook practice activities" (p. 4). Furthermore, to a statistically significant extent, students who had participated in CIRC met the criteria to exit the bilingual education program.

Humanist psychology

Maslow (1968), a leading humanist psychologist, proposed a hierarchy of needs that humans strive to satisfy. He divided these needs into two types: *maintenance needs* and *growth needs*. The maintenance needs must be fulfilled in order for growth to take place. Among these maintenance needs is the need for interpersonal closeness. Growth needs include the need to know and understand, aesthetic needs, the need to realize one's potential, and the need to connect with something beyond oneself. Rogers (1979) also stressed the role of positive interpersonal relations and empathetic understanding, arguing that the support they provide is essential for students' psychological growth.

In conjunction with affective concerns, humanists emphasize the unique-ness of each individual and the need for self-initiative as opposed to one-size-fits-all and teacher-fronted instruction. This emphasis on the individual might be seen as being in contradiction with cooperative learning, which focuses on interaction between people. However, on a continuum from teacher lecture to self-study, cooperative learning represents a major step away from dependence on teachers and toward greater reliance on self and peers. Further, the purpose of cooperative learning is not to get everyone to think alike, but to get everyone to think and to share and to develop their own thinking through engagement with others. This view is seen as supportive of democratic practices, which stress participation of the individual for the larger good (Daniels 1994; Ruddock 1991).

Second language educators have been influenced by humanist psychol-ogy (Brookes & Grundy 1990; Moskowitz 1978). The importance of groups for creating an atmosphere that promotes individual development is high-lighted by Moskowitz (1978: 2), who states that a key purpose of humanistic second language learning activities is "to help build rapport, cohesiveness, and caring . . . to help students to be themselves, to accept themselves, and to be proud of themselves." Links with cooperative learning seem clear in the introduction to the resource book of activities for humanistic language learning by Puchta and Schratz (1993: 3–4):

1. To be successful, students need the skills and attitudes for "cooperative inter-dependence in learning."
2. Because cooperative interdependence takes time for students to develop, teachers must continually be helping students toward this goal.
3. Cooperative interdependence entails the development of empathy and toler-ance for others.[1] (The sharing of feelings aids this development.)
4. Constructive, nonjudgmental feedback is vital.
5. Students should share power in deciding on instructional matters.
6. The development of collaborative skills should be combined with the devel-opment of language skills.

Prapphal (1991: 37) reports a study with an English class at a Thai univer-sity organized according to humanistic and cooperative learning principles. Based on informal evaluation by the students and their teacher, Prapphal notes that cooperative learning "appears to facilitate the learning process both cognitively and affectively." However, it is important to point out that how cooperative learning may interface with a particular culture is,

---

[1] However, we would rather submit "acceptance of others" as we believe this phrase is in better accord with the goals of cooperative learning.

of course, something that deserves consideration, as cultural dispositions toward learning a second language have been shown to be different (e.g., Crago 1992; John-Steiner 1985; McCafferty 1992), a topic that will be taken up in Chapter 2.

Global education

Closely related to the humanist perspective is a belief in connecting what happens in the classroom to the world outside (Dewey 1966; Freire 1970); educators have a responsibility to help students develop not just in subject area but as active citizens of their school, country, and of the world. They should grow into people who are willing to address problems and make appropriate changes. Toward this end, an area of education has arisen, sometimes known as *global education* (Bergstrom 1987; Pike & Selby 1988). Components of global education include peace education (Reardon 1988), environmental education (Knapp 1988), development education (Fountain 1995), and human rights education (Shiman 1993). Crucial to the goals of global education is that students realize that positive interdependence exists between themselves and their fellow Homo sapiens, as well as with the other species inhabiting the planet. Starting at the level of the small classroom group, cooperative learning helps students put this realization of positive interdependence into action. Cooperative learning promotes among students the ability and the inclination to work together beyond the classroom by making cooperation not just part of the how of learning but also part of the content (Jacobs 1997; Sapon-Shevin & Schniedewind 1991).

Global education has also appeared as a trend in second language education (Cates 1990; Ghaith & Shaaban 1995a; UNESCO 1987).[2] Additionally, as part of a trend toward content-based and theme-based language teaching (Crandall 1987), entire textbooks for second language students have been devoted to global issues (Abraham 1998; Brown & Butterworth 1998), as well as appearing as one among many themes in L2 textbooks (Jacobs & Goatly 2000).

---

[2] For instance, global issues special interest groups exist in the International Association of Teachers of English as a Foreign Language (www.iatefl-gisig.org) and the Japan Association of Language Teachers (www.jalt.org/global/).

2 Connections between cooperative learning and second language learning and teaching

George M. Jacobs and Steven G. McCafferty

In this chapter, we discuss theoretical perspectives and concepts from the literature on second language learning and L2 teaching that link with cooperative learning. Specifically to be considered are the input hypothesis, the interaction hypothesis, the output hypothesis, sociocultural theory, content-based instruction, individual differences, learner autonomy, and affective factors. (See Kagan & McGroarty 1993 for an earlier treatment of the links between cooperative learning and second language acquisition.)

The input hypothesis

In the 1970s, Stephen Krashen posited that second language acquisition (SLA) is driven by *comprehensible input*, that is, language that is read or heard that is just a little beyond what the learner already has acquired, a notion Krashen stated in theoretical terms as *i+1*. Moreover, following Chomsky, Krashen believed that this process takes place within the so-called language acquisition device in the brain. As such, it must be remembered that i+1 has to do with individual psycholinguistic processing. Thus, it should not be viewed as a process by which a learner in conjunction with another person tries to "find" the right level of vocabulary, for instance, as is commonly misconstrued (Dunn & Lantolf 1998).

This perspective does not immediately appear to have much in common with cooperative learning, especially as the theory accords no role for interaction as leading to SLA. In fact, the only benefit of *production* (speaking and writing) according to the theory is essentially bringing forth more input. However, in relation to cooperative learning, Krashen and Terrell (1983: 97) argued that despite the fact that in interaction learners may hear incorrect forms of the L2 from each other, student production should nonetheless be used as one part of the curriculum for their methodology, The Natural

18

Approach, arguing, "our experience is that interlanguage [intermediate forms of the L2] does a great deal more good than harm, as long as it is not the only input the students are exposed to. It is comprehensible, it is communicative, and in many cases, for many students it contains examples of i+1."

The interaction hypothesis

The interaction hypothesis (Hatch 1978a; Long 1981) emphasizes the role of the learner in social interaction, how he or she is able to exert agency over language input. However, research on this perspective has been limited primarily to dyadic and not to group interaction. The theory also has roots in work on linguistics. Of particular significance are Hymes's (1972) notion of *sociolinguistic competence*, as opposed to only grammatical competence, and Halliday's (1970) analysis of language in terms of the functions it is used to achieve, rather than looking at language as a thing in-and-of-itself, isolated from the purposes it serves.

Researchers who support the interaction hypothesis stress the need for communication by expanding on the *nativists'* (those theorists who believe language acquisition to be an innate process) emphasis on input only (as found above with the input hypothesis). Through the *negotiation for meaning* (Oliver 1998; Pica 1996; Schinke-Llano & Vicars 1993), the amount of comprehensible input is thought to increase. Ways of negotiating meaning include the listener asking for repetition or clarification, as well as the speaker checking to see that others have understood. Rulon and McCreary (1986: 182) held that groups promote negotiation of meaning because "the more intimate setting provides students with the opportunity to negotiate the language they hear, free from the stress and rapid pace of the teacher-fronted classroom." Also, Varonis and Gass (1985) reported more negotiation of meaning in dyads composed of two nonnative speakers than when a nonnative and a native speaker were paired, something to be considered in the forming of groups in mainstream classrooms such as those found in the United States, for example.

Furthermore, it should be understood that negotiation for meaning is not the only way that modification or restructuring of interaction can take place. Other forms include self, other, and collaborative repair (van Lier 1991); completion of utterances by others; and topic shifts. Also, negotiation is not the only way that interaction aids SLA. Finally, as with the input hypothesis, this theory of SLA has almost no role for production of the second language as leading to acquisition; that is, only the changes in input that result from negotiation are thought to lead to acquisition.

The output hypothesis

Postulating another role for interaction, Swain (1985) proposed the output hypothesis, which states that in order for learners to increase their second language proficiency, they need to produce language via speech or writing, and to receive feedback on the comprehensibility of their output. As such, the output hypothesis posits that comprehensible input is a necessary but not sufficient condition for SLA. This view is based on research in settings such as long-term L2 immersion programs in Canada in which Swain (1991) found that nonnative speakers did as well as native speakers on measures of receptive skills, but significantly poorer on measures of productive skills. Swain (1993) suggests four ways in which output might aid SLA that input alone could not:

1. *Promoting fluency via meaningful language use.*
2. *Pushing learners to engage in syntactic processing of language.* Just because learners can decode certain forms does not mean they can produce them. Semantic and pragmatic knowledge may often be sufficient for understanding, whereas in language production, syntactic processing must play a larger role, as learners need to formulate the words and sentences needed to express their thoughts. Kowal and Swain (1994) make this point by quoting Krashen (1985: 66): "In many cases, we do not utilize syntax in understanding – we often get the message with a combination of vocabulary, or lexical information plus extralinguistic information."
3. *Allowing hypothesis testing as to what works in the L2 in terms of appropriacy, correctness, and understandability.* When interlocutors cannot understand learners' utterances, this provides a kind of implicit negative evidence that something may be amiss with their use of the language (Long 1996). For instance, Freeman and Freeman (1994), native speakers of English, recount that the puzzled looks they received when trying to communicate in Spanish in Venezuela let them know that what they had said needed to come closer to conventional Spanish to be understood.
4. *Providing opportunities for feedback from others, in such forms as negotiating meaning or supplying missing words.* Indeed, Pica et al. (1989) found that negotiation of meaning led to modified output, although Foster (1998) found much less negotiation and fewer resulting modifications than in previous studies.

Of course one of the major concerns of cooperative learning is the opportunity for groups to work together, for students to talk to one another. Long and Porter (1985) found that in an L2 class of 30 students, under typical teacher-fronted, or lockstep, procedures the average time that a student spoke was only 30 seconds per 50-minute lesson. However, when students worked in groups of three for just one quarter of a 50-minute period, the quantity of student talk increased more than 500 percent. Kagan (1992) called this boost in production the *simultaneity principle*; that is, with lockstep teaching only one person at a time talks, but with group activities, potentially at least one person per group is speaking at the same time. Other research on L2 classrooms also supports this claim of more learner talk during group work (Deen 1991; Doughty & Pica 1986; Long et al. 1976). Furthermore, Magee and Jacobs (2001) found that when tertiary-level students of Mandarin as an L2 studied in three modes – teacher-fronted, unstructured group, and cooperative learning (Jigsaw activity) – they took significantly more turns and produced significantly more speech in the two-group modes compared to the teacher-fronted mode, and in the cooperative learning mode as compared to the unstructured group mode.

All the additional learner language production generated by groups might be thought to contain more errors, as students might be less concerned about form when the teacher is not always there to monitor them. However, research has not found this to be the case (Bruton & Samuda 1980; Jacobs 1989; Pica & Doughty 1985; Porter 1983). Also, not only does the amount of student output increase when groups are used, so too does the variety of language functions that students perform (Davis 1997; Long & Porter 1985). In the lockstep classroom the teacher often monopolizes the *speech acts* involved in such matters as inviting others to speak, making suggestions, and checking for understanding. On the other hand, groups provide a setting closer to real life, in which students have the opportunity to practice aspects of communicative competence such as conversational management (Long & Porter 1985). Freeman and Freeman (1994: 153) maintained that because "language develops in contexts of functional use," teachers should "create situations in which all their students use language for a variety of purposes and with a variety of people."

As part of investigating the output hypothesis, Swain and her colleagues have looked at tasks that might encourage interaction with regard to form. One such task is *dictogloss* (Wajnryb 1990), in which groups of students work together to reconstruct a text their teacher has read to them. (Specifically, a text is read aloud to students only twice and at normal speed while the students take notes. Then, using their notes, small groups of students collaborate to rebuild the text, finally comparing their versions with the original.) Kowal and Swain (1994, 1997) and Nabei (1996) all found dictogloss to be effective for encouraging student-student interaction about form.

Sociocultural theory

In recent years, a number of second language researchers and theorists (e.g., Coughlan & Duff 1994; DiCamilla & Anton 2004; Frawley & Lantolf 1985; Lantolf 2000; Lantolf & Appel 1994; McCafferty 1998; Platt & Brooks 1994; Roebuck & Wagner 2004; Takahashi 1998; Thorne 2000; Van Lier 1996) have applied the ideas of Lev S. Vygotsky (see Chapter 1) and related scholars to second language learning. This approach focuses on how people mediate learning of an L2 in accordance with contexts and experience.

At the between people, or interpersonal, level, Vygotsky's concept of the zone of proximal development (explained in Chapter 1) has received a good deal of attention. (See for example: Guerrero & Villamil 1994; Donato 1994; Dunn & Lantolf 1998; Kowal & Swain 1994; Swain & Lapkin 1995.) Additionally, there has been a reexamination of the ZPD. (See Kinginger 2002 for an overview.) For example, McCafferty (2002) cites Newman and Holtzman (1993), who believed that for Vygotsky the ZPD is a "tool *and* result." That is, the ZPD transforms the user too. For example, the ZPD shows how gestures can be mutually appropriated by conversational participants in a quasi-tutorial setting. Over time their interactions transform with regard to second language learning (McCafferty 2002), and as such, go beyond instrumentalist conceptualizations of the ZPD (tool *for* result).

Also consider the following important point regarding the ZPD and cooperative learning when working with children with disabilities:

Vygotsky's strategy was essentially a cooperative learning strategy. He created heterogeneous groups of . . . children (he called them a collective), providing them not only with the opportunity but the need for cooperation and joint activity by giving them tasks that were beyond the developmental level of some, if not all, of them. Under these circumstances, children could create a ZPD for each other, something not possible if one takes developmental level as the basis for learning (Newman & Holtzman 1993: 77).

As applied to L2 students, this passage indicates that students at the same proficiency level can help each other. However, at the same time, it needs to be recognized that creating these circumstances may prove difficult in some settings. For example, Sullivan (2000: 121) found that for L2 learners of English in Vietnam, grouping was seen as dividing up the class, not bringing it together; as such, she argued that forming groups runs counter to the "Confucian roots" of that culture. From this point of view, we are profoundly affected by our particular cultural-historical circumstances. This is not to suggest that we are psychological "mirror images" of what we experience at the interpersonal level: What we internalize at the psychological, or intrapersonal, level and how we do so has much to do with our own orientation to the world as embedded in our histories, expectations of the moment, and other contextual elements.

For example, Coughlan and Duff (1994) made the valuable but often overlooked point that a task that teachers or researchers ask students to carry out cannot be seen as fixed. Instead, students construct their own versions of the task based on their orientation toward it in conjunction with others. In their study, Coughlan and Duff gave each L2 participant the same task instructions: Describe a picture to an interviewer. Yet each person interpreted the task differently and in relation to what they thought the interviewer "meant" or "wanted" them to do. For instance, one tried to name as many things in the picture as possible, while another focused on relating events in the picture to her own personal experiences. In addition, the same participants when asked to do the same tasks at a much later date, did not simply repeat what they had done previously – their orientation to the task had changed despite receiving the same instructions.

Also, Platt and Brooks (1994) remarked on how the orientation of students – this time engaged in pair and group work – can differ from teacher expectations, noting that sometimes the L2 students in the study simply conformed to their assigned roles with little engagement, or in some cases much of what they said was in fact directed to themselves (*private speech*) in their efforts to both come to understand and carry out a group activity despite the presence of others. Platt and Brooks also address *intersubjectivity* (creating a temporarily shared social world) and how this can be a key element in determining joint orientation in activity.

Therefore, in regard to L2 classrooms and cooperative learning, sociocultural theory emphasizes the social nature of learning, that symbolic, physical, and mental space are mediated through interaction in culturalhistorical contexts. Students utilize themselves (their own histories), each other (as in groups), artifacts (especially language and other forms of communication), and the environment in their efforts to make meaning of and in the L2.

Content-based instruction

One manifestation of the overall trend toward communicative approaches to L2 instruction has been the growing use of content- and theme-based language teaching, in which the goal is to learn both the language and content. For example, "desert environments and the people who inhabit them" might be part of a social studies class. Many advocates of such an approach recommend the use of cooperative learning techniques for the reasons discussed previously both in this chapter and Chapter 1 (Chamot & O'Malley 1994; McGroarty 1992; Olsen 1992). For instance, cooperative learning is a central aspect of the Cognitive Academic Language Learning Approach (CALLA), which is specifically designed to promote L2 learning in relation to content-based L2 instruction (Chamot & O'Malley 1994).

Chamot and O'Malley classify cooperation as a social / affective strategy that students implement by "working with peers to complete a task, pool information, solve a problem, [and] get feedback" (63). To organize students, Chamot and O'Malley employ many considerations from cooperative learning, such as how to structure tasks to encourage positive interdependence. These ideas will be dealt with in greater depth in the next chapter.

Content teachers often complain that they have a great deal of material to cover with no time left for such matters as teaching collaborative skills or debriefing group effectiveness, and that more can be covered in a teacher-fronted instructional mode. Chamot and O'Malley respond by suggesting a "less is more" approach to covering content, in which the emphasis is on high-priority content that is studied in depth (178). Reducing content area load provides teachers more time to help students develop their collaborative skills, which can help students not just in one course but in many.

Individual differences

A central tenet of communicative language teaching[1] is a focus on learners, not teachers. From this perspective, teachers should be facilitators. One aspect of this learner-centered focus is the idea that learners differ from one another in terms of intelligences and learning styles. Kagan and Kagan (1998) advocate three ways in which instruction should be shaped in light of these differences. First, instruction should sometimes match the way that students prefer to learn. Second, because we want students to be able to learn

---

[1] As described by Richards and Rodgers (2001), CLT is based on a view of language as communication, not as a system of grammar rules or vocabulary lists. Fluency, not just accuracy, is valued (Nolasco & Arthur 1988). The goal of CLT is communicative competence that includes grammatical competence and also encompasses the ability of learners to use the language appropriately socially (sociolinguistic competence), to use it for larger frames of discourse rather than simply at the sentence level (discourse competence), and to find ways of gaining access to language forms through asking different types of questions (strategic competence) (Canale & Swain 1980).

in a variety of ways, instruction should sometimes place students in contexts outside their comfort zones so that their learning repertoire stretches beyond their preferred means of learning. For example, if some students seem to learn best via activities using music and rhythm, such activities should form part of the class's methodological repertoire. But because we want students to be able to learn in a variety of ways, instruction should sometimes place students in contexts different from their profiles so that their learning repertoires get stretched. For example, if some students always need visual clues to understand and learn, they should also gain experience learning without the aid of such clues. Third, students should come to recognize, understand, and value the diversity that exists among them.

One way of valuing these differences that also has to do with learning concerns the idea of multiple intelligences – the view that there are different types of intelligence, and that they can be developed through various types of exposure (Christison 1995; Gardner 1983). One form of intelligence often overlooked in traditional classrooms is *interpersonal intelligence*. This involves showing respect to others and knowing how to understand and interact successfully with peers.

Overlapping with the area of intelligences is work describing how learners have a variety of second language learning styles (Reid 1987). These differences result in the utilization of multiple strategies to learn and use second languages (Oxford 1990). Instruction is believed to help learners develop effective strategies (Wenden 1997). Included among effective language learning strategies are social strategies involving collaboration with peers and others (Kinsella 1996; Scarcella & Oxford 1992). Social learning strategies include asking others for help and speaking together in the target language.

Cooperative learning activities allow students opportunities to develop and practice such strategies for learning and using language. However, Reid (1987) and Kinsella (1996) note that students with certain learning styles – analytical, for example – may react negatively to group activities. To overcome these objections, Reid and Kinsella recommend clear aims and directions, activities that require cooperation, feedback from the teacher, and the use of group activities as only one of a variety of instructional modes.

Another area related to differences among learners involves the role of culture. In particular, the suitability of group activities for learners from Asian cultures has been a topic of investigation (Flowerdew 1998; Jacobs & Ratmanida 1996; Tang 1996). Despite the fact that respect for authority and power has been noted in many Confucian-influenced Asian cultures by researchers such as Hofstede (1980), Flowerdew (1998) argues that beyond respect for authority and power, three other important Confucian values – "face," cooperation, and self-effacement – can facilitate effective group activities. A recent edited volume (Kluge, McGuire, Johnson & Johnson 1999) focuses on cooperative learning in second language education in Japan, an Asian country known for maintaining elements of traditional culture. However, recall the findings of Sullivan's (2000) study of an English language classroom in Vietnam (as mentioned earlier in this chapter). The findings indicate that there may not be a cultural preference for group work for all Asian cultures; there can be important cultural-historical differences as well.

Learner autonomy

Another implication of the focus on learners in second language instruction is the concept of *learner autonomy*, the idea that students should develop into life-long learners by enhancing their abilities and their inclinations to plan, control, and evaluate their own learning (Wenden 1991). Learner autonomy does not necessarily mean that each student learns alone or without a teacher (Little 1990; Reid 1993). Rather, the collaboration that occurs in cooperative learning groups fits well with notions of learner autonomy as students are given a large role in controlling their own learning process (Macaro 1997). Also, Freeman and Freeman (1994) argue that in groups, students are more likely to take responsibility for their own learning. Similarly, for van Lier (1996), autonomy goes well beyond learners being able to work alone, and includes taking part in choosing "the what" and "the how" of curriculum. Hand in hand with this increased autonomy comes the responsibility for the learning of those with whom one interacts. Van Lier links this rendering of autonomy with Vygotsky's (1978) concept of self-regulation and Csikszentmihalyi's (1990) concept of *flow* (when there is a positive confluence of elements involved in doing an activity so that it becomes both enjoyable and seemingly effortless).

The idea that the best choice as to the "how" of one's own learning will often involve collaboration finds support in the work by cognitive psychologists who have studied the scholarly processes of successful scientists (Scardamalia & Bereiter 1996). In connection with this research, certain cooperative learning approaches foster a high degree of learner autonomy because they provide students with the freedom to explore their own interests and to organize group activities. For example, group investigation (Sharan & Sharan 1992) has student groups choose their own topics and decide how to research them in preparation for sharing what they learn with the entire class.

However, many learners are unfamiliar with group activities or may have had unsatisfactory experiences with them. Both these factors may lead L2 students to believe that the teacher-centered classroom offers the best learning environment (Brookes & Grundy 1990). Thus, they may resist when teachers encourage them to take more responsibility for their own learning (Cotterall 1995). To help students appreciate the advantages of becoming more independent, second language educators can explain their rationale for using groups to structure peer interaction in order to make it more productive at the level of individual learning (Brookes & Grundy 1990).

Peer feedback on writing represents one such practice that has seen a good deal of application (Amores 1997; Carson & Nelson 1994; Connor & Asenavage 1994; Guerrero & Villamil 1994; Jacobs 1987; Leki 1990; Mangelsdorf & Schlumberger 1992; Yoshihara 1993). Peer feedback came to prominence in second language education as part of the adoption from L1 pedagogy of a *process approach* to writing instruction (Moffett 1968; Murray 1968). Peer interaction can be utilized in all phases of the writing process – prewriting, creating multiple drafts, and revising – with peer feedback being particularly useful in the revision phase. One reason for this use of student-student interaction in writing instruction is the belief that students need "to practice the process of writing in class and talk about it to peers" (Brookes & Grundy 1990: 11). Reid (1993: 135), who has written extensively on second language writing, states that "students learn at least as well and as much from peers as they do from teachers."

Affective factors

Many affective elements have been proposed as important to SLA. Two of these, anxiety and motivation, will be taken up in this section. Although anxiety can be either facilitating or debilitating (Scovel 1978), too often L2 classrooms produce the debilitating variety (Brookes & Grundy 1990; Horwitz, Horwitz & Cope 1991). Citing research by Barnes (1973) in L1 classrooms, Long and Porter (1985: 211) suggested, "In contrast to the public atmosphere of lockstep instruction, a small group of peers provides a relatively intimate setting and, usually, a more supportive environment in which to try out embryonic SL [second language] skills." Indeed, Tsui (1996) found student-student collaboration to be an effective means of reducing debilitating anxiety among her L2 learners. Long and Porter believed that this "more supportive environment" may also increase motivation. They cite studies with L2 learners by Littlejohn (1982) and by Fitz-Gibbon and Reay (1982) to support this assertion.

Dornyei (1997) maintained that the affective domain represents an essential element in the success of cooperative learning leading to SLA. He attributed this positive interaction to the interrelated roles played out in group dynamics and heightened motivation derived from peer cooperation. Dornyei made a clear link between his theory of L2 motivation and the work in social psychology on groups as found in the general education literature (for example, Johnson & Johnson 1995). For instance, although his terms are different from Johnson et al. (1993), his suggestions for enhancing group cohesiveness are similar to those of Johnson et al. (1993) for increasing positive interdependence (Dornyei 1997: 485–6):

1. Proximity, or physical closeness (Johnson et al. call this "environmental positive interdependence".)
2. Contact in situations where individuals can meet and communicate (Johnson et al. call this "face-to-face promotive interaction" but also see a role for computer-mediated communication.)
3. Cooperation between group members for common goals (Johnson et al. call this "positive goal interdependence"; see also Alport's (1954) notion of the need for a common goal.)
4. The rewarding nature of group experience for the individual (Johnson et al. call this reward or celebration "positive interdependence".)
5. Intergroup competition, for example, games in which groups compete (Johnson et al. call this "external challenge interdependence," which also includes nonanimate competitors, such as students competing to beat their past average on quizzes. Also, it should be noted that Dornyei, as do many in cooperative learning, cautioned against the possible negative consequences of "us vs. them" attitudes that competition can cause.)
6. Group legends involve building up a kind of group mythology, giving the group a name, and inventing characteristics for the group. (This would fall into two of Johnson et al.'s categories of positive interdependence: identity and fantasy.)

Two other similarities between Dornyei's ideas and the mainstream cooperative learning literature deserve mention. First, Dornyei talked about the need for team building in order for groups to get to know each other and develop the trust and skills to work together. In the cooperative learning literature, Kagan (1995) urged that team-building activities be done not only when groups are first formed, but at regular intervals as well. Second, Dornyei, like Chamot and O'Malley (1994), believed that group functioning can be improved if groups regularly take time to evaluate how well they are working together. Johnson et al. (1993) list this, which they call *processing group interaction*, as one of their five essential components of cooperative learning.

This chapter has explored the connection between cooperative learning and different perspectives on second language learning. Although clearly cooperative learning is aligned more with social theories of learning and cognition than those that take a strictly cognitive view, one dimension or another of all of the second language approaches covered in the chapter was found to interface positively with cooperative / collaborative learning, lending strong support for its use as a technique in L2 classrooms. However, of course, how it is used in relation to specific contexts is of critical importance in promoting language learning – as will become apparent in the narrative chapters in the second part of the book.

3 Issues in implementing cooperative learning

George M. Jacobs

The previous two chapters have provided background on cooperative learning in terms of its history, key principles, and place in general and second language education. This chapter examines some of the more practical issues involved in implementing cooperative learning. Indeed, when implementing cooperative learning, teachers typically face a number of questions, each of which usually has many possible answers. Ultimately, answers about putting cooperative learning into action will be context dependent and accord with teachers' personal beliefs about teaching and education.

In Chapters 4–9 to follow, teachers across the spectrum with regard to both grade level and geographical location offer insights into their experiences with cooperative learning, including some of the questions they asked themselves and the options they chose. This chapter is divided into four main sections, each concerned with a principal aspect of implementing cooperative learning.

1. *Forming groups*. Groups are the core of most cooperative learning activities. Many questions arise about group formation. How often should cooperative learning be used? How many students should be in a group? How should group seating be arranged? How long should groups stay together?
2. *Functioning as a group*. Once groups have been formed, attention must be paid to how well they are functioning. A variety of questions merit consideration. Should collaborative skills be taught? Should groups spend time processing how well they work together? What is the teacher's role when students are working in groups?
3. *Cooperative learning principles and group activity*. In part, groups exist to carry out tasks. Attention should be paid to how tasks promote cooperation among group members. How is positive interdependence fostered? How are students encouraged to feel individually accountable for their own and their group mates' learning?
4. *Teacher collaboration*. When teachers collaborate with one another, they model cooperation and enhance their effectiveness. However,

questions need to be addressed in order for this cooperation to be successful. How can teachers work together to implement cooperative learning? How can teachers collaborate to learn more about cooperative learning, and how can they share their knowledge with others?

Forming groups

How often should cooperative learning be used?

No one advocates that cooperative learning be the only teaching strategy used in a classroom (Rogers 1978). Rather, the point is that cooperative learning can usefully come to take a regular and significant place in teachers' repertoires. Teacher-fronted and individual learning also play important roles in instruction, and can be easily combined with cooperative learning, as can group activities that are not structured along cooperative learning lines. It is also important to note that many cooperative learning techniques include the use of teacher instruction, for example, STAD (described in Chapter 1), while in other cooperative learning techniques, students spend some time working alone. Thus, there is more flexibility to cooperative learning than is commonly assumed, and no reason to believe that a lesson cannot include some element of cooperative learning even if the main focus is on some other mode of instruction. Indeed, it is expected that cooperative learning serves some pedagogical functions better than others, and it is up to the teacher to decide when it is best implemented. However, it also needs to be kept in mind that cooperative learning is not easy or simple to use. Thus, teachers just beginning to experiment with this approach will want to start slowly, using a greater variety of cooperative learning techniques as they master the skills of teaching via groups. Moreover, remember that students who are unfamiliar with cooperative learning may need a while to adjust to this new format for learning as well (Reid 1993).

How many students per group?

As stated in the introduction, even a pair is a group. Indeed, in some ways, two is an ideal size because greater participation is encouraged (Kagan 1994; Kowal & Swain 1994). Also, smaller groups are easier to coordinate owing to the interaction of fewer people. For this reason, some teachers prefer to start with groups of two until students become comfortable with working with each other in these circumstances (Kleiner-Brandwein 1995). However, larger groups have advantages as well, because for more complex tasks there are more people and perhaps cooperative learning has a wider range of skills and knowledge from which to draw. Larger groups also offer the possibility of differing opinions and perspectives in relation to experience. Additionally, larger groups make it easier for teachers to monitor each of the groups in a classroom, there being fewer of them.

In choosing a larger group size, four members seems to be the most popular size, especially because a foursome can be divided into two pairs. For instance, in Write-Pair-Square (Kagan 1994), each student first writes alone, then compares what he or she has written with a partner before sharing with the two other members of the foursome. (Squares have four sides, thus the name for bringing back together the two pairs of a group of four.) There are few references in the literature to groups larger than six.

Which students will be in a group together?

Four main options exist for forming groups: 1) Students can decide. In this way students are likely to feel more comfortable in their groups and possibly to share a similar working style. 2) Groups can be formed on the basis of some commonality: those who like a particular type of music or a particular musician in the case of a writing assignment on music; those with a similar problem in their writing; those with the same assignment for another course; or, on the other hand, those holding different views on the same issue, thus providing each other with a skeptical audience to endeavor to win over (Reid 1993). 3) Groups can be formed at random. This will usually result in some degree of heterogeneity but in unpredictable ways. The advantages are that random groups are quick and easy, and it seems fair to students to be selected in this way. 4) Teachers can decide. This is the option recommended in most of the cooperative learning literature, which advocates that teachers place students in groups that are heterogeneous in such characteristics as language proficiency (to promote peer tutoring); first language (to encourage second language use); ethnicity and gender (to break down barriers and provide different perspectives); and on-task behavior (to provide positive models). Ruddock (1978: 59) nicely states one of the arguments for heterogeneous grouping as a means of helping students see a variety of perspectives.

Marcel Proust, the great French novelist, once said that the only true voyage would be not to travel through a hundred different lands with the same pair of eyes but to see the same land through a hundred different pairs of eyes. Small group work is about learning through different pairs of eyes. In the same vein, Freeman and Freeman (1994: 154) noted, "When students work collaboratively, diversity is an asset to be celebrated since the varied experiences, knowledge, and interests students in each group bring to the task at hand add to the potential for learning."

Brookes and Grundy (1990) argued against the use of teacher-selected groups, believing that such a directive approach goes against the humanistic philosophy they advocate. They suggested, instead, that groups be formed based on some trivial commonality or dissimilarity, for example, the period of the year when students were born, or something a bit more consequential, such as childhood ambition, similar experiences, or, conversely, differing interests.

The use of heterogeneous groups according to academic proficiency is one of the more contentious issues in cooperative learning (Allan 1991; Slavin 1991); some researchers fear that high achievers when mixed with low achievers will end up feeling bored and the low achievers will feel intimidated. However, Johnson, Johnson, and Holubec (2002) argued that when high achievers help their lower-achieving group mates, they also help themselves in several ways. First, they may enjoy greater feelings of belonging, acceptance, and caring as they work for group rather than individual success. Second, the rehearsal and elaboration involved in teaching others may also aid their memory and deepen their understanding. Many teachers experience this, finding that high achievers understand the material much better once they have had the opportunity to teach it. Finally, working in this way with group mates prepares high achievers for professions that involve various forms of teaching others, such as being a doctor, lawyer, manager, and of course, being a teacher.

Equally important, research suggests that lower achievers benefit as well (Johnson et al. 1991). In heterogeneous groups in which students feel positively interdependent, low achievers receive help not just from their teacher but from their peers. Additionally, the high achievers can provide useful models of how to go about successfully undertaking tasks. Moreover, low achievers may feel more motivation / investment to try because if they fail, their whole group suffers along with them. Another reason that motivation may increase is that cooperative learning encourages each student to feel individually accountable; it does not allow students to simply sit back and let others do the task for them.

However, if the high achievers always do the helping, and the low achievers always receive the help, status issues may arise that might hamper group effectiveness. To attempt to ameliorate such problems, Kagan and Kagan (1998) urged the use of tasks that involve a wide range of intelligences. For example, music and drawing could both be included in language lessons (Bassano & Christison 1992; Murphey 1992). Those students who are currently weaker than their group mates in the L2 may be stronger in another area, thus potentially changing their status from receiver of help to giver of help. Cohen and her colleagues (Cohen & Lotan 1997) have used sociological theory to explore status differences and have developed what they call multi-ability tasks and other means of attempting to level relations within cooperative learning groups.

How should group seating be arranged?

Physical arrangement of the group is important for four primary reasons: 1) If students are close together, they are more likely to communicate with one another, and it is easier for them to do so. Sometimes, teachers can see from across the room that a group is not functioning well because one of its members is sitting apart from the rest. 2) Students sitting close together can use quiet voices, thus lowering the noise level of the classroom. 3) The room needs to be arranged so that teachers can monitor all the groups. 4) Consider the role of mirror neurons in the brain. (These neurons fire when we see others perform a significant physical action, when we perform one ourselves, and when we imagine engaging in such an action.) Mirror neuron behavior suggests a strong biological connection between both communication and learning for the role of what others do in an embodied fashion (Gallese & Goldman 1998). Therefore, it would seem that having students all facing forward, looking at the backs of each other's heads is highly antithetical to how people normally learn and communicate with one another.

One obvious exception to this injunction, however, is computer-mediated collaboration. The development of computers has opened up many new avenues for student-student interaction in education generally (Koschmann 1996; Wegerif & Scrimshaw 1997), as well as in second language learning (Beauvois 1998; Kern 1995). More specifically, ideas have been generated as to how second language learners can collaborate via e-mail (Soh & Soon 1991), networked computers, and chat rooms (Rankin 1997). For instance, Warschauer (1997) cited studies of the social dynamics of computer-mediated communication, which suggest that it leads to more equal participation among interlocutors, even when status differences exist among them (Sproull & Kiesler 1991). In a study of his own, Warschauer (1996) found that computer-mediated communication was also associated with greater diversity of views among interlocutors. However, the distance of distance education can be problematic as well, as writing is not the same as meeting face-to-face in a group for discussion purposes, although certainly satellite communications are improving this situation, and, of course, there are circumstances where meeting face-to-face is not necessary nor perhaps even the best choice.

How long should groups stay together?

An individual activity can be as short as a few minutes. For example, in Timed-Pair-Share (Kagan & Kagan 1994) each member of a pair speaks for a given time – perhaps a minute – and then students share their partner's ideas with the class. An activity can last as long as a few months. For example, in Group Investigation (Sharan & Sharan 1992), groups of students choose topics to research and present to the rest of the class. Moreover, even though a given cooperative learning technique may be brief, groups can remain intact for long periods of time and thus do many activities together.

There are a number of issues that relate to how long groups should remain together. For one, changing groups helps students get to know everyone in the class. Second, long-term groups allow time for building group identity (via group name, flag, motto, handshake, and so on), and for work on in-depth projects. They also help students establish support networks. Further, students have more reason to overcome difficulties they may have in working with certain group mates if they know their group will exist for weeks or months. For instance, Gerow (1997) recounts that when students asked to be changed to another group because they could not get along with a group mate, she would only allow them to change when they had demonstrated the ability to work well in their present group.

Long- and short-term groups can be used simultaneously. In other words, students can be a member of two groups at once. *Base groups* (Johnson & Johnson 1994a) are long-term groups that last at least a semester and preferably for a number of years. Their principal purpose is not to work on projects or prepare for tests. Instead, they provide support and motivation, meeting regularly to see how each member is doing in school. Base group members are considered to be like good friends with an academic focus. So, for example, if a student misses class, a base group member is expected to collect the handout and homework for the student. One figure for how long groups should be together often seen in the cooperative learning literature is six weeks. This gives students time to learn how to work with their group members, thus emphasizing the importance of allotting time for groups to discuss how well they are functioning and how they can function better. As previously mentioned, many experts on cooperative learning (for example, Dishon & O'Leary 1993) urge that groups be formed heterogeneously. It takes a while for teachers to organize such groupings, and we would not want to have to do that every week. If students already know which group they are in, teachers do not have to spend as much class time getting them organized. When long-term groups disband, students can hold some type of closing activity, for example, giving each other small presents or writing each other thank-you notes or letters of reference for their next group.

Functioning as a group

Once groups have been formed, some teachers believe that in order to enhance their functioning it is necessary to spend class time helping students feel comfortable learning together and helping them develop the attitudes and skills they need to interact effectively. The argument is that students may not have learned how to work with others from family, previous schooling, or elsewhere (McGrath 1998). Working together can be especially diffi-cult when students are placed in heterogeneous groups with classmates with whom they have not collaborated previously. One means of encour-aging groups to work well together lies in fostering the feeling of positive interdependence among group members. This is the basis of the following discussion.

Collaborative skills

Although they vary according to the ages of the students and the cultural context, collaborative skills can include asking for help, giving reasons, speaking at an appropriate volume level, disagreeing politely, paraphrasing, asking for repetition, listening attentively, making suggestions, encouraging others to participate, checking that others understand, keeping the group on task, asking about feelings, praising others, and so on. However, this does not mean that students must always get along, as this is not realistic. Moreover, in second language contexts it is important for students to learn how to interact in argumentative circumstances, that is, how to assert themselves in the L2, as well as how to acquiesce.

The development of collaborative skills may best take place when inte-grated into regular classrooms instead of one-time workshops (Maag 1990) because students need many opportunities for naturalistic or seminaturalis-tic practice in which they can see the benefits of positive behavior (Hawkins & Weiss 1983). Research suggests that cooperative learning accompanied by collaborative skills instruction can change the social ecology of the class-room, providing an environment more conducive to facilitative peer inter-action (Schneider 1993). For example, Mesch et al. (1986) found greater peer acceptance and liking for students identified as socially isolated and learning disabled, as well as higher achievement, when a group of American students worked cooperatively on French, Spanish, and mathematics tasks after being taught collaborative skills. Moreover, Bejarano et al. (1997) con-ducted a study in which one class of EFL students was given instruction concerning interaction strategies while another class at an equivalent L2 proficiency level was not. The researchers reported enhanced interaction among those classes where students participated in cooperative learning groups as compared to classes where this was not the case.

Many means exist for teaching collaborative skills. Johnson et al. (1993) suggested the following six-step procedure:

1. The teacher first helps the students understand why a particular skill is necessary.
2. Next the class discusses what the skill involves.
3. Students practice the skill in isolation.
4. Students utilize the skill in the group activities they do as part of the regular curriculum.
5. After some time, students discuss how well they are using the skill.
6. Finally, the teacher builds the skill into future activities, helping students to become better versed at using it.

One common way of implementing Step 4 above is with roles. An example of using roles to incorporate collaborative skills would be that one group member can be the facilitator, another the encourager (in charge of encouraging others to participate), another the praiser, and the fourth member can play the role of checker, asking to see if everyone has understood.

Should I spend time discussing how well groups work together?

Some experts of cooperative learning (for example Johnson et al. 1993), recommend that a regular feature of the use of cooperative learning should be that groups spend time during or after activities discussing how well their group is functioning and how they might improve in their future collaborations. Johnson et al. (1993) called this *processing group interaction*. Such processing is often tied to a particular collaborative skill upon which the class has been focusing. Various other forms that processing of group interaction can take include:

1. A simple thumbs up, down, or sideways to respond to an item such as, "I asked questions when I did not understand."
2. A Likert-type scale item, for example, "Hamida gave reasons when she made suggestions or gave answers: 5 (Always), 4 (Usually), 3 (Sometimes), 2 (Seldom), 1 (Never)."
3. A sentence completion item, for example: One thing our group did well was _____. We did it by _____ and _____.

4. One student can act as observer during the group activity and report findings to the group. For example, to examine the number of turns taken by each member during a particular episode of group work, the observer can simply put a check next to the name of the member each time this happens.

As can be seen in these first three examples, processing can involve group members evaluating their individual contributions to the group, the overall contribution of a fellow group member, and / or the effectiveness of the entire group.

Some educators feel that explicit attention to collaborative skills is not necessary and that students will develop them through working together on well-designed activities. They worry that explicit attention to building group cohesion may be an unwise use of time and that students may see it as unrelated to what they are supposed to be learning. Two arguments raised in support of devoting class time to work on group functioning relate to long-term benefits and career goals. First, promoting group efficiency by focusing on collaborative skills could in the long run lead to more learning because groups work together better. Second, teaching collaborative skills helps prepare students for the work world where a growing trend exists toward the use of groups (Hilt 1992; Huckin & Olsen 1991; Jacobs 1994; Tjosvold & Tjosvold 1991).

For example, Mawer (1991: 5) studied the changing needs of ESL learners entering the work force in Australia. She contrasted traditional and contemporary workplaces. Traditional workplaces stressed a strict hierarchical organizational structure with narrowly defined jobs and isolated tasks for workers. In contrast, information age workplaces prized worker initiative and the ability to work and communicate closely with others.

Although the two reasons already given for spending class time on group functioning apply to cooperative learning in any subject area, second language educators may also find that devoting time to group functioning fits into their language curriculum (Kramsch 1981). For instance, collaborative skills instruction fits well with teaching language functions, and cooperative learning activities provide a meaningful context for practicing these functions (Coelho 1994; Jacobs & Kline-Liu 1996).

What is the teacher's role when students are working in groups?

Teachers play an essential role in helping groups function well. As Edge (1993: 70) points out, "The teacher is not asked to *give up control* in order to use pair work and group work. The teacher is asked to *exercise control* in order to use pair work and group work" (emphasis added). In other words, it may actually take more skill for a teacher to be a facilitator, a guide on the side, than it may take to use teacher-fronted instruction, being a sage on a stage. First, skilled facilitators need to help students prepare to do the group tasks. This involves knowing the proper procedures and possessing the necessary content and language knowledge.

Then, while students collaborate with one another, the teacher needs to monitor how the students go about the task and whether they seem to be understanding and using the target language well. Observing student groups provides teachers with a window into students' minds, one we do not enjoy when we stand at the front of the class talking to students (Edge 1993). This is also an opportunity for teachers to give extra help to students or groups that are having special difficulties. At the same time, teachers should resist over-supervising group work. Groups should be allowed to try to overcome difficulties on their own before the teacher intervenes. One mnemonic for this idea is TTT, or Team Then Teacher.

Cooperative learning principles and group activity

Of course, the heart of cooperative learning is the group activity. Positive interdependence and individual accountability, discussed in the Introduction, are the two concepts that everyone in cooperative learning agrees are at the core of what makes cooperative learning activities different from just putting students in groups and asking them to work together.

How is positive interdependence fostered?

Another way to describe positive interdependence is the feeling of a group that understands they all "sink or swim together" (Johnson, Johnson & Holubec 2002). Positive interdependence is missing when students do not seem to care about helping one another to learn. Educators working with cooperative learning have developed many different ways of fostering positive interdependence among students. Seven categories to remember for encouraging this feeling of one-for-all and all-for-one follow. Any particular cooperative learning activity will have one and usually more of these means of encouraging group solidarity.

POSITIVE GOAL INTERDEPENDENCE

The group shares a goal or goals. For instance, they have to decide what to take with them on a trip to the moon, or they have to write a new ending to a story they have read.

POSITIVE REWARD INTERDEPENDENCE

There is a link between the reward that one group member receives and that which others receive. However, this is one of the most controversial areas in cooperative learning. First, there is the debate, which has raged for years in education, about which is more important, extrinsic or intrinsic motivation (Crookes & Schmidt 1991; Kohn 1992; van Lier 1996). Also, two other areas of controversy arise for those who believe in or have no choice about using extrinsic rewards: Should peers take part in assessing their group mates (Cheng & Warren 1996), and should students' grades be linked to those of their group mates?

Reasons for supporting group grading include the following (Johnson et al. 1993): 1) In the world outside the classroom, such as at the workplace, groups often succeed or fail together. Group grades prepare students for such situations. 2) Group grades may motivate students to help one another and to develop their collaborative skills. 3) A student's grade need not be based solely on the average grade of his or her group. Other possibilities include the group's average as a percentage of each group member's grade and bonus points if the group's average increases or is above a certain score.

Reasons for opposing group grades include the following (Kagan 1995): 1) Two students can do equally well but receive different grades because their group mates performed differently. 2) Parents, university admissions offices, and employers have more difficulty interpreting grades because they do not know how much of the grade was based on the student's own work and how much was based on their group mates' work. 3) Group grading may demotivate students by blurring the link between student effort and grades, thereby violating the key cooperative learning principle of individual accountability. With group grades, students may be encouraged to freeload, knowing that their group mates' efforts can raise their grade. By the same token, normally hardworking students may feel less inclined to try hard, knowing that their best efforts may be pulled down by a freeloading group mate. 4) Group grading is a key reason for opposition to cooperative learning among parents and others, and could potentially result in legal problems for teachers and schools.

Kagan (1995) recommended a number of alternatives to group grading as a means of motivating students to study hard and to help others: 1) Use content that is motivating by itself so that grades will not be needed as a tool to motivate. 2) Provide written feedback, apart from grades, on the work of individual students and of groups. This feedback can come from group mates and other students, in addition to the teacher. 3) Have students establish goals for themselves and, with the help of teachers and peers, assess their own progress toward those goals. 4) Use nongrade rewards, such as recognition in class, newsletters, and notes from teachers. 5) Give separate grades on the use of collaborative skills.

POSITIVE ROLE INTERDEPENDENCE

Each group member has a role to play in helping the group achieve its goals. Roles include *facilitator* (coordinating the group's work), *observer* of collaborative skills (checking if group members are using a particular collaborative skill deemed important to the group's interaction), *scribe* (recording what the group has accomplished), *keyboarder* (entering the group's decisions into a computer), *timekeeper* (helping the group stick to deadlines so they stay on schedule with other groups), and *reporter* (telling others about the group's work). Roles should rotate so that each student has opportunities to develop in a well-rounded way. Thus, care should be taken so that lower proficiency students do not always have nonacademic roles, such as collecting markers and scissors for a group project.

POSITIVE RESOURCE INTERDEPENDENCE

Each group member has only one portion of the information or equipment that the group requires to do the activity. Jigsaw is a good example of an activity in which each student holds unique information and must share it with group mates for the group to succeed. In Jigsaw, the information is usually given to each student by the teacher. However, information can also come from student research, as when each member researches a different aspect of a topic, or from their own experiences and opinions, as when students survey each other about how much electricity they use each day or about their favorite movie star. Dividing equipment among students also encourages positive interdependence. For example, if students are at a pond collecting data for a biology project, one can have the camera, another can hold a notebook, and a third can use testing instruments to measure the water quality.

POSITIVE IDENTITY INTERDEPENDENCE

Group unity is heightened when group members develop a group identity. This same concept is used by countries, sports teams, and schools to promote solidarity. For instance, students can invent a group name, create a group motto, write a group song or poem, or draw a group flag.

POSITIVE FANTASY INTERDEPENDENCE

Group members imagine that they are different people and / or in a different time or place. For instance, students preparing to study biology in a second language can pretend to be Charles Darwin and his imaginary team of colleagues on the Galapagos Islands in the nineteenth century. Role-playing situations (Ladousse 1987), games (Omaggio 1982), and simulations (Crookall & Oxford 1990) are popular means of encouraging fantasy interdependence in the second language classroom.

POSITIVE OUTSIDE CHALLENGE INTERDEPENDENCE

Group members compete against other groups, just as basketball teams compete against other teams or against a target or just as swimmers try to improve their best times. An example of competing against other groups would be if there was a prize for the group with the greatest improvement over their past average on a weekly quiz. As seen in the example of the swimmers, an outside challenge does not have to involve other people. Groups can try to beat their own past best total score, the average of last year's class, or some other target created by the students and teacher. Additionally, groups could try to defeat a problem, for example, drink containers being thrown away rather than sent for recycling.

How are students encouraged to feel individually accountable for their own learning and that of their group mates?

For groups to succeed, every member must feel a responsibility to learn and participate in the group, and students must demonstrate their learning. An oft-heard complaint about using groups is that some students will try to get a free ride, to leave everything to others, or, alternatively, that one or more group members will try to do everything, not allowing others to participate and learn. Many ideas for encouraging individual accountability can be found in the cooperative learning literature. (Note that some of these overlap with ideas for encouraging positive interdependence.) 1) Use tasks and topics that are so motivating that all group members will want to participate and learn. 2) Have designated, rotating roles for each member to play. 3) Have unique information or equipment for each member. 4) Start individual assessment after students have had time to collaborate. 5) Call upon group members at random to give their group's answer and to explain it. 6) Each group member takes primary responsibility for one part or aspect of the group's work. For example, if the group is writing a research report, one person writes the first draft of the literature review, another does the methodology, and another the results and discussion section. 7) Activities are structured to promote equal participation. An example of structuring for equal participation is the cooperative learning technique RoundTable (Kagan & Kagan 1998). In this activity, each group member has one piece of paper. Each writes an idea, paragraph, etc., on the group's topic and then passes her or his paper to another group member who reads it and comments on the idea, continuing the story. The spoken version of RoundTable is RoundRobin, in which each member speaks, one at a time, going around the group.

Another point to bear in mind is that although the concepts discussed thus far are primarily applied to small groups of students, positive interdependence, individual accountability, and other cooperative learning concepts can be applied to a whole-class setting or to an entire school as well. Indeed, they apply at the workplace, in the family, and anywhere else people come together. Thus, although this takes us beyond the scope of this book (but see Johnson & Johnson 1997; Sapon-Shevin & Schniedewind 1991), the ideas underlying cooperative learning have a great deal of relevance in many situations of life.

Teacher collaboration

The successful use of cooperative learning depends not just on what happens within the four walls of the classroom. What goes on outside in the rest of the school, as well as beyond the school grounds, powerfully affects our ability to facilitate student-student interaction.

Cooperation provides benefits not only for students but for teachers as well (Cooper & Boyd 1994; Edge 1992; Nor 1997). Teacher-teacher collaboration offers psychological support, the possibility of action research, new ideas, greater power, enhanced motivation, and a reduced workload. When students know that their teachers are working together, students are supplied with a model of collaboration in action. In this way, when teachers ask students to work together, it is not a case of "Do as I say, not as I do." Also, the use of cooperative learning in preservice and in-service courses is a means of helping teachers experience it from the student perspective (Ghaith & Shaaban 1995b; Hughes Wilhelm 1997). Furthermore, research on change in education suggests that change, such as the trend toward the use of cooperative learning, can only be sustained when teams of teachers take part (Fullan, Bennett & Rolheiser-Bennett 1990).

A key to ongoing teacher-teacher collaboration lies in administrative support (Johnson & Johnson 1994a). Administrators need to help establish a culture of cooperation throughout the school. Such a culture encourages teachers to work with one another and to make cooperative learning a regular part of their teaching rather than viewing it as a way that lazy teachers escape their real job: imparting knowledge to neat rows of quiet students. In an interview in *Educational Leadership* (Brandt 1987: 11) David Johnson said:

> If teachers spend five to seven hours a day advocating a competitive, individualistic approach – telling students, "Do your own work, don't talk to your neighbor, don't share, don't help, don't care about each other; just try to be better," those are the values the teachers are going to have in their relationships with colleagues and their administrators. On the other hand, if teachers spend five to seven hours a day saying, "Help each other. Share, work together, discuss the material, explain," and make it clear that "you're responsible not only for your own learning but for the learning of your peers" – if they promote cooperation among students – they will look at their colleagues as potential cooperators.

How can teachers work together to implement cooperative learning?

Some teachers attend workshops or courses on cooperative learning and go away enthused, but months or even years later, they still are not implementing it regularly. One reason they give is that it takes too much time to prepare. In part, this problem can be overcome with time, because as teachers become more familiar with various cooperative learning techniques, they more quickly know which ones are appropriate to which situations, and they and their students are more adept at figuring out what needs to take place for groups to swing into action (as attested in the narrative chapters to follow). Another way to overcome the planning problem is via teacher-teacher collaboration. Teachers can collaborate on cooperative learning implementation in many ways. For example, teachers who teach the same or similar classes can plan lessons together that utilize cooperative learning and can create and share materials to use in those lessons (Bailey, Dale & Squire 1992). Even teachers with very different classes but similar students can meet to discuss using the same technique or focus on the same collaborative skill. In addition, teachers from different subject areas can collaborate on integrated lessons. Projects especially lend themselves to this (Kagan & Kagan 1998). Finally, if schedules permit (an infrequent luxury), teachers can not only plan lessons together but actually be in the same classroom teaching together (Shannon & Meath-Lang 1992).

*How can teachers collaborate to learn more about
cooperative learning, and how can they share their
knowledge with others?*

Teachers who already feel committed to using cooperative learning can help
each other learn more and can share with colleagues in several ways. For
example, teachers can observe each other's classes and provide feedback
(this also can be done as part of action research projects as well). Additionally, those experienced with cooperative learning can invite teachers who are
less experienced to visit their classes. For instance, at the English department
of one Singapore secondary school, teachers who had been using cooperative learning organized a "cooperative learning week" prior to which they
circulated to colleagues a list of the classes in which they would be using
cooperative learning and the techniques that would be employed. Colleagues
signed up to observe.

Furthermore, teachers who attend courses or workshops, discover useful
ideas in books or on Web sites, or have taught successful cooperative learning lessons can conduct sharing sessions for colleagues. In addition, groups
of teachers can meet regularly to discuss implementation, and finally, teachers can share with educators beyond their school or district via conference
presentations, Listservs, and journal articles, for example. (The narrative
chapters to follow illustrate many of these forms of collaboration.)

However, some colleagues may be unreceptive to cooperative learning
due at least in part to their beliefs about education. Educators' beliefs affect
their attitudes toward curricular innovations generally (Richards & Lockhart
1994), as well as in the specific case of cooperative learning (Johnson &
Johnson 1994c; Rich 1990). For instance, Rich (1990) believed that two
aspects of teachers' belief systems affect their willingness to use cooperative
learning. The first relates to beliefs about how learning occurs. Does learning
take place by teachers transmitting knowledge to students in a way similar
to what occurs when water is poured from a pitcher (the teacher) into a glass
(the student)? Or, as was discussed in the Introduction, does learning take
place by learners constructing their own knowledge? One metaphor used
to illustrate this latter view is that of teacher as gardener helping the plants
(the students) to grow. The other aspect concerns whether teachers focus
solely on building students' academic knowledge or whether they also feel
that part of their job is to aid students' social and personal development.
Teachers with the latter view would value cooperative learning as a means
of helping students learn to collaborate.

Cuban (1987: 26) noted, "Teacher-centered instruction has been a creative response by teachers [to enable them] to cope with workplace

conditions, conflicting expectations, and structural arrangements over which they had little influence." Thus, it is important to take teachers' views into account. Also, if we reflect on the teachers in our own past, we may easily be able to recall some very good teachers who used an exclusively teacher-fronted approach. The point is that we need to understand why others may resist using cooperative learning and to see this strategy as a means of supplementing the good teaching practices they already utilize.

Conclusion

The purpose of this and the preceding chapters has been to lay a foundation for the second half of the book: the narratives of six second language classrooms. Chapters 1 and 2 looked at the question of *why* teachers use cooperative learning. The present chapter dealt with questions of *how* cooperative learning is used. Also, in addition to the works cited in Part I, many books written specifically on second language teaching offer useful advice as well (for example, Hadfield 1992; High 1993; Nolasco & Arthur 1988).

PART II:
TEACHER NARRATIVES

Introduction

The second part of this book consists of six narrative chapters that describe the uses of collaborative learning in particular second language classrooms around the world. It can be divided into three pairs of two chapters each based on the educational level of the students. The first two chapters, Chapters 4 and 5, deal with elementary / primary school classrooms; Chapters 6 and 7 address secondary school classrooms; and the final two chapters, Chapters 8 and 9, are concerned with postsecondary / tertiary classrooms.

Cooperative learning at elementary / primary schools

Students at the elementary school level have special needs that their teachers must address. These students are less familiar with schooling and with society in general. Thus, socialization is often an accepted aspect of teaching at this level. In the case of cooperative learning, socialization involves the teaching of how to work with others and explicit attention to fostering prosocial skills among students. Although these matters are addressed in all six chapters in this second part of this book, they receive particular attention in Chapters 4 and 5. One area of contrast between the two chapters lies in the fact that Chapter 4 illustrates a sociocultural approach to teaching, whereas Chapter 5 depicts a perspective on teaching that uses positive reinforcement via group contingencies as a key element.

CHAPTER 4

In this chapter, DaSilva Iddings and McCafferty describe the use of cooperative learning in DaSilva Idding's mainstream (English- and Spanish-speaking students) kindergarten class in the southwestern United States. The chapter emphasizes the laying of the groundwork for successful group activities by promoting an environment based on student-centered learning. This groundwork includes building ties with students' families and involving them in the learning process, increasing students' confidence and skills in various literacy tasks, and crafting a spirit of community within the classroom by such means as recognizing and labeling specific episodes of caring, sharing, taking turns, encouraging, and other social skills.

Particular attention is paid to forming groups and giving clear step-by-step instructions so that students are able to collaborate successfully. These groups worked on a variety of activities involving a full range of language skills. These activities are described in detail, with particular attention paid to students' language output, including excerpts from transcripts of group interaction. The teacher's role of providing scaffolded assistance to students as they worked together is also illustrated.

CHAPTER 5

In Chapter 5, Ghaith and Kawtharani discuss how, with help from Ghaith, Kawtharani and his fellow teachers used cooperative learning to teach English to primary school students in Lebanon. The chapter begins by describing how cooperative learning was introduced to Lebanon in the early 1990s, a time when the country was emerging from a civil war, as part of a larger effort to promote a communicative, integrated skills approach to language teaching and to address noncognitive goals in order to create a culture of harmony, empathy, and cooperation among students.

The authors provide details and examples of how they developed materials for and implemented two well-known cooperative learning techniques: Student Teams-Achievement Divisions (STAD) and Jigsaw II. Recall from Chapter 1 that STAD promotes positive interdependence via the use of team recognition based on how group members perform on quizzes for which they had studied together. STAD also fosters individual accountability based on each student taking the quizzes and receiving grades determined solely by his or her own scores. As described in the chapter, team recognition includes certificates or other forms of praise and acknowledgment for teams that reach or exceed a set standard. Jigsaw II encourages positive interdependence because each group member becomes the group's only expert on a particular text. In addition, recognition is awarded to groups based on individual quizzes students take on all the texts. Individual accountability is promoted because students need to teach their texts to their group members and take the quizzes individually and receive grades determined solely by their own quiz scores.

The authors also describe a number of class-building and team-building language activities used with the primary school students. Class-building activities are designed to foster a relaxed, trusting atmosphere among classmates, while team-building activities are designed to do the same within individual groups. Such class-building and team-building activities lay an important foundation for successful collaboration within and between groups.

Cooperative learning at secondary schools

By the time students reach the secondary school level, they are generally seen as being capable of greater independence. At this age, peers become even more important in their lives. The two chapters in this subsection illustrate the use of cooperative learning with such students. Chapters 6 and 7 are similar in that in both cases the authors provide detailed descriptions of the cooperative learning techniques they used and their reasons for using the techniques. Also, both chapters describe ways in which fellow teachers collaborated to promote cooperative learning.

CHAPTER 6

In Chapter 6, by Jones and Taylor, one aspect that stands out is that many of the cooperative learning techniques described were developed by the authors themselves. This chapter is also unique in that it is the only one that describes the teaching of a language other than English (i.e., French) as taught to native English speakers in Canada. Many of the cooperative learning techniques that Jones and Taylor depict involve the use of higher-order thinking skills, such as generating ideas and classification. For instance, in one technique, students create and describe an imaginary friend, and in another they form concepts based on the categorizing of exemplars from a data set. Another means by which Jones and Taylor promote thinking skills is via the use of graphic organizers such as mindmaps.

Three other points from the chapter deserve highlighting: 1) While they were learning about cooperative learning themselves, Jones and Taylor participated in Cooperative Learning Tuesdays, in which teachers at their school would meet to discuss their experiences in the classroom using this approach. 2) Rather than groups always reporting to the teacher and the whole class, sometimes they would share only with other groups. 3) Because cooperative learning involves students in speaking and listening to one another, it is ideal for integrated skills activities. The authors illustrate such activities.

CHAPTER 7

In Chapter 7, Wee and Jacobs discuss the use of cooperative learning with secondary school students in Singapore. The chapter begins by describing

Wee's early use of groups. Next the chapter explains how she dealt with some of the details of organizing student-student interaction: seating arrangement, group size, group composition, getting students' attention when they are working in groups, and giving directions. Then Wee and Jacobs describe a step-by-step procedure for the explicit teaching of collaborative skills.

The chapter includes descriptions of how cooperative learning was used to teach various language skills. For instance, cooperative learning was combined with the phases of the process approach to writing. Accounts are given of how students worked together to generate ideas, how they used guidelines to give peer feedback, and how computers added a new venue for collaboration on writing. Reading instruction and cooperative learning is also considered. For instance, the authors describe how Wee encouraged students to ask and answer higher-order thinking questions.

Positive interdependence is a key component of cooperative learning. One way Wee promoted this feeling of one-for-all and all-for-one within a group or class was to encourage students to unite to meet a shared challenge. In the case of Wee's students, the challenge was not a person or persons but an external exam that students were to take near the end of the school year.

Finally, the chapter presents some of Wee's experiences as head of her school's English Department in attempting to persuade colleagues to use cooperative learning. Among the methods she tried were sharing of work load, such as joint lesson planning, and observing each other's classes.

Cooperative learning at the postsecondary / tertiary level

Teaching students at the postsecondary level offers its own set of advantages and challenges. Whereas students have greater cognitive skills and knowledge, including greater familiarity with schooling, they also tend to have fixed views of student and teacher roles. In response, teachers need to carefully explain their rationale for promoting student-student interaction. This inflexibility in student attitudes may problematize the use of unconventional methods, such as those of collaborative learning.

Returning to the positive side of the ledger, tertiary level students are often most ready for independent work, such as projects. Both the chapters in this subsection describe project work. Chapter 8 illustrates global issues projects in which students worked in groups and then presented to the class, while Chapter 9 narrates how a university ESL class worked in groups to prepare performances and exhibits for the benefit of preschool students. Additionally, both authors devote attention to how their personal philosophies of education have developed and how these shape their use of cooperative learning.

CHAPTER 8

In Chapter 8, Joritz-Nakagawa explains how she used cooperative learning in a year-long reading course at a university in Japan. During the year, students worked in groups to do two projects, each of which involved global issues. Joritz-Nakagawa illustrates how the first project helped students develop their language and collaborative skills in preparation for greater independence on the second project.

The author explains her evolution as a cooperative learning practitioner. She demonstrates, as she gained experience, how her use of cooperative techniques expanded and how the planning of such lessons became easier and less time-consuming. Part of what Joritz-Nakagawa learned was the need to do class-building and team-building activities in order to build a classroom environment in which students felt safe and were willing to take risks. (There is conscious attention to creating such an atmosphere running through all the narrative chapters.)

Attention to group functioning was not something that the author did just the first couple of weeks of the course. Instead, she monitored how groups were working. For example, she observed whether the participation of group members was equal via observations, journals, and meetings with groups. However, like the other authors, Joritz-Nakagawa's use of cooperative learning did not mean that she stopped being a language teacher and devoted herself exclusively to the social life of the classroom. Indeed, she details approaches she used so that students became more proficient in the language as they collaborated.

Grading is a controversial issue when group activities are used. Joritz-Nakagawa presents the carefully thought-out system she used. This involved individual and group components, as well as teacher and peer assessment. The chapter also discusses how this system worked with students who lacked motivation.

CHAPTER 9

In Chapter 9, Wilhelm describes her use of collaborative learning with a class of high-beginner ESL students from a variety of countries who were studying at a midwestern U.S. university. A unique aspect of this chapter is the students' participation in authorship events in which they create something of their own for an audience beyond the teacher and the other class members. In this particular case, what was created were Story Theater presentations and exhibitions in the form of learning stations for preschoolers.

For the purposes of describing the course she taught, Wilhelm divides it into three phases, with her role as teacher changing with each phase. The first phase featured a good deal of teacher-centered instruction and focused on enhancing language skills, clarifying course objectives and procedures, and crafting a cooperative climate. In the second phase, Wilhelm's role shifted toward becoming a facilitator as students began their projects. In the final phase, the teacher's role again shifted, this time to that of constructive critic, coparticipant, and encourager. During this phase, students presented their projects, reflected on the course, and celebrated their accomplishments.

In Chapter 7, Wee was both teacher and department chair. In Chapter 9, Wilhelm was also both a teacher and an administrator. Like Wee, she used her role as administrator to promote collaboration among teachers. This took such forms as mentor teachers coaching others on the use of a cooperative approach, weekly seminars for novice teachers to this perspective, and perhaps most important, making sure that teachers had time to collaborate on curriculum design and to discuss their teaching.

In this part of the book, many innovative approaches to second language instruction are detailed and connections to second language learning, particularly from an interactive perspective, are drawn as well. Also, as these chapters are narratives of the teachers' experiences with collaborative approaches, they represent a valuable collection of insights into how to adapt cooperative practices to second language classrooms; what considerations need to be in place before implementing these approaches; how cooperative learning works with students in other cultures; how group and individual efforts can be evaluated; and how teachers can structure groups and activities to produce effective interactions among group members, among other things. Also, each of the chapters entails a good deal of reflection concerning what the teachers learned about themselves as teachers and about their students, and the art of second language teaching through making cooperative learning a part of their practice.

Also, we want to bring attention to the tasks and discussion points following each of the six chapters in this section. We hope that they will stimulate greater understanding of what we consider important aspects of the chapters. We also want to point out that there is a Conclusion to the book, in which DaSilva Iddings focuses on some of its significant offerings, and there is an Appendix that provides step-by-step instructions for many of the cooperative learning activities found in the narrative chapters.

4 Cooperative learning in a multilingual kindergarten

Ana Christina DaSilva Iddings and Steven G. McCafferty

Background

This chapter describes cooperative interactions in my (Chris's) half-day kindergarten class in a public school located in a metropolitan area in the southwestern United States. The school operated on a year-round schedule with students provided breaks throughout the year. As the surrounding community changed over time, staff members were faced with the challenge of meeting the needs of second language speakers of English while maintaining the inclusion of all students in heterogeneously grouped classrooms. In this particular classroom there were 30 students, all of whom were about 5 years old. Native speakers and second language (L2) learners were present in relatively equal proportions (14 students whose primary language was Spanish, and 16 who were monolingual speakers of English). There are both positive and negative consequences that result from this multilingual situation. One of the positive consequences is that students have opportunities to recognize the importance of working together toward cooperative goals despite differences in first languages and cultural backgrounds.

This chapter is specifically concerned with forms of cooperative interactions between second language learners and native speakers of English in an English-dominant classroom. The focus is on how students were developing English as they set out to do the tasks that were presented in class. That is, emphasis was placed on the students' activities or processes while performing the tasks I designed, and not so much on the product.

On several occasions during the course of one semester, as the students carried out the tasks, another teacher videotaped them. Approximately eight hours of video were recorded and examined as part of my doctoral research project for which Steve served as supervisor. As a result of these recordings, I am able to present the cooperative activities in this narrative accompanied by examples of student discourse, which illustrate the effectiveness of cooperative interactions in relation to L2 learners.

The underlying assumptions that guide my teaching practices are derived from sociocultural theory (see Chapters 1 and 2) – from the view of learning that knowledge is coconstructed, and from the concept of mutuality, which can be described as the different "selves" that arise depending on the contexts of a given interaction. Overall, I take the position that a language-integrated classroom can be successful in meeting the needs of L2 learners, provided second language learners are well supported by adult mediators, by more advanced peers, and by the kinds of instructional approaches and curricular adaptations that will be suggested herein.

The school and community

The school I worked at was one in which brightly painted walls and numerous flowerbeds created an inviting appearance. There were no fences; the grounds were well kept and adjacent to a public park, which had been renovated around the time of the project. The school also had undergone renovation, and a new building was constructed to accommodate the ever-increasing student population. There were brand-new computer labs and clean bathrooms. The hallways were filled with student artwork. The classrooms were loud, and generally, the children seemed to be engaged and happy. The faculty was friendly and cohesive. Administrative issues were handled through a site-based governance model of school management, which included the participation of staff, faculty, parents, and students, as well as members of the community, in the decision-making process.

The community surrounding the school was undergoing rapid transformation. A stable, mostly white, middle-class neighborhood was becoming increasingly diverse as immigrant families settled in. Small Mexican restaurants and Latino food markets had begun to make their way into the neighborhood. The long-time residents were for the most part not pleased with the changes, and they often complained that the neighborhood was losing its character. Many of them had put their houses up for sale, and others had already moved away.

Likewise, the school was not well prepared for the changes brought on by its increasingly diverse population. Its faculty members were almost all white and had little experience with diversity. Many of the teachers encountered frustration in dealing with cross-cultural differences. Some resented having to make adaptations to the curriculum to accommodate diversity in the classroom, although only some admitted that they didn't have the training or the knowledge to be able to meet the needs of language minority students. Issues of poverty, parenting styles, biculturalism, and language learning were largely misunderstood by the faculty and the community. However, in view of the rapidly growing, diverse population, through the site-based governance decision-making process, it was decided that address-ing the educational needs of second language students should be a priority for the school. How this was done will be described in the next section.

School programs

My school was representative of schools in the southwestern United States and across the country in its struggle to keep up with population shifts. During my six years at the school, there were numerous attempts to address language minority issues, but little progress was really made. These efforts failed largely because the school lacked specialized faculty and training ses-sions for classroom teachers. Only during the last year I was there did we get an allocation for an English Language Learners' Facilitator, or ELLF. However, due to the many obligations delineated in the job description for this specialist (such as placement testing), instructional decisions concern-ing how best to meet the needs of second language students still fell upon the classroom teacher. Good intentions and lack of preparation generated much confusion and frustration on the part of both the language minority students and the teachers. Newly arrived immigrant students do not quite understand how U.S. schools work. These students often have different expectations than their teachers, a different sense of pace, and different views regarding authority figures. For example, Latino children often confuse the friendli-ness of teachers with permissiveness. Teachers, on the other hand, frequently characterize Latino students as uninterested, irresponsible, and even lazy.

Parent involvement also becomes an area of difficulty for teachers who do not feel they can adequately communicate with the parents of their lan-guage minority children. There is a stereotype among some teachers that parents of second language learners are uninvolved in their children's edu-cation, that these parents view achievement as unimportant, and that this attitude is the primary cause of the children's lack of academic responsibil-ity. However, research in this area indicates that parents of English-learning students perceive school as an essential vehicle for obtaining successful positions in society (Delgado-Gaitan 1994; Heath 1986; Lewis 1988).

This disparity between teachers' perceptions and research findings may be seeded in sociocultural issues. In the Latino culture, for example, cooper-ative behaviors are valued above competitive ones. This characteristic may be detrimental to second language learners because measures of achieve-ment are often competitive in nature. Similarly, notions of responsibility may be culturally conflicting. Social responsibilities (e.g., caring for younger siblings, cooking for the family, cleaning the house) often take priority over academic responsibilities (e.g., homework and developing study habits). Furthermore, the perceived lack of involvement on the part of parents of second language students may stem from the fact that they trust that the American educational system will provide their children with the necessary tools to ensure them a hopeful future. Also, in many instances, parents of second language learners stay away from schools because they feel that they do not have the right to a voice; language and cultural differences can constitute a great barrier.

In view of all these obstacles, language minority children were often not adequately served. In many classrooms, little or no accommodations were made in the delivery of instruction or in the curriculum itself. Instead, teachers often directed their classes at the proficiency levels of the average mainstream students.

Classroom practices

At the elementary school, practices greatly differed across classrooms. There was no overarching philosophy or any particular instructional model that was prevalent at the school. For the most part, teachers adhered to their own individual styles. For example, in many classrooms a lot of group work went on, but in others teachers still relied solely on whole-class instruction. Generally, as with most elementary schools, the curriculum focused on developing literacy skills; students who were not progressing with their literacy in accordance with teacher expectations were sent to participate in a reading recovery program based on Clay's (1985) research on strategies for preventing reading failure at the emergent level. This program is designed to increase children's perceptual awareness of phonological, semantic, syntactic, and pragmatic aspects of the written language through the use of leveled picture books. Activities such as picture description, choral reading, and phonics skills lessons through using story books, as well as strategies to increase student self-monitoring and reading for meaning and fluency, are modeled by an adult mediator and practiced by the students. Even though language minority students seemed to profit from this approach, comprehension skills continued to lag behind decoding skills, perhaps because the books used for reading instruction usually did not follow a typical narrative structure, and many of them used contrived vocabulary.

In all classrooms, the language of instruction was English. Teachers often paired the more linguistically advanced non-English-background students with those who were at beginning levels of learning English so that the former could interpret the teacher's explanations for the latter. Even though it was beneficial for these children to be paired up, problems remained. First, teachers had to assume that the more advanced peer had understood the explanations enough to convey them to the other student in their native language. Second, often more advanced English learners did not have the vocabulary in their native language to be able to convey such concepts – translating is not a simple task. Third, more advanced peers sometimes resented having to translate as they felt put upon, having to do something that other students did not. Moreover, the more advanced students lost part of the teacher's explanations because they were busy translating when the teacher was talking. So, the dilemma of how to provide equal access to education for language minority students at the school remained largely unresolved.

My practice

Within a variety of collaborative activities involving small-group and whole-class formats, I aimed to provide each student with many ways to be an active participant and valuable contributor. It is through dialog and through purposeful interactions that knowledge becomes meaningful, relevant, and interesting. At each step, my goal was to make all classroom-learning activities accessible to all students by creating an inviting social-emotional environment in which students were able to continuously build confidence in their abilities and grow from their experiences. Specific episodes of caring, sharing, taking turns, encouraging, and other social skills were frequently recognized and labeled as they surfaced within our interactions as we continually aspired to attain a deepening interpersonal sensitivity and understanding.

Once this climate had been established, collaboration was more apt to happen. In kindergarten, particularly, many activities focus on the integration and development of oral language, listening, prereading, and prewriting skills. All of these activities were structured so that they promoted interdependence, shared leadership, and individual accountability. Individual differences were accommodated, and in the case of students whose first language was one other than English, an effort was made to place them in a group with at least one other student from the same language and cultural background so as to offer linguistic / cultural support. I tried to avoid the problem of burdening the more capable students with the task of always translating to less proficient students by not asking the students to translate, but rather by allowing spontaneous code switching while working together. Code switching involves using different languages interchangeably in such a way as to form a hybrid language. Also, the use of visual aids, concrete objects, and direct experiences provided access to instructional purposes and to the language that conveyed them.

At the heart of all learning tasks that I proposed to my students was an emphasis on arousing curiosity so that each day they came up with new questions and new ideas. Perhaps one of the most important lessons I gained in my experience was the fact that all children, as they arrive at school for the very first time, come with strong cultural and personal histories already in place. These must be respected and can be utilized as a powerful resource, therefore, special care was given to make instruction meaningful to these students by proposing activities that in some way reflected their experience, such as Sam's Diary and Group Dialoging, described later in the chapter. Personal agency / choice is an important element in trying to engage students in lessons; therefore, I tried to provide ample opportunities for students to choose among activities and select those that they found interesting and meaningful.

My role as a teacher was to guide students to complete their tasks, to elaborate on their thoughts, and to help them further their discourse by asking probing questions. The highly interactive nature of my kindergarten class allowed us to come to know each other well beyond the superficial level of just being in the same class. Another critical part of what I did was to assess instructional success.

For assessment, I used a variety of measures, emphasizing day-to-day observation of students' progress and the development of portfolios to document growth over time in all academic areas. Also, I recorded, with proper permission, videotapes of the students performing tasks I had proposed. The analysis of these tapes allowed me to observe what actually took place as the students performed the tasks, and it provided me with significant insights into the students' cognitive and linguistic processes (discussed later in this chapter). Additionally, as I assessed my students' progress, I had the opportunity to reflect upon and evaluate my own instruction in relation to particular students. In so doing, I became both a teacher-researcher and a critical self-observer. Through my action research in the classroom, I gained an increased awareness of student needs, and I was able to connect particular instructional methods with student learning. In the course of this process, I often found that I had to question my assumptions or perhaps try doing things a little differently. On a larger scale, I found that these reflections also led to transformations – that I expanded my knowledge and skills as a teacher.

Groundwork for cooperative interaction

Perhaps the most difficult part of implementing cooperative learning is setting the stage. In the first weeks of kindergarten, I believe it is important to establish a climate of collaboration and to build a cohesive whole-class identity within the classroom. In this way, we can all become enriched by each other's presence, and we can come to envision ourselves as part of a community of learners. Particular attention has to be paid to the development of collaborative skills, which enable cooperative behaviors in the classroom as children broaden their social circles and embrace a larger "we." Skills such as sharing, taking turns, and providing encouragement are instituted as an integral part of the classroom climate through constant modeling and through verbal identification and recognition of these behaviors. For example, when one student stopped to listen to another, I usually recognized it aloud by saying either to the group or to the whole class (depending on the situation), "Ana stopped talking because John has the turn now – she *is taking turns.*" In this way, cooperative behaviors became embedded in the language used in the classroom, and therefore discursively constructed rather than imposed on the children as just a series of specific lessons.

It was only after several weeks, when the class began to exhibit more collaborative behaviors and cohesiveness, that groups were formed. I took the initiative to form the groups myself to ensure that factors such as proficiency level, collaborative and behavioral skills, gender, cultural background, race, first language, and socioeconomic status were mixed within each group. However, as participation in some activities was subject to student choice, groups occasionally got formed on the basis of students' mutual interests. For example, there were some small-group activities that had become children's favorites and thus became established at permanent *centers*, which children could choose to go to. These included the sand table center, where students filled different-shaped containers and then compared the amount of sand in each of the containers, and the paint-a-portrait center, where the students painted each other's portrait and then compared physical features.

Classroom structure

As I strove to create an environment in which cooperative interactions underlay most of the activities that I proposed to my students, I set up my classroom with objects and materials that would stimulate awareness of the students' own interdependence. Handmade quilts made by the families of our class community hung from the walls, reminding us that we were all a part of a whole. I also covered entire walls with dry-erase board panels on which children could freely write messages or draw pictures to each other; flannel boards on which they could tell and retell stories to each other using cloth puppets derived from the books used in class; and peg-boards where building materials such as Lincoln Logs™, Lego®, and small blocks hung in bags within the children's reach. Also, a painting area, a science exploration station, and numerous learning centers were set up in the classroom to be visited daily by students working in pairs or triads. Due to all of the autonomous activity centered around the activities described above, there was hardly ever silence in the classroom. Instead, one would hear children verbalizing their thoughts as they worked cooperatively to make sense of the proposed tasks, to negotiate ways to approach them, and to offer each other direction.

Throughout the school year, parents and / or people from the community often actively participated in our classroom. The bilingual adults served not only as translators but also as group facilitators. These adults helped create equal chances at participation among students in groups that included L2 learners by providing guidance and feedback and by monitoring turn-taking behaviors. This ensured that the L2 students had equal opportunities to express themselves. With the help of these facilitators, children's individual needs were addressed and their strengths were often recognized. By establishing true alliances between home and school, we became unified and supported in our goals to promote student achievement and to foster growth.

I have found through my experience that a highly interactive, cooperative classroom environment, with its focus on the development of individual accountability through interdependency, provides an excellent context for L2 development. For example, in one activity in which the students draw the sequence of events involved in the growth of a plant, each student draws one of the growing stages and then places it in order next to others on a board. Through their conversations about how to place the pieces that they draw (i.e., what the correct sequence is) students can arrive at a shared understanding. Such cooperative activities are generally highly contingent on verbal interaction; they encourage students to express themselves naturalistically through the use of many different language functions, such as suggesting, inferring, hypothesizing, generalizing, and disagreeing. This approach is in direct contrast to what happens in more traditional, teacher-directed classrooms, in which comparatively little interaction takes place.

Managing cooperative groups

Most of the groups in this kindergarten class were small. I rarely formed groups of more than four students. Larger groups tend to be too distracting for students at that age. Also, small groups better benefit L2 students by increasing their opportunities for communicative interaction.

To identify cooperative groups, I used a pocket chart hung on the wall and colored index cards with the name of each student. Different colors indicated the different groups. At the top of the chart, I had a pictorial representation of the activity assigned to each group so that the students could identify their tasks. In the beginning of the year, I also placed colored dots (corresponding to the group color) on children's shirts to help them find their group mates. For activities based on mutual interest, for which I did not assign groups, the students had wooden tongue depressors with their respective names written on them, which they placed inside cups with taped pictures representing the different activities. No more than four tongue depressors were allowed inside a cup; therefore, no more than four individuals could participate in a given activity.

As kindergarten students need clear, step-by-step directions, in addition to explaining orally, I made up task cards with pictorial clues that helped the children to keep track of the directions and sequencing of steps. Also, along with some students, I modeled the activity and then had other students demonstrate a sample activity before I gave the whole class a chance to try it themselves. During the activities, my role and the role of the other adult facilitators in the room (if there were any) was to scaffold the groups by asking probing questions, by elaborating on students' thoughts, and by helping students to further their discourse.

In the following section, I provide a description of the oral language, reading, listening, and writing activities regularly used in my class. Excerpts from actual interactions recorded in the classroom are also provided to illustrate how these activities aided language gains. Two of the students who participated in the interactions depicted spoke Spanish as their first language, and even though they were both classified as beginning students, their level of English proficiency differed. Nancy was more proficient than Leticia. The third participant, Blake, was an English-speaking monolingual boy who had been exposed to Spanish through his grandparents, who came from Spain and lived in the same household.

Speaking

Shared Story Box

For this activity, I read a story familiar to the students and then asked them to use different objects contained in a box to retell the story. As the students retold the story, they placed the objects in the box in the same sequence as revealed in the story.

The following example illustrates the interaction among Nancy, Leticia, and Blake as they endeavored to retell the story of *The Very Hungry Caterpillar* by Eric Carle, using puppets and other realia. The students started by jointly sorting pieces of fruit referred to in the story, and then, while Blake looked at the book for support in narrating the story, Leticia placed the pieces of fruit inside the box. Nancy used the caterpillar puppet to illustrate its metamorphosis into a butterfly:

1. Leticia (NNS): Esa va con ésta (that one goes with this one).
2. Blake (NS): The worm came out. He ate one apple. He ate two pears.
3. Nancy (NNS): Two pears.
4. Blake: Three plums, he ate . . .
5. All: Four strawberries, five oranges.
6. Blake: One pickle.
7. Nancy: What's this? (holding a plastic piece of salami)
8. Blake: Salami.
9. Nancy: Oh! Yeah! Salami.
10. Blake: One lollipop.
11. Leticia: No, the lollipop [is already] inside [the box].
12. Blake: One cupcake, one watermelon, one pizza.
13. Leticia: No, we no have pizza.
14. Nancy: What pizza?
15. Blake: Is this a pie? (pointing to the picture in the book)
16. Leticia: That's a pizza.
17. Nancy: No, we don't have [any] pizza; it's a pie.
18. Blake: Then he had a tummy ache. Then he got fat. Then he was a beautiful butterfly.

In a related activity, I read a familiar story, and then the students, assembled into their cooperative groups, retold the story through dramatization, including the use of puppets, props, and drawings. Focus was placed on vocabulary use and story structure. Later, the groups created a different setting for the story and retold it once again. All groups shared their work with the class, and then the class discussed how the different settings changed the stories. Illustrations in the books, the different context clues, the repetition of a narrative structure, and the interaction with others all greatly contributed to vocabulary gains for the second language students as determined both through my observations and by more formal means of assessment.

Sorting and ranking activities

For ranking and sorting activities, the groups were given a variety of pictures, which they were asked to sort in a logical manner and then to rank order according to a given criterion. The groups were then asked to explain their thinking to the rest of the class. For example, first the students would sort the pictures that were alike according to function. For example, Leticia, Nancy, and Blake would separate pictures of tools from pictures of eating utensils, and then they would rank order both piles according to those used most frequently. This activity seemed more difficult for the beginning English students like Leticia and Nancy than for Blake, but it still generated a lot of discussion. Often, some teacher mediation was necessary for them to complete the task. Even though I used mostly English to mediate, some first-language mediation was necessary for Leticia and Nancy when working together, as they seemed comfortable switching codes to convey their ideas. However, when they had to explain their thinking to Blake they reverted to English.

Group Dialoging

During Group Dialoging, as a whole class, the students sat in a circle on the floor inside the classroom and shared experiences such as events and things that had happened to them, or they talked about people in their immediate communities. After the sharing of the students' personal narratives, we jointly decided on one story to write for our "daily news activity." Once we had written the daily news on the chalkboard, we discussed various conventions of print contained in the stories, such as quotation marks and exclamation marks. This activity served to illustrate relationships between voice and print. Because the stories that we wrote came directly from the students' experiences, there was a clearer connection between written and oral language than with the books we read in class.

Group Dialoging was a whole-class activity that helped prepare students for student-student interaction in small groups. For instance, in order to instill turn-taking skills, we used a wand to stipulate whose turn it was to talk. Whoever held the wand had the turn. The students passed the wand to each other without much guidance from the teacher. The wand also served to reduce anxiety. As the students learned how to take turns, the wand was removed and the conversation became more fluid, and the discourse became more socially constructed.

Universal stories activities

Universal stories are those that are present in many different cultures, such as folktales and fairy tales. These are stories that the students, in many instances, had already heard or read, and thus, they could easily identify the plot. I used these stories to further develop students' understanding of the concepts involved in narrative structure. For instance, in one such activity I read two versions (from different cultures) of a familiar story such as "Cinderella" to the students. They assembled into groups and discussed the differences and similarities between the two versions. Using a Venn diagram and flannel board pieces to characterize the stories, each group placed the respective elements of each story in the diagram (students had the choice of whether to use their books for reference). A bit later on, the groups were asked to use elements of both stories to make up an altogether different version. Then each group shared its story with the class.

This activity is designed to reinforce universal story scripts and to facilitate understanding for second language and other students. By using familiar stories, bilingual students may be able to apply their previous knowledge of the same or similar story in their native language to better comprehend the story and to attain greater understanding of story structure. Vocabulary learning is also enhanced by the transfer from the two versions of the story told by the teacher to the new, student-created versions.

Writing

Sam's Diary

This activity involved a teddy bear (Sam) and a small traveling bag. A different student would take the bear home each day. The bear accompanied the child in her / his activities throughout the day. Parents and child collaborated in writing a journal entry describing the bear's activities with the child. They also drew or took pictures illustrating the entry. The next day, the child brought the bear back to school, and she or he read the journal entry to the other students. In that way, Sam's Diary became a living book that continuously evolved. It provided insights into the daily lives of all the students so that they came to understand, and with the right climate, appreciate, each other's similarities and differences across cultures. Such insights can foster more harmonious interactions when students collaborate in small groups. Also, Sam's Diary allowed for parent-child collaboration on the same product, and it brought a greater awareness of the relationship between voice and print as the students narrated their stories to be written by a caregiver. In the case of caregivers who could not write in English, I usually wrote the story in the diary as the students told the class about their experiences with Sam.

Listening

Listening activities are helpful for improving second language students' receptive vocabulary and also for allowing students to link new information to prior knowledge. In one such activity, I would read a page of a story but not show students the illustration for the page. After they listened attentively in their cooperative groups, they were encouraged to draw a collective picture to illustrate that page. The students then shared their drawings with the class and compared their pictures with the one in the book. Benefits to second language learners included participation in problem-solving interactions as the groups decided what to include in their drawing. Also, drawings offer a tangible representation of what is happening in the story, aiding comprehension of the linguistic representation.

Other activities I used that started with listening included dramatization of a story or poem. For example, I would read a few familiar stories to the class. Then each group was assigned a different story. However, the title of the story was not disclosed to the other groups. Each group was to dramatize the story so that the other groups would be able to guess which story it was. Each group had to discuss strategies that would best convey the title of the story to the rest of the class and cooperatively work out the skit. All members were encouraged to act.

This activity offers students the awareness that nonverbal forms of communication are also a tool to convey meaning and that nonverbal forms differ cross-culturally. Moreover, the nonverbal aspect of the task gives L2 students an opportunity to demonstrate their abilities to make meaning through other communicative channels, often a welcome change from the emphasis on speaking.

In an example of a related activity, I would detach the illustrated pages of a picture book that the students had heard only once before, and give them the pages that illustrated the prepositional phrases (e.g., *over* the haystack, *around* the pond, *across* the yard). Each group would receive the same set of pictures. Students were then asked in their cooperative groups to place the pages in some reasoned order, and to explain their reasons. The excerpt below illustrates how this activity helped prepositional usage for Nancy:

1. Blake (NS): Well, Rosie went for a walk across the yard, over the hill (looking up for approval), over the haystack, through the fence . . .
2. Nancy (NNS): On? . . . Into? . . . the beehive [gesturing under].
3. Blake: No. *Under* the beehive.
4. Nancy: Oh! Yeah! OK! *Under* the beehive.

After each group had arranged the pictures, I would read the story one more time and ask the students to rearrange the pictures according to the sequence of events in the story. This activity is a useful tool in evaluating students' listening and comprehension skills. However, this task can be very demanding for students at low levels of English proficiency, who, even though they are present, may not actively participate in the problem solving. For instance, in the example above, the native speaker (Blake) had a very dominant role and seemed to intimidate the others, a point that will be taken up in the following section.

Further considerations in forming a cooperative environment

From the observations already described, I came to realize the importance of analyzing students' interaction in relation to the complexity of the contexts in which an activity takes place. To discuss collaborative practices, the overall sociocultural dynamics in the classroom need to be noted as elements that contribute to the establishment of a sense of community.

The emphasis on creating a whole-class identity and the implementation of participatory approaches that stress connections between the classroom and the specific communities to which students belong (such as noted in Sam's Diary and Group Dialoging) were instrumental in developing a sense of community within the class. In addition, the daily practice of interactive activities, such as those described in this chapter, contributed to changing exclusionary patterns (often found in more traditional settings) to patterns of collaboration. Also, and of particular importance, active parental involvement had a pronounced effect. Through a variety of organized events and activities (such as literacy nights, class picnics, and parent information nights) we were able to establish relationships that went well beyond the classroom. The collaboration of parents in the classroom helped the children to establish a sense of trust in school and to attain a greater awareness of what was expected of them.

The organization of classroom space also played a key role in the establishment of a collaborative environment. My room was organized so that it fostered free mobility, increasing independence from the teacher, and a sense of responsibility because the students had ample access to each other and pedagogical materials. There were purposely no seating assignments in order to allow flexibility of groups and to encourage students to sit near those with whom they had an affinity. Also, all materials such as crayons and pencils were shared to provide a greater sense of community and to further opportunities for communication. All together, I found that these factors lowered students' anxiety levels and increased autonomy in their behavior.

However, it seems somewhat utopian to try to create an environment in which everyone cooperates with mutual intentions and to an equal degree. There are inescapable asymmetries in interpersonal relationships, especially in situations in which some group members are second language speakers of the dominant language. However, at the same time, such complex webs of interaction provide opportunities for L2 students to negotiate a sense of identity in relation to the group and to occupy a variety of positionings in the community.

Paper Bag Share provides an example. Students are encouraged to place a toy from home inside a paper bag and bring it to school to share with a partner. They take turns drawing what they think is in their partner's bag based on feeling the size and shape of the object. After showing each other their drawings derived from these tactile observations, students are encouraged to share their respective toys with each other. The interaction below between Ana (nonnative speaker of English) and Laura (native speaker of English) shows how Ana positioned herself within the activity as an expert:

1. Laura (NS): What are you making [drawing]?
2. Ana (NNS): airplane (gesturing: vroom, vroom).
3. Laura: It doesn't look like an airplane (sitting down on the chair).
4. Ana: I [was] sitted there.
5. Laura: You don't know everything.
6. Ana: Yes, I do.
7. Laura: No, you don't.
8. Ana: I know everything.

Even though this excerpt shows more conflict than cooperation, Ana was able to negotiate her identity within that interaction by positioning herself as someone who "know[s] everything." By taking up Laura's sentence that was previously uttered in a negative form (*you* don't *know everything*), and reconstructing it as an affirmative sentence (*I know everything*), Ana asserted herself in the situation.

Although the purpose of this chapter is to make evident the fact that collaborative interactions aid second language learning, at the same time, it must be acknowledged that an environment where the participants are engaged in what they are learning, helping each other understand what is needed, and working toward a mutually agreed upon goal is not easily attained. In addition, true dialogical activities can be difficult to implement. One aspect of this stems from the makeup of the groups themselves because the dynamics within a group may lead one person to dominate or another to say virtually nothing. Although such factors can be controlled to some extent by the interventions of adult mediators, typically they cannot be managed to the degree that the entire class is happily situated within perfectly functioning groups.

During the classroom interactions described in this chapter, a number of arguments broke out within the student groups, and sometimes the children seemed quite angry. Often these altercations had little to do with the activity itself, but rather revolved around the behavior of one or more participants in the group. Utterances such as "Stop! You're not sharing" and "She won't let me have the brown [crayon]" are examples. At times, students requested teacher intervention to help resolve such conflicts, and generally, I tried to serve more as a mediator than a referee. These incidents point out that there may not be the level of cooperation with kindergarteners that is expected of older children. However, these interactions were still an important part of social development – one of the major goals of cooperative learning. Second language learners can benefit from such conflicts because, obviously, they need to be able to manage themselves and others in exactly these situations. This is an important part of developing a personal sense of identity in the second language.

Conclusion

While the most logical inference that can be drawn from the observations presented in this chapter is that students who are learning a second language need to have ample opportunity to use it, there are more subtle realizations that come to the surface. For example, although almost any interaction is believed to promote opportunities for L2 learning, the context in which those interactions occur is as important as the interactions themselves when promoting language learning. The learning environment that was created in my classroom played a critical role in shaping not only the larger discourse, but also the understandings achieved. As the discourse began to reflect attitudes of caring, commitment, encouragement, and collaboration, I then began to see greater linguistic gains for my L2 students. For example, when Leticia and Rob (a new classmate, also at a beginning level of English proficiency) engaged in a dispute over some scissors, Leticia explained: "We share, . . . see, you first, then me." "You need crayon too?" "[Here] is a blue." "I get the book, we can see [the] color of [the] house, then we [will] color [the house]. . . ."

I found greater linguistic progress when my second language learners were provided with occasions to use a variety of modes of expression, to present their work to others and receive feedback, and to choose the interactions in which to participate. Through group interactions, L2 learners borrow and build on each other's abilities as they make successive advances in reaching higher levels of proficiency. However, it is important to note that groups composed of students of similar backgrounds, with small differences in proficiency levels, may be better able to provide guided support to their peers because of shared understandings and an ability to communicate in a like manner, which includes resorting to the L1.

Another observation stemming from my classroom is that the role of the teacher remains important through providing scaffolded help, particularly to beginning students. It seems that in some instances perhaps children lack the linguistic sophistication to be able to provide the type of guidance necessary for effective scaffolding. Therefore, in a collaborative setting, the role of the teacher is to structure activities so as to promote participation from each and every class member, to monitor student interaction, to allow for meaningful exchanges, and to promote more symmetrical relationships among peers.

Teachers have to be aware that even though there must be genuine concern for the individual learner and for the variations that individuals bring to a task, they must be attentive to the fact that their role is also to create a context that can be conducive to collaboration. That is, focus should be placed on the process of how languages are learned: not primarily through the memorization of rules and structures, but through participation in dialogical practices. A favorable environment for the development of social and linguistic competence is intertwined with creating a classroom community that shares a commitment to caring, collaboration, and dialog. In this setting, students should be encouraged to develop their own identity, interests, and abilities. In this way, each student is valued as an important contributor to the whole.

However obvious these conclusions may be, predominant classroom practices still favor *lockstep instruction*, where teachers control the discourse and students are not provided the opportunity to interact meaningfully. In many instances, native languages are not allowed in a school setting, and learners are not encouraged to associate because teachers often fear the occurrence of uncorrected errors or the modeling of nonstandard language. In other words, the main focus of teaching still seems to be on the product rather than on the process of language learning. This incongruence between research and practice may be attributed to the fact that a truly collaborative environment might be threatening to some teachers, as they may take it to mean a loss of control over their students' learning. Also, authentic learning activities are often not valued as legitimate instructional practices, particularly in low-income areas where scripted lessons, transmissive approaches, and recitative methodologies are favored by many teachers above more holistic ones. It is hoped that the recent attention given to the study of the effects of social interaction on second language learning will redefine and minimize asymmetries of classroom roles, subvert old myths associated with language learning, and also establish the classroom as a place to foster and nurture social and linguistic growth.

Discussion points and tasks

1. What advantages and disadvantages are there when a class contains both L1 and L2 learners? How does DaSilva Iddings seek to maximize the advantages? What other ways might also be used?
2. Much of the literature on cooperative learning emphasizes that when more capable peers help their group mates, they themselves benefit as well. Yet the chapter describes how this helping hand can also be a burden for the more capable group members. How can teachers create an environment in which more proficient students enjoy and benefit from helping their peers?
3. One way that DaSilva Iddings tries to develop collaborative skills among her students is by calling attention to and labeling times when students demonstrate collaborative behaviors, such as caring, sharing, taking turns, and encouraging others. How else might you promote collaborative skills among students, and why would you want or not want to do this?
4. Conflict is inevitable when people come together. Many educators hope to decrease the amount of conflict that arises among students, yet DaSilva Iddings and McCafferty talk about the benefits of conflict.

What do you see as the potential benefits of conflicts among group members? What role does the teacher have in helping to achieve these benefits?

5. DaSilva Iddings and McCafferty state that although the advantages of student-student collaboration may seem obvious, in their experience, lockstep instruction is still the predominant mode. Cooperative learning is not a new idea. For instance, in North America, educators have been talking about it for more than 20 years now. Given the evidence in support of the use of cooperative learning found in the first chapter of this book, how do you explain the continued predominance of lockstep? Based on your explanation, what can be done to promote a more balanced use of a variety of modes of classroom interaction?

5 Using cooperative learning with primary school students

Ghazi Ghaith and Anwar Kawtharani

Background

Arabic is the native language of most people in Lebanon. Foreign language instruction (French or English) starts with the beginning of schooling, irrespective of whether the students are enrolled in the private or public sectors. According to recent statistics published by the Lebanese National Center for Educational Research and Development (NCERD), there were 2,671 schools in Lebanon during 2000–2001. The percentages of private and public schools were as follows: 50 percent public schools, 14.1 percent subsidized private, and 35.9 percent private schools. Moreover, there were 891,520 students during 2000–2001 distributed as follows: 347,498 (39 percent) enrolled in public schools, 111,200 (12.5 percent) enrolled in subsidized private schools, and 432,822 (48.5 percent) enrolled in private schools. Of these students, 67 percent studied French as a foreign language (FFL) and the remaining 33 percent studied English as a foreign language (EFL). Furthermore, in relation to this chapter, for those students studying EFL, instruction begins in kindergarten and continues through secondary school, but the number of hours assigned to EFL decreases gradually as students gain proficiency.

Learning about cooperative learning

In this chapter, we discuss how we came to know about cooperative learning, following which we will illustrate our applications of cooperative learning in grammar and reading classes. We will also explain how, as we gained more experience, we expanded the application of cooperative learning into the areas of building team spirit and collegiality.

Shortly after the end of the Lebanese civil war (1975–1989), I (Ghazi) joined the American University of Beirut (AUB) Department of Education. About that time, the department started a series of in-service teacher training workshops in collaboration with the university's Center for English

Language Teaching and Research (CELTR). The goal of these ongoing workshops is to help English language teachers keep up-to-date with recent developments in the field of ESL / EFL and to introduce practical and innovative techniques into their classes. I have served as coordinator and presenter of several workshops, which brought together teachers with various backgrounds from all over the country. Some of the teachers had been teaching for many years while others had just joined the profession. Some came from private schools whereas others came from public schools. Some had participated in previous teacher training programs although for others, the workshop was their first such experience.

Problem

In the early 1990s, feelings of tension, skepticism, and self-consciousness prevailed among EFL teachers in Lebanon. Perhaps this was mainly due to the civil war that had a tremendously negative impact on schooling in the country, leading to absenteeism, destruction of school facilities, distrust, and sharp declines in standards. Some workshop participants expressed worries about their personal and economic security. Furthermore, considerable numbers of the participants were not in touch with developments in the field of second language teaching, and most of them felt that their institutions were not interested in their professional development. They mistrusted workshops in general, believing that workshops offered only a series of boring lectures. Worse still, some participants felt inadequate as teachers and feared that the workshops might expose their inadequacies to others.

Solution

Solving the above problems required us to design workshops that would create a tension-reducing atmosphere, help boost the trainees' egos, and show trainees that learning can be enjoyable. Consequently, we first thought of group work as a possible framework for presenting and applying activities selected from the affective-humanistic approaches to second language teaching, such as Suggestopedia and Community Language Learning as well as those methods that emphasize learning by doing, such as Total Physical Response. In addition, we thought of emphasizing purposeful, authentic, and communicative tasks for teaching the four language skills of listening, speaking, reading, and writing separately as well as in integrated form.

Our plans began to materialize during the summer of 1992. At that time, the university organized its first major post-civil war conference in Larnaca,

Cyprus. The theme of the conference was conflict resolution, and it attracted participants from all over the Middle East, Europe, and the United States. At the conference, I (Ghazi) presented a paper on peace education in the EFL / ESL classroom in collaboration with Professor Kassim Shaaban, who had organized and participated in several workshops that had included some applications of cooperative learning for the language classroom.

The conference included several sessions specifically on cooperative learning and sensitized me to its effectiveness and viability as a mechanism for maximizing students' interaction in the language classroom. I saw its potential for increasing motivation, enhancing social skills, providing opportunities for language practice, combining language and content learning, and boosting achievement in a stress-reduced and supportive environment. I found that cooperative learning offered an attractive set of techniques that correlated with various approaches to second language acquisition, creating a positive classroom climate and bridging social and academic language.

Fortunately, I had a chance to experience firsthand some cooperative learning applications immediately following the conference because Robert Slavin of Johns Hopkins University gave a four-day workshop to the faculty members of the AUB Department of Education present at the conflict resolution conference. Slavin made a strong case for using cooperative learning in various subject areas, including language learning, based on empirical evidence that strongly suggested its superiority over traditional instruction in increasing the cognitive and noncognitive outcomes of schooling. He further drew a distinction between generic cooperative learning methods, namely Student Teams-Achievement Divisions (STAD), Teams Games Tournament (TGT), and Jigsaw, which can be used to teach all subjects at all levels of instruction, and subject-specific methods, which have been designed for teaching a particular subject. Team Assisted Individualization (TAI) for teaching mathematics is one example. Slavin also demonstrated the procedures for assigning students to heterogeneous groups based on gender, ethnicity, and achievement, and concluded the workshop with practical applications of the dynamics of the STAD and Jigsaw methods.

Upon returning to Beirut, my colleagues and I decided to share what we had learned in Larnaca. Thus, we started a regular series of workshops. Three years later, in September 1995, Anwar participated in a four-day workshop on cooperative learning. First, I demonstrated two ways for assigning students to heterogeneous groups (to be explained later). Then the components of STAD were shown in a video produced by the Association for Supervision and Curriculum Development (ASCD 1990). The teachers then observed the components in action as I demonstrated them, following which participants successfully developed and demonstrated lesson plans applying STAD to their own curriculum.

That workshop was the beginning of my cooperation with Anwar and his fellow teachers, a cooperation that has continued and deepened over the years. Shortly after the workshop, Anwar invited me to talk to the teachers at the branches (sites) of his school about the applications of cooperative learning in the language classroom. There were eight full-time teachers of English in the first branch and ten teachers in the second. The students ranged from 4 to 12 years of age, and they were all learning English as a foreign language. In 1998–1999, the school enrolled a total of 1,000 students in the first branch and 1,100 students in the second branch. The school is located in the suburbs of Beirut and enrolls Lebanese learners from various socioeconomic backgrounds. The curriculum adopted by the school emphasizes the goals of learning EFL for communicative and sociocultural purposes as well as enabling students to pursue further education at English-medium schools. There is also an emphasis on enhancing students' ability to live in harmony and work with others. As such, Anwar and his colleagues perceived cooperative learning as a natural choice because it correlated with their goals and the needs of their students.

The school administrators graciously agreed to open their school as a research venue to me as I had expressed interest in testing empirically the effects of cooperative learning in EFL classes, with particular attention on the variables of linguistic achievement, affinity to subject matter, and affinity with classmates and school. Consequently, Anwar and I conducted several training sessions specifically for the teachers at his school. Many of them have been participants in the cooperative learning research program at the school. These workshops have covered the dynamics of the STAD and Jigsaw techniques (Slavin 1995) in addition to a wide variety of other cooperative learning techniques described by Kagan (1994).

Teachers of English at the school applied various forms of cooperative learning in their instruction. In the subsequent sections of this chapter, Anwar will describe his experiences in teaching language rules and mechanics, reading, and building team spirit and collegiality.

Implementing cooperative learning at the primary school

Shortly after I (hereafter, Anwar) attended the workshop organized by Ghazi, I decided to use STAD in my teaching of English rules and mechanics.

STAD is a relatively simple cooperative learning technique. It consists of five major components: class presentation, teamwork, quizzes, individual improvement scores, and team recognition. The class presentation component involves direct instruction in the form of a lecture-discussion and can also include audiovisual presentations. The second component (teamwork) involves working in heterogeneous teams based on academic achievement, gender, or ethnicity, in order to study or complete worksheets, discuss problems together, and make sure that all team members learn the material. The third component (quizzes) requires students to take individual quizzes without helping each other. Thus, every student is responsible for knowing the material and for helping group mates to know it. The fourth component (individual improvement scores) is based on the idea of giving students a performance goal that can be achieved by working to perform better than their past achievements. That is, students' quiz scores are compared to their past achievements (base scores) to award their team improvement points. Finally, the team recognition component involves giving certificates or other rewards to teams if their average improvement scores exceed a certain criterion. (Further details on implementation follow.) It should be stressed that each student's grade is based solely on his or her own score. The improvement score is used solely to calculate whether a team should receive a certificate.

I chose this method because research suggests that STAD is among the more effective cooperative learning methods for improving students' learning of clearly defined objectives in areas such as language rules and mechanics. Our school curriculum emphasizes language skills and grammar based on the assumption that developing the necessary linguistic threshold is important in enhancing language use. Consequently, we place stress on students' ability to develop automaticity in language processing in addition to building their linguistic and grammatical competence.

Some people question our use of extrinsic motivators, such as certificates and other rewards, to motivate students to collaborate. However, we see the rewards as a kind of standard that we provide our students. This is similar to a group of runners training to beat their previous best time in the 400-meter relay. By encouraging teams to help each member improve on his or her previous average, the scoring system in STAD offers students clear goals that they must work together to achieve. When teams earn points, they can see for themselves the benefits of collaboration and gain confidence in the efficacy of their efforts, both as individuals and as a team.

Before I was introduced to STAD, my classes were rather teacher-centered and perhaps not conducive to learning or to students' motivation to acquire a language that is orthographically and structurally very different from their own. In fact, my typical lessons were lectures followed by workbook drills completed individually by students to practice the teaching points under study. Consequently, I saw in STAD an attractive alternative to teacher-centered instruction based on the assumption that using this new method would promote my students' learning by creating maximum opportunity for communicative and meaningful classroom interaction in a low-risk and stress-reduced environment. I expected such an environment to result in success because students would work together in small groups and encourage each other, in contrast to a whole-class setting where the teacher is, more often than not, the center of attention. But what attracted me most to this method was that it provided me with a technique for diversifying activities within each class period as we moved from teacher presentation to team study, individual quizzes, and finally, to improvement points and recognition of teams.

In implementing STAD, I had to make decisions regarding classroom setting, group composition, and material development and adaptation, taking into consideration the limits and possibilities of my classroom. In the next section, I describe the decisions I made concerning these factors and why I made them.

Classroom setting for cooperative learning

At my school, the fourth- and fifth-grade students with whom I work remain in the same classroom for the entire day and are taught by at least four different teachers, depending on the school schedule. As such, there are no classrooms specifically designed for teaching English or any other school subject. Furthermore, every two students share a fixed desk, which creates a problem when using groups of more than two. I partly solve this by having pairs of students turn around in order to face the students behind them and form a heterogeneous team of four members. Turning around is a little bit awkward, but the students do not seem to mind, and I think that the benefits outweigh the awkwardness.

I have placed several posters and charts on the walls of the fourth- and fifth-grade classrooms in which I teach to remind the students of certain procedures and class rules. I used to remove the posters when I first started teaching with cooperative learning, but now I use a permanent bulletin board on which I place the posters as needed. The teachers of other subjects also have their bulletin boards. This makes the classroom a colorful and constantly print-rich environment. Figures 5.1a, b, and c show examples of my posters.

- Work in your team and make sure that all team members have learned the material.
- Talk softly.
- Ask your teammates before you ask the teacher.

Figure 5.1a: Classroom rules

Quiz Score

Improvement scores

More than 10 points below base score	0
10 points below to 1 point below base score	10
Base score to 10 points above base score	20
More than 10 points above base score	30
Perfect paper (regardless of base score)	30

Figure 5.1b: Rules for points

	Base score	Quiz score	Improvement points
Ahmad, S. (all names are pseudonyms)	80	68	0
Khalid, Y.	82	79	10
Hassan, M.	75	83	20
Reem, F.	80	92	30
Samar, N.	91	100	30

Figure 5.1c: Example of the distribution of improvement points

Group composition

In applying STAD, I assign students to groups of four and encourage them to work together according to the principles of positive interdependence, heterogeneous grouping, individual accountability, and equal opportunities for success. Positive interdependence signifies a feeling among group members that they sink or swim together. This feeling promotes support within groups. Positive interdependence is encouraged primarily through creating opportunities for resource, identity, environmental, and role interdependence among students. Resource interdependence is promoted by having students use the same pen to complete the same worksheet. To promote identity interdependence, students develop team banners and celebrate their successes, thus experiencing a sense of themselves as a team. Environmental interdependence is encouraged by students meeting in a specific work area and by sharing resources, such as pens and worksheets. Different roles within the team (e.g., group leaders, checkers, secretaries, and encouragers) promote role interdependence.

In addition, I strive to promote individual accountability and equal opportunity for success. Individual accountability is encouraged by keeping group size relatively small, having students endorse and accept responsibility for finished work, and giving individual quizzes and grades. Likewise, the improvement points system explained earlier encourages students to feel they have an equal opportunity for success because the points are awarded based on the students' past achievements (base scores) rather than on class norms. As previously mentioned, points won by a team are separate from the grade students receive on their report cards.

The number of teams in a class is determined by dividing the total number of students by four. In the particular English grammar class (the class studied for this chapter), this process resulted in five teams. Four teams had four members each and one team had five members. Students were assigned to their teams according to the following procedure:

1. Students were ranked from highest to lowest based on their past achievement on measures of knowledge of language rules and mechanics (base scores).
2. A letter (A, B, C, D, E) was assigned to each team member.
3. The letters were matched to the names of students, arranged in a descending order from highest to lowest base scores of students. Thus, the highest-achieving student (number one on the list) was assigned the letter A, the second highest the letter B, and so forth. The order of letter assignment was reversed and repeated starting with number six on the list until all students were matched with letters in an effort to form relatively equivalent teams.

Finally, I made a few changes in the composition of teams in order to ensure the gender heterogeneity of the teams as well, as there were fourteen males and seven females in class. Ethnicity was not an issue as all the students were Lebanese.

Materials development and adaptation

My colleagues and I prepare the necessary worksheets for practice, quizzes, and answer keys for students to check their own work. These are based on the class readings and textbooks adopted by the school. This preparation for STAD was a little time-consuming when we first developed the materials. However, we have saved time as we started storing and using the same materials year after year, with some changes for fine-tuning and new instructional ideas. We have also needed to increase the school budget allocated for photocopying and materials production. In addition, we use available team forms (Slavin 1995) as well as encourage students to design their own forms as part of their art activities. (Certificates are awarded to all the members of all high-performing teams.)

Implementation

I use the following STAD procedure as described by Slavin (1995). During the Teacher Presentation stage, I present the material under study in the same way as I used to before I started using STAD. This stage lasts from 10 to 50 minutes, depending on the nature and complexity of the material. After the introduction of materials, I involve students in Team Study to complete the handouts or to do the exercises in their textbooks in order to reinforce learning (Figure 5.2).

I also administer individual quizzes during which students work alone in order to check their learning of subject matter and to encourage individual accountability. Figure 5.3 shows a quiz I give after a STAD lesson on singular and plural nouns.

After the quizzes, I ask students to individually correct their own work using answer keys prepared specifically for this purpose. This provides them yet one more reinforcement opportunity. The students then determine their improvement points based on comparing their performance on quizzes to their past performance (i.e., base scores, as explained earlier). Finally, the students determine the team improvement points by computing the average improvement points of team members. That is, the improvement points of individual team members are added up, and the total is divided by 4 or 5 depending on the number of students on a team. At the end of quizzes, the members of high-scoring teams are given certificates as Good Teams, Great

Complete this worksheet in your group.

A. Write sentences on the lines below as indicated in parentheses.

1. (Declarative) —————————————————————

2. (Interrogative) ————————————————————

3. (Imperative) —————————————————————

4. (Exclamatory) ————————————————————

B. Change the sentences below from statement to question or from question to statement.

1. Is Sydney a port city in Australia?

————————————————————————————————

2. Have you found your notebook?

————————————————————————————————

3. His friend was walking with him.

————————————————————————————————

Figure 5.2: Grammar handout

Teams, and Super Teams according to the following guidelines suggested by Slavin (1995). Members of the teams that achieve an average of below 10 improvement points are not given team certificates. This is done in order to encourage students to do their best to earn points for their teams. When teams improve from 10–14 points, they are awarded a Good Team Certificate, 15–20 improvement points receives a Great Team Certificate, and an improvement of 20–30 points gets the Super Team Certificate. Teams do not compete against each other; for instance, all teams can be Super Teams.

Teaching reading

Although we use STAD to teach grammar and mechanics, my colleagues and I use another cooperative learning technique, Jigsaw II (Slavin 1995) to teach reading. This is the procedure for Jigsaw II:

1. Students form heterogeneous teams of four or five members (home teams), exactly as in STAD. Each person receives either a text that has been divided into four subtopics or four texts all on the same general topic.

Work alone to answer the following.

A. Change the following nouns to the plural form. Then use them in meaningful sentences.

1. Deer (_____)

_____

2. Photo (_____)

_____

3. Ox (_____)

_____

4. Wife (_____)

_____

5. Lady (_____)

_____

B. Underline the nouns in the sentences below and write the plural forms.

1. The song had the best verse. _____

2. The composer repeated the line several times. _____

3. My friend sang in the concert. _____

4. The cowboy had lost the fastest horse. _____

5. He follows the animal through the bush. _____

Figure 5.3: Grammar quiz

2. Students leave their home teams and form expert teams of no more than four members. Each expert team is assigned a subtopic of the larger topic the class will be reading about.
3. Students meet in their expert teams to first comprehend the reading material specifically assigned to the expert team and then to plan and rehearse how to teach it to the members of their home team.
4. Experts return to their home teams to teach their teammates.
5. Students take individual quizzes covering all the subtopics.
6. Home teams receive recognition as in STAD.

We chose Jigsaw II because it enables students to experience active listening and speaking as they read and discuss the assigned material in their expert groups and then return to their home teams to teach their home team members.

Read the selection below in your expert group and complete the following handout.

Reading A: Chimney Presents on New Year's Eve

1. New Year's Eve is not celebrated in Armenia as it is celebrated in other countries. For youngsters, this evening is the most pleasant of all evenings. It is an occasion of a real good time for everybody. Each family celebrates at home. After dinner, we make a fire and keep it burning until after midnight. This fire symbolizes life, and by keeping the fire burning, we express our wish that our family life will be continuous and bright.

2. In the center of the room, we put up a large table and fill it with dishes of raisins, nuts, and sweets. The boys and girls eat what they can. Then we fill our pockets with what is left. As the celebration is going on, the neighbors lower through the chimney a basket full of goodies. No one knows who our Santa Claus is. After distributing the contents of the basket, it is now our turn to lower a basket for our neighbors. Every family has a Santa Claus.

Reading A Expert Sheet

A. Write (T) if the statement is true, (F) if it is false, or (?) if you can not find the answer in your assigned reading.

   1. Armenia celebrates New Year's Eve like other countries. _____

   2. Armenian youngsters enjoy New Year's Eve. _____

   3. Armenians consider light the sign of life. _____

   4. Armenians exchange goodies on New Year's Eve. _____

B. Find words in the reading that match the meaning of the words below.

   1. Children _____

   2. A time when something happens _____

   3. Enjoy oneself _____

Figure 5.4: Jigsaw II handout

I have developed reading expert sheets for students to use in their expert teams. The purpose of the expert sheets is to help students comprehend their reading and to prepare them to teach it to their home team. For example, in one Jigsaw II lesson students read about New Year's celebrations in four different countries: Armenia (Reading A), Scotland (Reading B), Lebanon (Reading C), and the United States (Reading D). Figure 5.4 includes extracts from the reading and expert sheets of the Reading A expert teams.

Implementing Jigsaw II does not necessitate any major adaptation to the nature of the reading selections assigned to students. First, each reading selection is divided into four sections. Then expert sheets are developed to help students comprehend each section. For this purpose, I developed exercises using a wide variety of graphic organizers (e.g., idea webs, T-charts, Venn diagrams, story sequence charts, main idea charts, problem-solution charts). On other occasions, expert teams read different selections about the same topic and then go back and report to their home team about them. For example, members of expert teams read about celebrating New Year's Eve in Armenia, Scotland, Lebanon, and the United States. Each team member reported to the home team what he or she had learned about celebrations in the countries about which the class had read. The teams then synthesized information and completed charts about what they had found.

The Jigsaw II procedure promotes reading and a great deal of active listening and speaking because the experts report to their teammates who listen to their reports and ask questions. However, this procedure creates considerable noise and can be a little confusing to the students at the beginning of its application. Consequently, I use the management technique of a Zero-Noise Signal to maintain an acceptable noise level. More specifically, I agree with the class that they should stop talking and keep their hands and bodies still whenever I say, "May I have your attention, please?" or when I flip the lights on and off. This works very well as the students are usually cooperative and willing to respond to either of these two signals.

Furthermore, as my colleagues and I gained more experience, we started to use more cooperative learning techniques in our instruction. Ghazi conducted another workshop at our school that focused on class building, team building, and mastery learning techniques. Our experience with these techniques follows.

Class-building and team-building techniques

The cooperative learning techniques of People Hunt and RoundTable were emphasized in the workshop for their use as class-building and team-building activities. Indeed, we have found these techniques, as described by Kagan (1994), extremely useful as ice-breaking activities, especially with new classes, new teams, or at a time when the class needs an energy boost. The techniques are relatively easy to use, as they do not require much special preparation of material. We have also found the techniques applicable at all levels of instruction. The procedures we follow in implementing the techniques are outlined next.

	Self	Friend
Favorite school subject		
Favorite ice cream		
Astrological sign		
Favorite TV show		
Dream car		
Favorite season of the year		
Eye color		

Figure 5.5: People Hunt handout

People Hunt (Kagan 1994)

Students circulate around the classroom looking for classmates who share common characteristics and preferences. For example, students who have English as their favorite subject write *English* under the "Self" column on the chart (Figure 5.5) in response to the first item. Then they ask the question about favorite school subject to classmates until they find someone whose favorite subject is English. Students then write the name of that classmate under the "Friend" column on the chart.

Students continue the process until all the cells on the chart are filled. Figure 5.5 shows an example of the chart.

Sequential RoundTable (Kagan 1994)

For this task, students form heterogeneous teams of four. Each team has one piece of paper and one pencil. Each team makes a list of related items as determined by a topic, for example: "What do you need for the first week of school?" Teacher recognizes the team with the longest list.

Mastery learning techniques

Mastery learning provides students with opportunities to learn the material under study according to certain standards. Based on Ghazi's suggestions, my colleagues and I implemented the mastery learning cooperative learning techniques of Mixer Review and Numbered Heads Together, as described by Winn-Bell Olsen (1992) and Kagan (1994), respectively. An explanation of Mixer Review follows. Numbered Heads Together is discussed in Chapters 7, 8, and 9 and in the Appendix.

Mixer Review

Material: A set of question sheets on previously studied material.

1. Students stand up and form two lines facing each other.
2. Each student should be facing a partner in the other line.
3. Partners discuss the first item on their question sheets. They may use notes or ask other pairs if they get stuck.
4. At a signal from the teacher, one line moves down one step so that everyone is now facing a new partner. New partners answer the next question, using the same procedure they followed in answering question 1.
5. The same procedure, "moving down one step," is repeated for each new question, until the question sheet is complete.
6. When all questions have been completed in this manner, students resume their seats and the teacher leads a discussion on the answers.

Conclusion

Our experience in using cooperative learning in the language classroom has been quite rewarding. Cooperative learning promotes opportunities for interaction among students, which is essential to language learning. A great deal of active involvement takes place because students work together on meaningful activities in a relaxed environment. Also, as the students experience the dynamics of cooperative learning – sharing their answers, earning points for their teams, and exchanging information with their classmates – they develop a feeling that they are a team both with their three or four other group mates, as well as with all their classmates. This enables us to address the noncognitive goal of creating a culture of peace, harmony, and cooperation among students. Working together in small groups to achieve common goals typically results in developing feelings of empathy, understanding, and liking of school and classmates. This, coupled with improvements in academic achievement, underscores the value of using cooperative learning in the language classroom, especially in postwar settings, where various forms of physical, psychological, and ecological violence may be exacerbated and where the need for constructive conflict resolution is pressing.

Furthermore, what we have found to be very useful when teaching with cooperative learning is that all students, irrespective of aptitude, are given equal opportunities to contribute improvement points to their teams when using the STAD and Jigsaw II techniques. This is made possible because improvement points in cooperative learning are determined based on past achievements (base scores) in comparison to current scores rather than in comparison to the performance of other classmates. This, in our view, is a healthy practice, as it encourages students to compete with themselves, not with their classmates, thus leading individuals to focus on actualizing their own potential. This form of teaching is consistent with student-centered instruction, which has been recognized as imperative to effectively learn a second language. It is equally important to us that cooperative learning provides excellent opportunities for diversifying instruction and the mode of dealing with material within each class period. Moreover, cooperative learning can be used to complement and not simply replace teacher-fronted instruction and individual work.

Finally, we would like to add that using the generic methods of STAD and Jigsaw II and the other aforementioned techniques does not necessitate adoption of any curriculum-specific packages, as we continue to use the same textbooks and address the objectives set by the school. At the same time, we have developed worksheets and answer keys in addition to team recognition forms based on existing curricula and textbooks. This was a time-consuming process at the beginning; however, as indicated earlier, it saved time eventually because we started storing and using the materials from one year to the next.

Discussion points and tasks

1. This chapter includes a section on teacher education about cooperative learning. The authors paint an initially gloomy picture of language teacher education, with teachers concerned about personal and economic security, disillusioned with workshops, out of touch with developments in their field, and self-conscious about their own perceived inadequacies. To what extent is this a picture of teachers in your area? How would you expect staff morale to affect teachers' ability to implement innovations such as cooperative learning?

2. Ghaith and Kawtharani discuss the use of affective-humanistic approaches. What do *affective* and *humanistic* mean to you? Does cooperative learning fit into your definition of affective-humanistic? If so, how? If not, why not? Does your answer depend on what particular cooperative learning techniques are used?

3. The authors mention, on one hand, generic cooperative learning techniques that can be used regardless of the subject area and, on the other hand, subject-specific cooperative learning techniques. What cooperative learning techniques do you think would not work in L2 classrooms or with certain types of L2 students? Conversely, what cooperative learning techniques might be only appropriate for language learning but not other subject areas, such as science or mathematics? What about using cooperative learning techniques with content-based language instruction (Echevarria & Graves 1997; Snow & Brinton 1997)?

4. The chapter mentions a research agenda that Ghaith planned to carry out along with the administration and teachers at the primary school. What are some research questions that you would like to investigate in regard to cooperative learning?

5. An explicit approach was used by Kawtharani to teach grammar rules, in addition to the more naturalistic learning that might take place during students' group discussions. What is your view of the best way(s) to build students' syntactic competence in the L2? How can cooperative learning fit with this view?

6. The authors use a good deal of extrinsic motivation in their application of cooperative learning. For instance, in the STAD technique, students are promised nongrade rewards if their team does well. Other chapters seem to put more emphasis on intrinsic motivation. What is your position on the issue of extrinsic and intrinsic motivation? Can the two be combined? Should they be? What can teachers do to affect the degree and type of student motivation? How do students respond in relation to different approaches to motivation?

7. The authors talk about cooperative learning promoting a low-risk and stress-reduced environment in the classroom. Is this necessarily the case? How might peers sometimes create more stress for students than an understanding teacher? Is peer pressure increased by the fact that in a technique such as STAD students feel individually accountable to their group mates to do well so that their team can earn a certificate? Is there such a phenomenon as good pressure or an optimal pressure level? How might an environment become too stress-reduced? What are the roles of teachers and students in achieving optimal environments within cooperative learning groups?

8. Ghaith and Kawtharani discuss the concept of equal opportunity for success. They implemented this concept by calculating the number of points that students earned for their team based on a comparison of each student's base score with her or his score on the most recent quiz, rather than on the absolute value of the score. How would this concept aid less proficient group members? What other ways could equal opportunity for success be implemented?

6 Using cooperative learning to teach French at the secondary school level

Pete Jones and Anne Taylor

Background

We (the authors) taught together for five years at a secondary school near Toronto, Ontario, Canada. Pine Ridge Secondary School is a high school with 2,000 students. The first-year French classes at Pine Ridge are available to students at the applied and academic class levels. Applied classes emphasize a more hands-on approach to the language, whereas the academic classes put more emphasis on concepts. Class sizes were approximately 25, and all students had studied French for four years before entering secondary school.[1]

In 1990, we attended workshops on cooperative learning offered by our Board of Education. Up to that point we had not tried many group activities in our classrooms, and the workshops provided us with a chance to break from our classroom routine. The workshops covered generic use of cooperative learning techniques, which we applied to create materials that applied cooperative learning to our French classes.

We had the opportunity to compare notes with colleagues on what we called Cooperative Learning Tuesdays. These meetings took place once a month on a specified Tuesday at lunch hour. Teachers using cooperative learning strategies would model and share with colleagues a strategy that they had recently used with their classes. After the presentation, we would discuss, analyze, and see how the strategy might be adapted for our different subject-matter classes.

In this chapter, we describe some of the cooperative learning techniques we adapted and some that we created ourselves. We have used them for many years. They are tried and tested and work well in our second language classes. Learning a language involves integrating listening, speaking, reading, and writing. We use cooperative learning activities to support second language development in each of these four areas. The activities described

---

[1] Canada requires that all students become bilingual in French and English.

in this chapter incorporate essential elements of cooperative learning such as positive interdependence, individual accountability, face-to-face interaction, and collaborative skills (Johnson & Johnson 1994a).

Our chapter is divided into four sections. The first three sections describe activities we created ourselves or adapted from our readings. In the first section, we present activities that focus mainly on oral / aural skills. The second section focuses on reading and writing, and the third section presents activities that integrate the four skills. The final section focuses on skills that facilitate effective group interaction.

Oral / aural skills

My Imaginary Friend

First, we would like to discuss small-group cooperative learning activities that enable students to develop their oral and aural skills in the second language. Our first technique is a great class builder. Class builders are important because they give students a chance to meet and feel comfortable working with a number of classmates before ongoing small groups are formed. Sometimes we assume, and incorrectly so, that all students in a class already know each other. Class-building activities help to break the ice, and thus, create a more relaxed atmosphere in the class.

This class-building activity we call *Mon Ami Imaginaire* (My Imaginary Friend). To begin the activity, we usually model what we expect the students to do. By modeling, we increase the likelihood of students performing the task the way we believe it will work best: We stand in front of the class and put our arms around some fresh air which is *mon ami imaginaire*. We then introduce this friend in French to the class by saying: "*Je vous présente Sophia. Elle a les yeux bruns et les cheveux noirs. Elle habite en Italie et elle est actrice. Elle est très grande et elle aime regarder les films au cinéma. Sa nourriture favorite est le poulet rôti et elle adore le vin blanc.*" (Translation: "I present to you my imaginary friend. Her name is Sophia. She has brown eyes and black hair. She lives in Italy and is an actress. She is very tall and likes watching films in the cinema. Her favorite food is roast chicken and she just adores white wine.")

We then invite students to give back a full description of *mon ami imaginaire*. Once this is done, students create their own *ami imaginaire*. Students must include a name for their *ami* and four or five details. We ask students to practice the description in their heads until they are completely comfortable with it. Now the fun part begins: Students stand up and locate another student to talk to, and then present their *ami imaginaire* to that student, who in turn presents her or his *ami*. Also, all students must be able to describe their partner's imaginary friend because they will describe that *ami* to a new partner. This activity reinforces many of the important points of the lesson and builds descriptive vocabulary as well.

Once this part of the activity is completed, students move again, but this time they have a totally new *ami imaginaire* – the one their classmate just introduced to them. Students typically can rotate four or five times exchanging friends. After the fourth or fifth rotation, we stop the activity and ask a student for the name of the original *ami imaginaire* she or he created. Let's say the name was Vincent. We then find the last person in the class to be introduced to Vincent and ask that student to describe him. It is really exciting to hear how close or far away the description of Vincent is from the original creation by double-checking with the student who first imagined Vincent.

We like *Mon Ami Imaginaire* because it includes face-to-face interaction as students are communicating directly with each other through this activity. It is important to note that, along with its advantages as a language learning activity, *Mon Ami Imaginaire* includes an important aspect of cooperative learning: individual accountability. This is built into the activity because students know in advance that they will have to present their new friend to their classmates in the target language.

Magic Box

In this class-building activity that we created, each student places three imaginary objects in his or her imaginary box. Then, the student presents what is in the box to as many classmates as possible during the time allowed, and at the same time, finds out the contents of other students' magic boxes, working in pairs, as with *Mon Ami Imaginaire*. We number each student's magic box in order to keep track of the boxes. Some of the fun things that have gone into the boxes are the winning lottery ticket, a pen that knows all the answers to French tests, and a trip around the world.

Inside-Outside Circles

We have also used Inside-Outside Circles (Kagan 1994) for class building. This technique works well with small or large groups and reinforces listening and speaking skills. Students begin the technique by illustrating (drawing or coloring) the following four things, one in each corner of their nametag. In the top right, students depict what they did on their last vacation; in the top left, they put their favorite color. In the lower right, they illustrate a leisure activity, and in the lower left they illustrate the subject in which they have the most homework.

Students then put their nametags on and the class numbers off (1, 2, 1, 2, . . .). The number ones are asked to come to the center of the room and form a circle with their backs facing in, and the number twos then form a circle facing the number ones. (If there is an odd number, one teacher becomes the missing partner).

Next, the students introduce themselves to the person facing them, and then the activity begins. The number ones explain the illustration in the top left corner of their nametag (their favorite color). After the ones have finished, the number twos explain their same illustration to their partner.

The next part gets a little tricky, so it is important to give clear oral instructions. The inside people (the number ones) rotate as a group so each faces a new number two. This time students explain the lower left illustration on their nametags to each other (the subject in which they have the most homework). The fun part is when we ask a student to explain what a partner has told the student. Like the activities already discussed, Inside-Outside Circle also emphasizes the need for careful listening and encourages everyone to be engaged in the activity.

We have also used this technique with literature. For instance, in the short story "L'Oeuf de Pâques," by Henri Crespi, there are two characters, Nadine and Simeon, who are wife and husband. The story is about an Easter egg that Simeon hides for Nadine each year. Inside the chocolate egg is a different surprise, one year a bracelet, another year a three-day vacation on which they rekindled the romance of their marriage. One particular year Simeon seemed rather preoccupied and left in the morning on a business trip. Nadine spent that day looking for the egg. She was upset thinking that Simeon had forgotten to hide the egg; she continued to search for the egg and finally found it. After the first bite she found a slip of paper and as she swallowed the remaining chocolate, she read "I don't love you anymore." Simeon had put poison in the egg that year and Nadine died.

Using this story and the technique Inside-Outside Circles, we ask the outside circle people to be Simeon and the inside circle people to be Nadine. The Simeons tell the Nadines what made them stop loving her, and the Nadines tell the Simeons what they liked best or worst about him. This allows the students to role-play and become the characters in the story. They try on a different identity, a different voice from their own. This can be fun because students are not representing themselves. The interesting aspect of this activity is the variety of responses from students with the same role. Again, it is important to ask individual students what another student said or did.

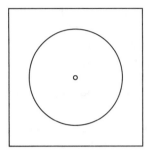

Figure 6.1: Circle and Square

Circle and Square

We believe that students need to trust their group mates before they can work together effectively. This trust provides a foundation for students to enjoy working together and to collaborate effectively. Thus, we conduct team-building activities when groups are first formed and at other times to strengthen the bonds among group members. One of our favorites is Circle and Square. Each group of four receives a page with the circle within a square (see Figure 6.1). Each person in the group picks a number from one to four. Inside the circle next to their corresponding number each person writes one thing that the other members of their group would not already know about them, passing around the form to each member. When everyone has finished, the group discusses each person's item. This offers the group an opportunity to get to know each other better. Also, after this, they make a list inside the square of eight or nine things that they have in common with each other.

Upon completion of the list, group members discuss what they have in common and, keeping those things in mind, create a team name and logo to represent their team. They also create a silent celebration for their team. A silent celebration is a celebration of their successes, whether it is the successful completion of an activity in class or a great effort that day by the group. This celebration could be anything from high fives, to a special dance, a chicken cheer (in which students flap their arms simulating a chicken flapping its wings), or a pat on the back for all. The key, and no doubt the best part, is that their celebrations are all SILENT!

When the team has prepared its team name, logo, and silent celebration, one member of the group (picked randomly according to number by the teacher) explains their choices. For example, one group had these commonalities: They all enjoyed chocolate, had visited Florida, were wearing watches, and were right-handed. As a result, their team name was

The All-Right St. Petersburg Candy Watchers. Students love to show off their new name, logo, and, of course, their silent celebration.

Flip It!

Another technique, which encourages oral / aural skills, is a pair technique that increases student-student interaction in the target language. On the overhead projector, we show a picture of a woman wearing a hiking outfit with boots, her hair done up with a band. On her back is a backpack and sleeping bag, and she is carrying a large walking stick. We then invite students to describe in French whatever they see in the picture. Once the class has done a full description, we ask them to go beyond the picture and to think about what the hiker's name is, where the scene might be, and what her favorite food / show / pastime / hobby / book could be. This sets the scene for what's to come later. Students then number off (1, 2 or A, B or Mr. Spock, Captain Kirk – whatever they want). We then give each group of two a laminated picture mounted on construction paper of a person or persons. Students have a couple of minutes to work alone to prepare their oral description of the picture.

We ask the Captain Kirks to start, in French, with a description of the picture – just as we did on the overhead projector. After ten seconds, we say "Flip It!" and the Mr. Spocks continue the story started by the first member of the pair. At all times, the picture is kept between the two students so that they can both see all of its details. After another ten seconds or so we say "Flip It!" again and the description reverts back to the Captain Kirks. This procedure continues for as long as it seems that the discussion is flowing well. Before the students get going on Flip It!, we tell them that the description has to be continuous with no breaks (this makes it more difficult for someone to get away with saying nothing). However, if someone gets stuck, they are allowed to repeat something that already has been said.

Next, one member of several pairs is called on to describe their picture to the class using the details the pair related to each other during the activity. Students do not know in advance who will be called upon to share their description with the class. It could be Kirk, or it could be Spock. Thus, individual accountability is promoted, as everyone is encouraged to pay attention and be prepared to participate.

In Flip It!, all students are actively engaged, and weaker students have a chance to practice and to learn from a stronger partner before being called on. Moreover, through this activity students have a chance to work on fluency, practice narrative structure, and develop descriptive language, all important aspects of learning a second or foreign language. The noise level in the class dramatically increases during Flip It! and other cooperative learning activities, but it is a good noise – the noise of the target language. We do not attempt to reduce the noise level because it is part of the technique and thus, very acceptable.

OTHER APPLICATIONS OF FLIP IT!

When we finish teaching a grammar point, for example, the imperfect tense and its formation, we use Flip It! to reinforce the verb endings. Instead of using a picture, students write five verbs (e.g., *chanter, écouter, parler, regarder*, and *téléphoner*) on a piece of paper and then conjugate them with *je, tu, il, elle, nous, vous, ils*, and *elles*, using Flip It! The Captain Kirks begin, and the pairs use Flip It! as described. Pairs that finish early sit back quietly and listen to others as they finish the exercise.

We also have students flip a story (or part of a story) the class has just finished reading as a way of enabling them to review what they have read. Also, we sometimes bring closure to other lessons by having students flip things that they did not know when they came through the door on any given day.

Think-Pair-Share

Think-Pair-Share (Lyman 1992) is a cooperative learning technique that quickly becomes a whole-class technique. Active listening and speaking increase and students feel more comfortable about responding in a large group setting after they have worked in a small group. Here's how Think-Pair-Share works.

The students are in pairs and one is Spock and the other is Kirk (or whatever they choose). We ask the students to engage in an activity, for example, "Describe three things that you did on the weekend."

Think Each student takes thirty seconds to think of his or her response to the question. (No talking is allowed during "think" time.)

Pair The Spocks share their responses with the Kirks. The Kirks actively listen because they will need to know what their partners have said. When the Spocks finish, the Kirks respond.

Share After each member of each pair has responded, we ask that a volunteer share three things her or his partner said. By asking for a volunteer, weaker students have more processing time for their answers and more models to choose from as presented by others. We then choose a few more students at random to share.

A	wrote	*My Canadian friend	sent	me
romantic	who lives	who is nineteen	box of	a
	in Toronto			
poem	letter	candies	chocolates	card
*I adore him!	last week	with roses	last Friday	*for Valentine's Day

Figure 6.2: English translations for Magic Sentences

We sometimes use Think-Pair-Share to begin a class in order to reinforce material covered the previous day or to introduce a new topic. We also use it during a lesson to exemplify a new concept. It is a wonderful way to get students involved and to give them the confidence they need through participating in a relatively relaxed manner.

Another benefit of Think-Pair-Share is that it allows students: 1) think time to formulate a response; 2) an opportunity to listen to their partner's response and use that response as a model for their own response; and 3) a one-on-one sharing session with a partner.

Reading and writing

Magic Sentences

This technique allows us to review the vocabulary and grammar structures of a new unit in a fun way. We have been amazed at how much writing our students do. Another thing we like about this technique is that it facilitates many types of positive interdependence: role, goal, and reward / celebration. Using Figure 6.2, we show how *Phrases Magiques* (Magic Sentences) works with a Valentine's Day theme.

First, students form groups of two. One student proposes two sentences using the words and phrases in Figure 6.2, and the other student writes them down. The person writing also checks the spelling. After two sentences, the roles of the creator and scribe are reversed, and so on. In order to compose, students start with the first starred phrase (**My Canadian friend*) and choose words or phrases that in combination form a grammatical sentence (for example: *My Canadian friend sent me a box of chocolates for Valentine's Day*). Students have to end their sentences with a starred phrase to earn two points. They might, however, compose the following sentence: *My Canadian friend sent me a card*. In that case they would earn only one point.

Students write the sentences on lines provided beneath the words. There could be 15 or more lines. Students, of course, are allowed to compose as many sentences as they wish and can simply turn over the page to do so.

We inform students that groups of two that write sentences equaling 20 points or more will receive a reward. Please note that is 20 *points* and not 20 sentences. The reward could be bonus points or one free homework check, meaning that a student would not be penalized for incomplete homework that day. We find that telling the students that the team that gets the most points will receive a reward is not such a good idea because this creates too much rivalry among teams. Once Pete told a class that the team with the most points would be the only team to receive a reward. This really upset the other groups because they realized that no matter what, they could not compete with a team with top French students.

Phrases Magiques is effective because students are actively involved, provide each other with peer support, and have fun manipulating new vocabulary and grammar. Also, as mentioned earlier, positive interdependence comes in the form of role interdependence because students take turns composing and proofreading the sentences. Moreover, incentive / reward interdependence can be promoted as well.

The Five Friends

Another technique, which allows us to emphasize reading and writing skills, we call *Les Cinq Amis* (The Five Friends). It allows students to work in cooperative groups of four. It, too, fosters positive role, resource, goal, environmental, and reward / celebration interdependence. Throughout the activity, the characters are linked together by their interests, traits, tastes, problems, and pastimes. Here's how *Les Cinq Amis* works: The students read and answer the clues in French (we have provided an English translation below), which are looped and linked in an intricate way. Patience is the order of the day! Students record the information on the worksheet next to the appropriate person and category. If their answers are accurate, there will be four blank spaces in the table. Figure 6.3a lists 19 clues for students. The student worksheet (Figure 6.3b) is an empty chart with the four questions listed after it. The answer sheet (Figure 6.3c) is for the teacher's eyes only! The theme of the example is media.

To move from a strictly reading / writing exercise to a listening / speaking exercise, students can create (and write) four additional questions based on other information in the chart. They might ask their questions to the whole class or to other groups of students.

As a follow-up to *Les Cinq Amis*, our students enjoy expanding the information they obtained on any given character by adding two serious and two silly details. Students then prepare a mindmap based on the character. The students do not know in advance who in the group will be selected to present

A. Student Clues
   1. Roger Radio likes to watch comedies.
   2. Emile Emission likes to read his horoscope in the newspaper.
   3. The girl who dislikes Pierre Publicity likes the ad for Red Lobster.
   4. Pierre Publicity likes to listen to the same music as the girl who likes to watch romantic films.
   5. The boy who likes to read his horoscope does not like the ad for Levi's.
   6. The boy who likes reggae also likes to do the crossword in the newspaper.
   7. Violette Videoclip is Roger's friend and Roger is her friend.
   8. The girl who likes to watch romantic films also likes listening to reggae on the radio.
   9. The boy who doesn't like the Levi's ad loves the McDonald's ad.
   10. Roger's friend likes cartoons on TV.
   11. Violette Videoclip does not like Pierre Publicity.
   12. Violette's friend adores the Red Rose ad.
   13. Emile Emission loves spy films.
   14. Florence Feuilleton likes watching romantic films on TV.
   15. The boy who likes the Red Rose ad also likes listening to heavy metal music on the radio.
   16. Florence Feuilleton likes reading the classifieds in the newspaper.
   17. The boy who likes watching comedies also likes reading the lonely hearts column in the newspaper.
   18. The girl who likes cartoons also likes listening to the latest hits on the radio.
   19. The boy who likes doing the crossword puzzles also likes the Bell Canada ads.

Figure 6.3a: English translations of clues for The Five Friends

	Roger	Florence	Pierre	Violette	Emile
Favorite show on TV					
Likes to read this in the paper					
Likes to listen to this on the radio					
Likes these ads					

1. Who likes the Swiss Chalet ads?
2. Who likes to watch the soaps?
3. Who likes to read the sports section of the newspaper?
4. Who likes to listen to jazz on the radio?

Figure 6.3b: Handout

	Roger	Florence	Pierre	Violette	Emile
Favorite show on TV			the soaps		
Likes to read this in the paper				sports	
Likes to listen to this on the radio					jazz
Likes these ads		Swiss Chalet			

Figure 6.3c: Answer sheet

the mindmap. We have them write the numbers 1, 2, 3, and 4 on pieces of paper that they turn upside down, randomly, in front of them. We then call a number and that student comes to the front of the class to make an oral presentation of the mindmap.

The oral description that accompanied the mindmap, including silly details, was something like the following translation from French: "I present to you Violette Videoclip. She likes reading cartoons in the newspaper, and she loves sports. She listens to the latest hit songs on the radio, and she likes the Red Lobster ads on TV. Her hair is red and orange, and she has an antenna in her head. She is always a happy person, and today she is wearing a pretty skirt."

Integrated skills

The techniques in this section integrate all four language skills: listening, speaking, reading, and writing. The following cooperative learning techniques are more complex in nature than those discussed thus far, but they are enjoyable to experiment with in the classroom.

Graffiti

Graffiti (Gibbs 1987) is a wonderful technique that is quick and easy to set up, and the results can be great. Together with the class, we choose a theme to begin the activity, for example, sports. We divide the students into groups of four. For each group, we write an unfinished sentence about the subject on chart paper (approximately 3 × 2 feet wide). For example: *Sports are necessary because . . .* or *Professional athletes make too much money. . . .* Each member of the group writes her or his own response to the unfinished statement. These responses could be ideas, feelings, reactions, and so on. Members write nonstop for one minute about the statement on the chart paper. When the minute is up, each chart is rotated to a new group, and the activity is repeated until all of the groups have responded to all of the statements.

When the final rotation is complete, each statement is returned to the group where it began. At this point, it is full of comments and expressions. Each group's task is threefold: 1) discuss the responses on their page, 2) pick the four they like the best, and 3) write a paragraph using the four responses they chose. It is also important to point out that each group member assumes a role for the activity: reader, scribe, timer, or reporter. The reader reads the statements given by the members. The scribe writes down the group's final paragraph. The timer keeps the group informed about time limits, and the reporter reads the final paragraph prepared by the group to the class.

Graffiti is a great warm-up technique as well as a way to promote equal participation among students. Equal participation comes about as students write their responses to the statements, discuss the responses from their peers, and report the final group product to the class. It helps student writing in French through a focus on synthesizing and integrating information in paragraph form.

Concept Attainment

Concept Attainment (Bruner, Goodnow & Austin 1967) is an instructional strategy that we learned about many years ago and that we have used ever since in our second language classes. We learned about this technique through an in-service workshop given by Barrie Bennett from the University of Toronto. Bennett introduced us to Concept Attainment and showed us how to wrap cooperative learning techniques around it to make them even more powerful. Students work in groups of two for Concept Attainment, and we wrap the cooperative learning technique Think-Pair-Share around it. Following is a complete lesson we have used successfully. The lesson is divided into the four basic steps: 1) focus statement, 2) presentation of data sets, 3) sharing thinking and hypotheses, 4) naming and applying the concept.

FOCUS STATEMENT

To begin, students see a series of statements. Some statements are blue and some are red. The students' task is to work in pairs to see if they can decide what makes the blue and red statements different from each other.

PRESENTATION OF DATA SETS

To demonstrate presentation of data sets, we usually have the statements cut out on cardboard strips, which we attach one by one under the blue or red

Bleu (Blue)	Rouge (Red)
Plusieurs langues dans le monde	Une seule langue dans le monde
Un crayon qui est jaune	Un crayon qui sait les réponses á un test
Un miroir qui dit la vérité	Un miroir qui vous rend plus beau
Un prof qui donne des devoirs	Un prof qui ne donne jamais de devoirs

Figure 6.4: Data sets

Bleu (Blue)	Rouge (Red) – they are so clever!
Un pingouin qui habite en Antarctique	Un pingouin qui sait bien parler français
Tom Cruise / Julia Roberts qui gagne un Oscar	Tom Cruise / Julia Roberts qui danse avec moi
Une vache qui nous donne du lait	Une vache qui distribue les oeufs de Pâques

Figure 6.5: Sharing thinking and hypotheses

column headings on the chalkboard using masking tape. A sample data set is shown in Figure 6.4. (The blue statements translate: *many languages in the world; a pencil that is yellow; a mirror that tells the truth; a teacher who gives homework.* The red statements translate: *only one language in the world; a pencil that knows the answers to a test; a mirror that makes you more beautiful; a teacher who never gives homework.*)

SHARING THINKING AND HYPOTHESES

In pairs, students first think about and then share their hypotheses concerning how the blue and red statements differ. Students use Think-Pair-Share to do this. We then continue by adding more examples to the existing data set. See Figure 6.5, for an example. (Translation of the blue statements: *a penguin that lives in Antarctica; Tom Cruise / Julia Roberts winning Oscars; a cow that gives us milk.* Translation of the red statements: *a penguin who can speak French; Tom Cruise / Julia Roberts dancing with me; a cow that passes out Easter eggs.*)

Students continue thinking about their hypotheses, and again share their thoughts with their partners. No one shares with any other group, and no one shouts out what the concept may be. We then continue with what are called *testers* for the data set. These statements are not written out in blue and red. They are all of the same color – whichever of the two we decide. One by one we hold up these statements, and the students guess if each statement conceptually belongs with the blue or the red category. Students can do this orally or nonverbally: thumbs up for red, thumbs down for blue, or thumbs parallel to the desk if students do not know. After students have indicated whether the statements are blues or reds, we place the statements accordingly on the chalkboard with the rest of the data set. Here are translations for some of the testers we have used for the current example: *a nonalcoholic drink, a rose with petals, it snows when it's hot, a book without pages, rain in the springtime, a supersonic jet, a house without walls, a purple apple, a zoo with no animals, a war without casualties, and the punch line is "Santa Claus!"*

NAMING AND APPLYING THE CONCEPT

Once the class agrees on what the concept is, it needs a name. Here, we call it "*Ça n'existe pas!*" (Things that don't really exist!). How we apply the concept is as follows: We tell the students that they are going to compose a poem called "*Ça n'existe pas!*" where they will talk about things that do not exist; but wouldn't the world be a wonderful, marvelous, unusual, strange, different place if they did! Here are some gems from our grade 11 students:

> *Les murs qui disent: "Ne vous appuyez pas sur moi!"*
> (Walls that say, "Don't lean on me!")
> *Et les chaises qui disent: "Attention, vous me faites mal!"*
> (Chairs that say, "You're hurting me.")
> *Ça n'existe pas, ça n'existe pas!*
> (Doesn't exist, doesn't exist!)
> *Une grenouille qui se transforme en prince*
> (A frog that transforms itself into a prince)
> *Sur un lac sans eau*
> (on a lake without water)
> *Ça n'existe pas, ça n'existe pas!*
> (Doesn't exist, doesn't exist!)
> *Des licornes qui se promènent avec*
> (Unicorns walking with)
> *des centaures dans le parc*
> (centaurs in the park)
> *Ça n'existe pas, ça n'existe pas!*
> (Don't exist, don't exist!)
> *Le monde sans guerre*
> (The world without war)
> *La paix pour tous*

(and peace for all)
Ça n'existe pas, ça n'existe pas!
(Doesn't exist, doesn't exist!)
Eh! Pourquoi pas!
(And why not?)

Concept Formation

Another technique we enjoy using in our classes is Concept Formation (Taba 1992), which is based on an inductive model of learning and encourages students to form concepts based on the categorizing of exemplars from a data set. The lessons we have created are enjoyable, and they encourage students to work together in their cooperative groups to reach consensus. There are three basic steps to Concept Formation: 1) The teacher presents the data set, thus providing a focus statement for students to categorize. 2) Groups share their thinking about the common attributes of the items within each set. 3) Groups apply the information generated by the categorizations in some creative fashion.

The example of a Concept Formation activity that follows was designed to introduce our students to the Canadian national anthem and to lead them to an understanding of its vocabulary and themes. The focus statement that we give to each group of students is as follows: "You are about to see a number of words that we would like you to arrange into different categories. There are no right or wrong categories in this activity. Please remember the importance of group consensus as you work through the activity." The students then receive the data set shown in Figure 6.6a.

Next, the students cut out the words, spread them out in front of themselves at their table, and begin the task of determining appropriate categories. Upon completion of the categories, students enter their categories on the classification sheet. Figure 6.6b shows a student example from this activity, which we have translated into English.

Once the classification has taken place, one member of the group remains behind at the home group table to explain the categories as the other members join the remainder of the class in a Gallery Tour (Kagan 1994). The Gallery Tour consists of each group visiting all of the other groups for an explanation of their categories. Each visit lasts approximately four minutes. When group members return from the tour they have time to change their categories if they so choose.

We then play the anthem and put up a transparency on the overhead projector that allows students to follow along. As an application, they are then

Canada	home	native	land	true
glowing	patriot	hearts	rise	north
strong	wide	stand	guard	far
keep	glorious	our	we	

Figure 6.6a: Translation of data set

COUNTRY	BODY	PRIDE
Canada	glowing	home
native	hearts	true
land	strong	rise
patriot	stand	keep
north	guard	glorious
wide	we	our
far		

Figure 6.6b: Words and categories classification sheet

asked to write a new verse for the anthem, or sometimes they are asked to use all of the words in one category, for example, from the pride category, in a paragraph, poem, song, or short story.

You Be the Judge!

This is one of the more complex activities we try. It is a Jigsaw activity (Aronson 1980). The example presented below is based on the fairy tale of Cinderella. (It could be based on any favorite story.) Pete designed this technique to increase student interaction and communication. We like You Be the Judge! because it enables students to be creative with higher-level thinking skills. Here's how it works. Students begin in their home groups of four. Each student is assigned a number (1, 2, 3, or 4). Based on that number, they assume the role listed on the activity pages for the assignment. Student 1 is Prince Charming, student 2 is Cinderella, student 3 is one of the sisters, and student 4 is the fairy godmother (boys and girls can take these parts).

Each student in the group takes her or his own character's question sheet and leaves the home group to form an expert group with three other Cinderellas, three other Prince Charmings, and so forth. In the expert groups, the four students answer the questions on their particular character sheet. The students must all agree on and write the same answer to each one of the questions. Once all of the questions have been answered by all the expert groups, students return to their home groups. In their home groups, all students take turns at being a prosecuting lawyer.

Whoever plays Prince Charming reads out the questions from the sisters' sheet, and the group will listen to and take notes on the answers the sisters give. Next, the sisters read the questions for the fairy godmother to answer. This continues until all the questions have been read and answered. The group then decides from the evidence assembled if Prince Charming and Cinderella are mature enough to get married and if they will regret their decision later on. Students continue to discuss their decision until each member of the group is able to explain the group's decision, knowing that one member of the group will be randomly chosen to present the reasoning behind the verdict to the entire class (individual accountability). If there is disagreement on the decision, it should be mentioned in the report. Following is a set of questions for one of the characters, in this case Cinderella:

1. Tell us a little something about yourself.
2. Did you receive a good education? Please explain.
3. How do you keep busy at the house?
4. What do you want to do in life? Please explain.
5. We have learned that you hallucinate about pumpkins being turned into carriages and about mice becoming coachmen. You have just returned from Vienna where even the great Sigmund Freud was unable to furnish a satisfactory answer to this problem. Do you have any remarks?
6. When you arrived at the ball, what attracted you to Prince Charming?
7. What did you talk about?
8. What qualities do you admire the most about him?
9. How do you plan on ending the jealousy you have aroused among the ladies of the court and your half sisters?
10. One day the prince will be king, and you will be the queen of the people from whence you came. What effect will all this power have on you?

Collaborative skills

We would now like to talk about collaborative skills and their evaluation. Collaborative skills are an integral part of the cooperative learning classroom. These skills help students interact successfully, not only with group mates but also in other situations in which they use the L2. How can we make sure that our students have the collaborative skills needed to participate in and to understand the expected behavior in our classrooms?

To help us decide which collaborative skills to teach our students, we began by looking at the list found in *Cooperative Learning: Where Heart Meets Mind* (Bennett, Rolheiser-Bennett & Stevahn 1991). We then decided to introduce and emphasize one skill every three weeks. Also, we made a conscious effort to model the collaborative skills we hoped to see our students use. These skills are also included in our reporting to parents, thus providing an effective way to evaluate our students and set expectations for our classrooms.

In teaching collaborative skills, first we explain to students why the skill we have chosen is important. Then, using a T-chart, we introduce the skill, for example: disagreeing in an agreeable way. We ask students what they would expect to see in terms of nonverbal behaviors if everyone was practicing disagreeing in an agreeable way. Student responses have included eye contact, people leaning toward each other, nodding heads, and furrowed eyebrows. We record these responses on the left side of the T-chart for later reference. Then we ask about the right side of the chart: What would we hear if everyone was practicing disagreeing in an agreeable way? Typical responses (translated from French) include "I like your idea; however, ... " or "That certainly makes sense but what if... ?" Once we have recorded responses on the T-chart, students are put to work on a cooperative activity, and throughout the activity, they are reminded to keep the collaborative skill in mind in terms of appropriate verbal and nonverbal behaviors.

For assessment purposes, a collaborative skills chart (Figure 6.7) was developed to record both the mark the teacher might assign for a particular day (represented by the *T* on the sample chart) and the student self-evaluation mark for the same day (represented by the *S*). All of the collaborative skills that we teach during a term are listed on the chart, but only one collaborative skill is evaluated at a time. Collaborative skills represent five percent of a student's mark for the term. The students inform the teacher of their self-evaluation by filling in a form where they justify the mark they have given themselves for a particular skill. Both teacher and student marks are combined to develop a final mark.

Conclusion

We spent five years teaching together at the same school before Anne became an administrator, and we were very comfortable visiting each other's

Subject											
Collaborative Skill	Student	T	S	T	S	T	S	T	S	T	S	Total
a. Taking turns												
b. Sharing material												
c. Encouraging												
d. Staying on task												
e. Staying with group												
f. Working quietly												
g. Participating equally												
h. Following directions												
i. Praising/No put downs												
j. Contributing ideas												
k. Being responsible												
l. Asking for help												
m. Criticizing ideas, not people												
n. Listening actively												
o. Being self-controlled												
p. Disagreeing in an agreeable way												

Figure 6.7: Collaborative interaction skills

classrooms to observe a variety of cooperative learning strategies being modeled at all grade levels. We had each attended cooperative learning institutes, and we were anxious to share with each other what we had learned and also what we had developed in the way of instructional strategies using cooperative learning. Our experience shows that it is important to have more than one teacher at a school trained in cooperative learning. We didn't feel lonely in our new endeavors. We learned a lot from each other and gained confidence. We gave each other constructive feedback, words of praise, and suggestions for improvement that we both incorporated into the same lesson the next time around. It is great to have a buddy like that when you travel into uncharted territory. The Cooperative Learning Tuesdays, which we mentioned earlier, helped us and other teachers gain more confidence using cooperative learning strategies. Thus, by working as a pair and with larger groups of teachers on our implementation of cooperative learning, we experienced for ourselves the advantages of cooperation. This experience, plus the positive reaction of students to cooperative learning, convinced us even more of the benefits of cooperation and encouraged us to share these with teachers beyond our school, as we have done via conference presentations, Web sites, and, now, this chapter.

Discussion points and tasks

1. At the school where Jones and Taylor taught, teachers would sometimes gather on Cooperative Learning Tuesdays to share ideas about
   their implementation of cooperative learning. What methods of
   teacher-teacher collaboration might you like to engage in?
2. Jones and Taylor did team- and class-building activities. Many books
   on cooperative learning advocate such activities as a prerequisite to
   successful group interaction. How might these activities be done in a
   way that builds L2 proficiency at the same time as building solidarity
   among the class and within groups?
3. Some of the cooperative learning techniques in this chapter, such
   as Think-Pair-Share and Graffiti, were taken from the literature on
   cooperative learning, but others, such as My Imaginary Friend and Flip
   It!, were developed by Jones and Taylor. Although there are well over
   100 cooperative learning techniques in the literature, no doubt more
   can and will be developed. What ideas do you have for cooperative
   learning techniques? They don't have to be completely new; they could
   be adaptations of existing techniques or a combination of elements
   from two or three techniques.
4. Jones and Taylor highlight the benefits of students talking with a partner before being called on to speak in front of the whole class. Among
   the benefits they mention are reduced anxiety and opportunities to use
   peers as a model. However, some educators fear that learners are more
   prone to be off task when working in groups than when whole-class
   instruction is used and that L2 learners are just as likely to pick up
   errors from their peers as they are to find correct models. What is your
   view on these two issues? What in your experience, either as a student
   or a teacher, leads you to hold these views?
5. The authors of this and other chapters discuss various ways by which
   they encouraged positive interdependence and individual accountability among group members. These two concepts are seen as critical
   to successful group activities (see the introductory chapters). What
   has been your experience with levels of positive interdependence and
   individual accountability for people when they work in groups? How
   would some of the ideas in this book be useful for increasing those
   levels?
6. One of the ways that Jones and Taylor attempted to foster positive
   interdependence and individual accountability was by having each
   group member take on a role. For instance, for the Graffiti technique,

roles in a group of four are reader, scribe, timer, and reporter. What are other roles that group members might take on? How can teachers help students prepare to perform these roles successfully?

7. Many advocates of cooperative learning maintain that it provides a forum for students to develop their thinking skills. Jones and Taylor highlight this in some of the cooperative learning techniques they describe, such as Concept Formation and You Be the Judge! What thinking skills would you particularly like students to develop? How can cooperative learning help with this? Also, how do you see thinking skills and collaborative skills building on each other?

8. Jones and Taylor, as well as the other chapter authors, made frequent use of cooperative learning. Would you be comfortable doing this? What to you would be the optimal mix of whole-class instruction, cooperative learning, and individual work? What factors might alter the composition of this mix?

7 Implementing cooperative learning with secondary school students

Sheila Wee and George M. Jacobs

Background

I (Sheila)[1] work at the Teachers' Network,[2] a part of the Singapore Ministry of Education (MOE) that promotes teacher-directed professional self-development. In this chapter, I describe my use of cooperative learning in the mid-1990s when I was teaching students in their final year at a secondary school in Singapore. At the end of this final year, students take a major exam that strongly affects whether they will continue their education and, if so, at what type of institution. This exam is either the Cambridge GCE (General Certificate of Education) "O" (Ordinary) level or the "N" (Normal) level exam. The school where I taught is classified as a neighborhood school. This is the most common type of Singapore secondary school. The other two types, autonomous and independent schools, are more selective in their admission criteria.

In Singapore, students enter secondary school at about age 13 and stay four or five years until the age of 16 or 17. Students are placed in streams based on examinations and past achievement. The three main streams are, from highest to lowest, Express, Normal Academic, and Normal Technical. Singapore has three major ethnic groups. In descending order of size of population, these are Chinese, Malay, and Indian. English is the medium of instruction for almost all courses in Singapore schools. Thus, by the time they near the end of secondary school the level of students' second language proficiency is higher than that of many students in other second language settings. Alongside the prominence of English in Singapore schools, the MOE also strives to help students with their mother tongue. Toward this goal of bilingualism, students take a language course in their first language.

---

[1] Although this account is written in the voice of the first author, both authors were involved in the writing of the chapter.
[2] www3.moe.edu.sg/tn

Teaching and group work

I have been using group activities ever since I started teaching, but I did not use them regularly during my first years of teaching. It was usually my special lessons that featured group work. Those lessons were special because the students came alive when they were given opportunities to work together. Having students work in groups appealed to me because I believe that students have much to learn from each other. I had done group activities such as Jigsaw Reading (although I did not know the name at the time). Also, I had asked students to work in groups to play the roles of characters in a novel when being interviewed by another student, a reporter. However, I inevitably ran into problems when using groups. These problems ranged from one or two group members not participating to conflicts in groups that resulted in students coming to me to complain that they did not want someone in their group and asking me if I would remove that person. Because I was doing group activities without any theoretical framework, I could not fall back on any principles to overcome such problems. My fellow teachers did not talk much about their classes, so I did not know how to get ideas from them about how to improve. Actually, I also suspected that my colleagues were not using groups regularly, in which case they would not have been able to help me anyway.

In this chapter, I first discuss how I came to learn about cooperative learning. Then, I illustrate how I set up the classroom for cooperative learning and how I used it in the teaching of three language skills: writing, reading, and oral skills in a Normal Academic class. In the chapter's final section, I explain how the teachers at my school cooperated with each other to make our work easier and more successful. In each of these sections of the chapter, I also talk about how the principles that I learned from the cooperative learning literature provided me the framework I had been missing previously.

Learning about cooperative learning

I took a course taught by George Jacobs, which met weekly for three hours a session over 10 weeks for a total of 30 hours. We learned many different principles and techniques in the course and also had opportunities to experience the techniques as students ourselves during the course sessions. There was also time to plan how to use the techniques with our own students. The fact that the course met only once a week gave us a chance to go back to our classes to try out the techniques we had explored at each session and then to discuss our experiences at the subsequent session. Such discussion was relatively easy for me because colleagues from my school, whom I saw every day, were taking the course at the same time and trying out the same techniques. Knowing what I do now about *action research*, what was happening as I experimented with cooperative learning could have been the beginnings of an effort to systematically inquire into my practice of using groups in class more effectively and confidently.

In the year after I took the cooperative learning course, I felt more comfortable using groups. Principles such as positive interdependence, individual accountability, and the teaching of collaborative skills were starting to make sense, and I was finding ways to apply them in this class. I discovered it was not difficult to use cooperative learning in nearly every lesson, even though some lessons only lasted 35 minutes. Many cooperative learning techniques are very versatile and can be used in brief periods of time.

One easy cooperative learning technique I started to use was Think-Pair-Share (Lyman 1992), and I soon found it to come in handy in many different settings. One way in which I used it was for generating ideas in the prewriting phase of the process approach to writing. Students had previously had great difficulty developing ideas for their compositions. So, after some preliminary whole-class discussion, I would have students first *think* alone to brainstorm possible ideas for writing. Next, they would *pair* with a member of their group to share and discuss their ideas. Then I would call on students to *share* their partner's ideas with the class. The sharing helped the class build up useful ideas for their compositions. Also, the fact that students might be called on to share their partner's ideas encouraged them to listen carefully and to clarify so that comprehension also took place, and of course this promoted individual accountability as well.

Also, at the end of a lesson, I would often use a variant of Think-Pair-Share to encourage students to confirm and consolidate their learning. The Pair and Share steps were the same, but in the first step, Write replaced Think. Students wrote in their English notebooks about two or three things they had learned in the lesson, paired with a partner to compare and check ideas, revised if appropriate, and then shared by passing in their papers to me. I like the Write step because it makes thinking visible, thus strengthening individual accountability by making students' work more accessible to others. Moreover, in the process of writing out their ideas, sometimes students develop new ones or clarify their thinking.

Using Write-Pair-Share at the ends of lessons helped students gain a clearer sense of what they had learned in class. For example, sometimes they wrote about how they could apply what they had been learning. Using their notebooks to document their emerging knowledge and skills built students' understanding of and conviction in how and what they could do to improve their command of English. In fact, so important was this notebook that it became their bible for English. Because we did not use a set textbook and we teachers generated many of our own worksheets, the notebook became a place where the students' learning was consolidated. I took great pride in my students' notebooks because they were also my accountability documents. As the Head of Department, I showed my students' notebooks to the other teachers and to my supervisors, thus demonstrating transparency in that I was walking the walk, not just talking the talk. I modeled the sort of practice I was encouraging in my department.

One more situation in which the class used Think- (or Write-) Pair-Share was at the beginning of a lesson to recap what had been covered in the previous class session. I find that a gap often exists (sometimes a Pacific Ocean-sized one) between what has been taught on the one hand and what has been learned on the other. When students have opportunities to discuss their learning with peers at the end of a lesson or at the beginning of the next one, this gap can be narrowed. Tony Buzan (1983) suggested that recall and review within a day increases learners' rate of retention of learning. As I listened in while students talked to their partners, I could see that they were not just learning the different skills of English in discrete pieces. Instead, as they reviewed each lesson, they increased their capacity to apply what they learned to other contexts, as well as to integrate the different language skills.

An example of the benefits of students collaborating to consolidate their learning was that as they learned to explain the meaning of different metaphors in the reading comprehension class, they would add the new metaphors to the word / description banks in their notebooks. When appropriate, they would also practice using the new metaphors in their compositions. Some even experimented with creating their own metaphors, which was very satisfying to me because it gave a freshness and uniqueness to their work.

As will be discussed later, I often encouraged my students to read each other's work, regardless of whether it was "good." It was wonderful to see that they learned the collaborative skill of giving praise and showed spontaneous appreciation for their classmates' work. In a way, what was being built or consolidated was a sense of class identity – that they were a community of learners striving and enjoying together. They could both critique and appreciate each other's work. They were learning from each other's mistakes and successes. This form of practice was my cooperative learning experience at its peak. With the GCE "O" level examinations collectively seen as the outside challenge, students felt more positively interdependent with their classmates, and thus, more committed to helping each other do well on the exam.

Getting ready for cooperative learning

In preparing the groundwork for groups to collaborate successfully, I had to consider and take action in a number of areas. These included seating arrangements, group size, group composition, designating groups, getting groups' attention, giving directions, and teaching and modeling collaborative skills.

Seating

In Singapore secondary schools, students stay in the same classroom for most of their classes and their teachers move from one classroom to another. This can create problems if one teacher wants students seated in groups, while another teacher uses whole-class, teacher-fronted instruction. My students sat at individual square desks arranged in rows for most of their lessons with other teachers. These desks were easy to move around and rearrange. What I did was to assign students to groups of four for an entire 10-week term and tell them that they should be in their groups by the time I arrived. The lesson before, I would tell them whether they would start the next lesson in groups of two or four. This way, classes were ready for group work the moment I arrived. If the next teacher was not going to use groups, the students would rearrange their desks at the end of my lesson with them.

Group size

I used groups of four for several reasons. First, four divides nicely into two groups of two. As discussed in Chapter 2, pairs offer the greatest amount of simultaneous interaction (i.e., the largest number of students overtly active at the same time, with 50 percent of the class potentially speaking at any one time). Then, after the pair has worked together, they can share what they have done with the other two members of their group of four. The way I used to use groups before I learned some cooperative learning techniques was for one group at a time to send a representative to the front of the class to share their group's work with the entire class. That takes a long time, and only one person at a time is speaking, but when pairs share with each other, 25 percent of the class is potentially speaking at one time.

Who works in which group?

Group composition was decided by me. My top priority was mixing students according to ethnic group in order to encourage the use of the target language. If, for example, all the students in a group were Chinese, they might be tempted to speak in Mandarin or another Chinese dialect. Mixing the groups ethnically discouraged this. My second priority was mixing students according to proficiency level. Although the students had been streamed, variations still existed. This mix of proficiency promoted peer tutoring. I also sought to form groups composed of even numbers of girls and boys, for two reasons. One, I hoped that mixing sexes would generate different perspectives. Two, I have found that sometimes students are more on task in mixed-gender groups. Setting up such groups was difficult because two-thirds of the class was girls, and some boys seemed to freeze up when grouped with girls. As with all less-than-ideal situations, we learned to make do. What I did was to form groups with two boys and two girls, until all the boys had been grouped, after which all-girl groups were formed. However, mixing girls and boys was only my third priority; so, I did not always keep to this formula.

Designating groups

Having a way of calling on a specific group can be useful. To facilitate this, I tried having students choose a team name, which also promotes positive identity interdependence and gives students a chance to exercise their creativity. However, I found the names confusing to remember, and groups seemed to jell well without them; so, we ended up just designating the groups by letter.

Giving directions

A classroom management technique I learned from other teachers helped me when I gave students directions for working in their groups. First, I would ensure that I gave simple, clear directions, and I gave the directions one step at a time if they were long. Then, I would call a number and ask the member of each group with that number to repeat the directions to their group mates. By walking around and listening in on these repetitions, I could see if the directions had indeed been understood. Prior to this method, groups would get confused and would be unsure what to do. I would end up wasting time, moving from group to group only to find my directions misunderstood and having to reexplain them. I did not mind if students modified the procedure a bit, but I wanted them to at least first understand the original procedure.

Teaching collaborative skills

To enhance interaction among students, I taught them collaborative skills. Among the skills I taught were basic social interaction skills, including saying "thank-you" and using greetings, such as "good morning" and "how are you today?" Of course, students already knew how to enact these skills in English. The point is that they very seldom used them, and I found that when they started using them, the atmosphere in the groups and in the class generally turned a bit warmer, and the winds blew in a bit more of a cooperative direction.

I also taught collaborative skills that directly helped students learn. These included the following:

1. Praising others for their good work: By giving specific praise, students could learn from each other more effectively.
2. Asking for elaborations: Often students' writing or answers were skeletal, and elaboration was needed to bring the skeletons some life.
3. Coaching others: By helping peers evaluate their own work, students helped everyone in the group to internalize the guidelines I provided for doing good work.

To teach collaborative skills, I would choose one skill and begin by helping students see why the skill was important. For example, when I taught them the skill of listening attentively, we first brainstormed several reasons for using the skill:

1. We can learn more from others when we listen attentively to them.
2. Listening attentively to others is the polite thing to do and promotes a gracious society, one of the Singapore government's goals.
3. People are more likely to listen carefully to what we say if we have listened attentively to them.
4. Arguments are less likely to arise if we listen attentively even to those with whom we disagree.

The next step in teaching a collaborative skill was to help students begin to develop a sense of what is involved in using the skill. One means of beginning this development is via a T-chart as shown in Figure 7.1.

The students enjoyed working on the T-chart because they had never thought about how such a simple thing as listening could look and sound.

Looks like	Sounds like
Eye contact	"yes"
Nodding	"ah, ha"
Smiling	"hmmm"
Note-taking	"what do you mean by?"
Frowning	"and ...?"
Leaning forward	"are you saying that ...?"

Figure 7.1: Listening attentively

Then, I tried to choose practice activities for the collaborative skills that would very clearly exemplify the importance of developing that skill. For example, we would do an information gap activity where partners had to listen carefully to each other in order to successfully complete the exercise.

For teaching the collaborative skill of listening attentively, Paraphrase Passport (Kagan 1994) was useful. In this cooperative learning technique, one person in the pair provides an idea. The second person paraphrases and the original speaker checks the paraphrase for accuracy. Once the paraphrase is approved by the partner, the second speaker gives her or his idea on the topic. Paraphrase Passport fit well with the collaborative skill of listening attentively because partners would not be able to paraphrase answers well if they were not listening carefully.

Since Paraphrase Passport is a little bit like a game with partners practicing the skill, observing each other's use of the skill, and then giving feedback, the class found the learning enjoyable. It was very satisfying to watch the students genuinely having fun as they learned together. Another reason I liked Paraphrase Passport was that it encourages equal participation in the groups – no one can dominate a discussion because each person gets a turn after paraphrasing what her or his partner had said.

Another way I helped students learn what was involved in using a collaborative skill was by modeling. When students were working in their groups, I would walk around and listen in. If I did not hear the skill I had selected being used, I would use it. The students generally liked commenting on my modeling, too. I was also glad that we were building a culture of teacher and students being learners together in the classroom. The students did not necessarily practice the chosen collaborative skill using all the steps in the six-step procedure outlined in Chapter 3, but I did persist in continually bringing a particular skill to students' attention, and I gave them feedback on how well and how frequently they seemed to be using the skill.

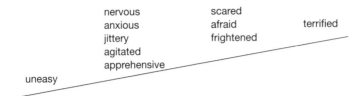

Figure 7.2: Word cline

Cooperative learning and the teaching of writing

I frequently used groups for writing instruction. In this section, I describe how groups were combined with the process approach to traditional writing and to writing with computers.

Generating ideas

Students used a process approach to writing to help generate ideas for their writing and to provide themselves more readers (i.e., peers) to respond to ideas. Before students wrote, they read model compositions of the same genre (e.g., stories about frightening experiences). For model compositions, I tried to choose passages that students had read for their reading compre-hension lessons so that the passages would be of the same genre and field as the texts students were later to write. To build vocabulary, we created *word clines* (Figure 7.2). An example of a cline might show words depicting dif-ferent levels of fear. The words that show a mild level of fear are written toward the low end of the cline, while those that show a high level of fear are written toward the high end. As students generated words and suggested where on the cline to place them, we would think about the actions and thoughts that might indicate the level of fear felt by a particular character in a familiar text.

To brainstorm synonyms for a word, we played a game similar to Scat-tergories™. Groups would work together to list as many appropriate words as possible. At the end of the time limit, each group took a turn to call out their lists, and repeated words would be struck off. Groups with the longest remaining list would win the game. This could generate a lovely long list of interesting words. In this game, positive interdependence within the groups was fostered via competition with other teams, but it was a friendly competition, so I was not worried about causing bad relations between members of different groups.

We then worked on putting the words generated on a cline according to intensity. As a follow-up to this exercise, we would also often look at how, for example, different levels of an emotion would be translated into facial or bodily expressions, so that in their compositions students could describe in greater depth how a character was feeling instead of simply telling the reader that the character was *afraid* or *excited*.

Integrating other skills with writing

One of the nice things about cooperative learning is that it affords so many ways to integrate the four language skills (listening, speaking, reading, and writing). In the writing lessons described in the previous section, students had already read the model compositions. One part of the assessment that my students were to take at the end of the year was an oral exam that included a conversation component involving listening and speaking. So as another prewriting activity, they had conversations in which they asked each other about past frightening experiences. After the reading, word cline, and conversations, we would do the Think-Pair-Share activity described previously as the last prewriting task.

Peer feedback

Students then individually wrote their first drafts at home. In the next class, we would do peer feedback on content in one of several ways. Sometimes, students used Simultaneous RoundTable (Kagan 1994) as a vehicle for that. The way it worked was that each person passed their double-spaced draft to the person to their right, who read it and wrote their feedback directly on the draft. If a student from the group did not bring the homework, four students would simply have to work on three drafts, with one pair reading the same draft simultaneously. This activity continued until each student had received written feedback from their group mates, at which point each author had a chance to discuss any of the feedback that they had received. I stressed that feedback should either be in the form of positive comments or questions, rather than criticisms. I wanted to avoid negative feedback for a few reasons. First, these students had a low self-image of themselves as writers; I wanted to boost their images. Second, I hoped that by looking for the positive, students could learn from their peers' strengths. Third, I wanted to change offering praise and affirmation from a novelty into a habit. As for students who did not do the homework, the penalty would fall directly on them because they would not benefit from any feedback from peers.

Feedback guidelines

There were specific guidelines for peer feedback. In the beginning, students focused on matters of grammar and mechanics. To help students concentrate more on other features of writing, I gave them guidelines on what to look for. These included:

1. Does the author *show* the readers what is happening, rather than *telling* them?
2. Does the author slow down the action to help readers see step-by-step what is taking place?
3. Does the author elaborate on what the characters are feeling, thinking, and doing?
4. Is there anything that is unclear or that you would like to know more about?
5. How did you feel as you were reading the piece?
6. What part grabbed you the most? How did the author achieve this effect?

For instance, in regard to showing instead of simply telling, students would read each other's stories and comment on whether the writer had shown enough through descriptions of thoughts and actions. I was particularly pleased with students' improvement in showing, not just telling. This made their stories come alive. They also started to enjoy playing the stories in their heads in a frame-by-frame way, as if they were directing a movie!

Next, students would write their second drafts at home. The following class period, peer feedback would be given on specified aspects of form. I limited the areas for feedback in order to make the task more manageable for students. The areas I selected were ones that I had taught recently, such as connectors or verb tenses. In pairs, students gave feedback on each other's compositions. Thanks to the peer feedback, I found that when students' work came to me, it was noticeably better: The content was improved and there were fewer grammatical mistakes. Furthermore, giving peer feedback helped students develop criteria for self-evaluation. To promote the development of these criteria (which were similar to performance rubrics), students kept a list in their English notebooks and referred to it when writing. When I handed back students' work, I would highlight particularly good examples and encourage other students to have a look at them, which students often did as they liked to see models written by their peers. The best work in the class represented attainable standards that gave the other students comfort and encouragement.

Writing with computers

Singapore is one of the world's most wired countries, and its schools are well equipped with modern hardware and software. Furthermore, the MOE has taken many steps to encourage the use of information technology in schools. With this impetus, process writing became even more convenient. Before we had computers, the students would make comments and edit their friends' work in green ink. (I told them that that was the color the chief examiners used in Cambridge; so, there was an added sense of importance given to the editing process.) Once we had computers, students could input their draft compositions. During editing sessions, students would display their written pieces on the monitor. Armed with the rubrics I had given them, students would then go from terminal to terminal inserting comments on their group mates' work, using the track changes and insert comments functions in Microsoft® Word. Track changes uses different colors to allow readers to differentiate between the original writing and parts added, altered, or deleted by an editor. The insert comment function allows readers to put an electronic message anywhere in the text without disrupting the flow of the writing. All the writer had to do after that was read the comments and suggestions and cut, paste, delete, add, and rephrase to end up with an improved second draft. This was much better than having to rewrite the whole composition, and I had the joy of marking more coherent, better-organized work. That the writing was beautifully typewritten was an added bonus!

Grading student writing

Students' grades were based solely on their own compositions; I did not give points or use any kind of group grade or a combination grade based on individual and group scores because students were willing to help each other without grades as a motivator. These students had known each other – in many cases for between two and four years – and in general liked each other. Indeed, they were willing to sacrifice themselves to help their group mates. One example of this that stands out in my mind was of three group mates who dealt most admirably with a group mate with whom it was difficult to work. The difficult student would display a temper over a poor grade for an assignment and kick the tables and chairs in the classroom, sometimes threatening worse when the poor grade was for a test. It was great watching the three group mates being especially nice – continuing to calm and encourage their group mate, despite continued rebuffs. Eventually, they did have some success, although the situation remained difficult. No doubt, the student's behavior would have been much worse without the group's support.

Group compositions

Not all writing was done individually. Sometimes, students wrote group compositions in their foursomes. I had hoped that by working in groups students could create more realistic writing. Too often they relied on movies they had seen, making their stories a strange concoction of Hollywood and real life. To build their store of realistic story ideas, students brought in newspaper articles to share with their groups. I would let them first tell their group mates the news story they had picked, and then together with the class, I would flesh out one of the news stories as an example. When it was the students turn to do the same with the other stories, they would practice describing what had happened from the perspective of one of the people in the news story.

In one particularly vivid article, an employee of Singapore's train system, when attempting to pick a piece of rubbish off the track, had to make a mad scramble for safety from an oncoming train that, unfortunately managed to catch her foot. The students went into how the woman might have felt as the accident unfolded. The key lay in giving a detailed, moment-by-moment account, including describing what the character was feeling, thinking, and doing.

Feedback from other groups

Each group would write a story based on a different article. Then groups would share with each other using the Stay-Stray technique (Kagan 1994). After the groups of four had finished their first drafts, three of the four members would leave and each go to a different group. These were the *strayers*. The ones left behind were the *stayers*. Stayers would read their group's draft aloud to the strayers, who had been given feedback guidelines, and the strayer would respond to the feedback. In addition to the feedback guidelines mentioned previously, others that were used at various times include:

1. What descriptors could be added to the story?
2. Did the group try to use all five senses to tell the story?
3. Was the action slowed down?
4. What was your favorite part of the story? Why?

After the stayers had listened and responded to the strayers' feedback, the strayers would return to their original groups, where the stayers informed the group about the feedback their draft had received. Stay-Stray promoted individual accountability because each member of the group had to be ready to explain the group's writing decisions in case their number came up to be the stayer. The strayers would pass on good ideas about writing they had picked up from other groups' drafts, another way that individual accountability was promoted. Then each group would write a new draft. Stay-Stray could then be repeated. When the groups submitted their final drafts, they all received the same grade for the work. This did not cause any protests from students, perhaps because they did not care that much about grades – the main thing on their minds was the end-of-year exam.

Another twist to collaborative writing was that sometimes after writing the first draft together, the students wrote individual second drafts. Because the students had fleshed out the stories together, the subsequent individual work was significantly better than work produced in isolation.

Cooperative learning and the teaching of reading

In addition to composition, another major element of the English curriculum in Singapore deals with reading comprehension. Cooperative learning helped here as well.

Higher-order thinking

The class would read a text and then students would answer questions on the text for homework. These included comprehension as well as higher-order thinking questions. I stressed to students that they should provide not only answers to the questions but that they should also explain the thinking behind their answers. Thus, asking for and giving explanations was a crucial collaborative skill. In order to accomplish this, I used Numbered Heads Together (Kagan 1994) to discuss the questions in groups. There are four steps to this method:

1. Students number off within their groups: 1, 2, 3, and 4. (We had already done this numbering off, and students had a regular number they used for all group activities.)
2. The teacher asks a question or gives a task. (I had done that already with the questions for the reading passage.)
3. Students put their heads together together literally and figuratively to answer the question and develop an explanation of the thinking behind their answer.

4. The teacher calls a number. The student in each group with that number gives and explains her or his group's answer if the teacher calls that group.

Promoting individual accountability

The virtue of Step 4 can be seen by comparing it to what I had been doing before I learned about cooperative learning. Students would work in groups, and then I would call on one group to give their answer. The problem with that was that the same student, the top one in the group, would usually answer. The other group members knew that they would not have to answer and thus often would not feel the need to be prepared to answer. At the same time, the top students in each group knew that because they would answer for their group, they did not need to help their group mates be ready to answer.

In contrast, Numbered Heads Together encourages all students to think about the question and to help their peers to understand the process behind their group's answer. The way we did this was for half of the students with the number I had called (1–4) to come to the board and write answers and explanations, after which the others with the same number would come to the board to evaluate the answers. Next, the whole class discussed which answers were good and why. At first, I offered points and food treats to encourage students to work hard in their groups, but it turned out that the students were sufficiently excited about coming up with a good answer and defending it; so, extrinsic motivators eventually were not necessary.

Summary writing

In Singapore, summary writing is taught as a reading comprehension skill. Writing summaries was a part of the GCE "O" level exam on which students seemed to do particularly poorly. They tended to just pluck points from the passage and string them together in haphazard ways.

This is how I used cooperative learning to help improve students' summaries. Students would come to class with their summaries completed as homework. In class and in pairs, they would take turns mentioning a summary point, using Paraphrase Passport (as previously mentioned) to check the clarity of their summaries. Paraphrase Passport helped students see that what they had thought they meant was not always what their partner had understood them to have said. This experience in speaking definitely proved to be useful practice for producing clearer, better-connected written summaries.

Cooperative learning and the teaching of oral skills

Almost any time cooperative learning is used, oral skills come into play. However, in this section I describe some ways that I used cooperative learning to specifically focus on oral skills.

Exam preparation

The oral exam my students took as part of their "O" level English paper had three components: reading aloud, picture description, and conversation. My strategy was to prepare my students for the oral exam in such a way that they could work outside class to improve their oral skills both individually and collaboratively. During teaching and practice in class, I would explain the exam rubrics to the students and point out the usual mistakes candidates make during the exam (e.g., commonly mispronounced words and sounds), as well as ways to engage the examiner in a lively conversation through the sharing of personal anecdotes. In class, the students always worked in pairs, taking the roles of tester and candidate in turn. The tester's job also included pointing out strengths and areas needing improvement. The pairs were, therefore, role interdependent. The exciting aspect of this preparation in class was that it empowered the students to become more independent from me by becoming more interdependent with their peers. I repeatedly encouraged them to work outside class on improving their oral skills, which they did, much to my delight. I was thrilled and gratified to find students staying behind after school, working together on benches the school provided in various areas outside the staff room or at the school canteen. They graded and coached each other. Sometimes they would come in their pairs to ask for an informal test with me to get my feedback. I always tried to hear the peer's feedback first before giving my own. Their peer assessments were fairly accurate.

Activities like this helped students to feel that they were responsible for their own learning instead of always depending on teacher feedback. This is why I gave them "handles" (something to hold on to) to create very clear guidelines about expectations, so that they knew how to improve. I also found that this increased responsibility increased students' confidence as well as self-esteem. For many of them, it was the first time they had truly understood the expectations of the exam and could perform appropriately. The exam was not, in fact, the kind of hit-and-miss affair that many of them had assumed it to be. They just had not understood clearly that they needed to improve, nor did they know how to do it. From primary school on, students had been told, "You cannot study for English." However, I guided them to see that, in fact, they could. Actually, the students were astounded at how much they could do to develop their oral proficiency not only on their own but also by working with their peers inside and outside of class. No longer did they feel helpless and at the mercy of some seemingly ruthless and arbitrary examiner!

Teacher-teacher collaboration

One of the things I like about cooperative learning is that I can see lots of application for cooperative learning concepts outside the classroom. For example, I found a lot of benefit in collaborating with other teachers.

Sharing the workload

Teacher-teacher collaboration was sometimes directly related to cooperative learning. An example of this was when another teacher, Daphne, and I worked collaboratively to build up teaching and learning resources for the same level of students. To support each other in materials preparation, Daphne and I would take turns to write or collate resources for different units of work. Since no one curriculum text could provide for the needs of our students, we spent a fair amount of time on material selection and preparation. Given our time constraints, we depended on each other for alternate units of resource material and ideas. Even when exchanging materials we would suggest to the other how we would use the materials, and after class we would share our successes and failures with one another. The feedback was the basis for modified worksheets being included in our resource packages. It was truly satisfying watching a tried and tested resource package grow collaboratively through the year!

In a very real way this working partnership also demanded a high level of individual accountability between us. The worksheets had to be professionally prepared and had to demonstrate our professional competence. Because the work was open to critique not only by each other but by other teachers in the level with whom we shared the material, I believe we both grew professionally in the process.

Observing each other's classes

While colleagues and I were taking the 10-week cooperative learning course mentioned earlier with George, we would informally talk about how it was going with implementing cooperative learning in our classes. We also did some of this as part of the cooperative learning course. In the course, ideas for professional sharing were presented from a book by Cooper and Boyd (1994). One of the ideas was to invite other teachers to watch us teaching via cooperative learning. So, I decided to organize a cooperative learning week. This was very unusual because it was the first time for many teachers to visit their fellow teachers' classes. Normally, the only visitors were the supervisors, namely, the principal, vice-principal, Head of Department, or someone from the MOE during a school appraisal exercise.

The way the cooperative learning week worked was that teachers taking the cooperative learning course were asked to offer demonstration lessons for the other teachers at the school to observe and learn from. The cooperative learning-trained teachers who were willing to let others watch their lesson stated the topic and level to be taught, where and when the class would be, and which cooperative learning technique(s) they would be using. I made this into a schedule on which teachers could sign up. Also, trainee / student teachers were encouraged to visit these classes rather than the usual practice of staying only with their mentors. Also, no more than three teachers, whether trainees or regular teachers, were allowed to sign up for any particular time slot. The week seemed to be a success as many teachers, including some from other departments, signed up.

We built on the cooperative learning week through adding a mentoring system in which teachers who had been using cooperative learning coached those who were just getting started. This mentoring not only helped those teachers who were the learners – my fellow mentors and I also benefited in terms of feeling pride in our enhanced teaching knowledge and skills. Further, being in the role of mentor gave us a gentle push to use cooperative learning more often and more thoughtfully, so as to set a good example for our peers.

The cooperative learning week and the mentoring that followed succeeded in promoting the use of cooperative learning among other teachers. However, without having taken a course and, instead, having simply adopted or adapted a couple of cooperative learning techniques, many of the novices' first lessons were a bit rough. Fortunately, however, about 25 percent of the colleagues in my school signed up for the cooperative learning course the next time it was offered.

Conclusion

In the second half of the year, after I took the cooperative learning course, teaching seemed much easier because the new techniques and the management devices were in place, and students were helping each other rather than depending on me. I had become more adept in using cooperative learning, and the students had become more accustomed to cooperative learning and had improved their collaborative skills. Of course, teaching was still, and always will be, a continual learning journey with many bumps along the road. The bumps keep me from getting too complacent and push me to learn more about cooperative learning and other areas of teaching.

Toward unconscious competence

A colleague of mine who had attended a workshop by Spencer Kagan told me how Kagan had explained that teachers go through four phases in becoming proficient at using cooperative learning. The first stage is *unconscious incompetence*, in which teachers are not aware of cooperative learning and have no competence in its use. That was the stage I was at when I started teaching. The next stage is *conscious incompetence*, in which teachers are aware of cooperative learning but do not yet know about it. I was at this stage at the time the teacher from my school took the course in cooperative learning and told me about it. The third stage is when teachers become *consciously competent* at using cooperative learning. At this point, we know about cooperative learning and can use it, but it takes a lot of planning to figure out how to bring cooperative learning principles and techniques into play as we organize our classrooms. This was the stage I was at during the year described in this chapter. Many teachers I have talked to at this stage worry that cooperative learning takes too much time to plan and prepare. Because of this, some of them are reluctant to use cooperative learning very often. Fortunately, I was moving toward the fourth stage, *unconscious competence*, in which I did not need to spend so much time to create cooperative learning lessons. My increased familiarity and skill meant that I could think of which cooperative learning techniques would go with which lesson content and objectives more quickly and easily. Also, I had a better feel for how to adjust to the particularities of each of my classes, bearing in mind key cooperative learning concepts. Thus, it seems that I now have the framework for group activities that I once lacked.

Needless to say, I still have much to learn about cooperative learning. My time at Teachers' Network is almost up, and I'm looking forward to returning to the classroom. While at Teachers' Network, I have picked up many good ideas about cooperative learning by working with other teachers on collaborative investigations of their teaching, using an action research model for investigation. It has been said that the more we know, the more we realize how little we actually know. I feel that way a bit about cooperative learning. The human interactions that go on within groups inside a language classroom are so complex, and with a whole other layer of complexity added by factors from beyond the classroom, I'm sure I'll never get it all figured out. Fortunately, I enjoy trying.

Discussion points and tasks

1. Wee and some of her colleagues took a course on cooperative learning that other teachers at her school had already taken. She points out that so many teachers knowing about cooperative learning made implementation easier. Teachers also observed each other's classes and shared in materials preparation for cooperative learning lessons. The literature on innovations in education (e.g., Fullan 1998) suggests that a key factor in the success of school innovations is that teachers work together in teams. If you implemented cooperative learning, how would you want to work with colleagues? Would you consider contacting colleagues at nearby schools or via the Internet?

2. After she was more experienced with cooperative learning, Wee found that it was not difficult to use cooperative learning in nearly every lesson, even though some lessons only lasted 35 minutes. Think about lessons you might teach that do not involve cooperative learning. How could you modify these lessons to include cooperative learning as at least a part of the lessons?

3. The author describes the large gap that often exists between what is covered by the teacher and what is learned by the students. She claims that cooperative learning can help close that gap. In your own experience as a learner (including what you learn as you teach), have you found that to be true (i.e., that by collaborating with others you strengthen and expand your learning)?

4. This chapter talks about how a group dealt with a member who was difficult to work with. Such situations arise not only among students but in all areas of life in which collaboration takes place. Have you encountered students who did not seem to like to work in groups or with whom no one wanted to work? How did you handle or how would you handle the situation? In the particular case described in the chapter, the other group members handled the situation fairly successfully. How can we prepare students to cope in such situations, both in terms of helping the one student and in terms of the other group members? To what extent should teachers intervene, and to what extent should students be left to sort things out on their own?

5. Sometimes when teachers conduct group activities, they attempt to motivate students by having groups compete against each other. In this chapter, we saw how an examination, rather than people, was used as an outside force to encourage collaboration in the groups. Some educators worry that if we have groups compete against each other, bad feelings may arise in the class. In contrast, other educators feel that intergroup competition makes the classroom a livelier place to learn. What is your experience with intergroup competition in education and elsewhere?

6. Wee assigned students to groups in an attempt to achieve groups that were balanced on a number of factors. However, the numbers of females and males was not equal, with females comprising two-thirds of the class. The solution adopted was to form groups with two females and two males, until all the males had been placed in a group, after which all-female groups were formed. Would you resolve this dilemma the same way, or would you try to have one male in every group, or would you try a different solution? Why?

7. The author explains how she worked to give clear instructions for the cooperative learning techniques. Would her way of giving instructions work with all students? If not, how might you adapt them? Wee also states that she did not mind if students changed the techniques a bit. Would you also be so flexible, or do you think it is important for students to follow the instructions precisely?

8. Wee gives a good deal of attention to students' collaborative skills, spending time to teach these skills explicitly. Is such attention warranted or is it time away from the syllabus? If you feel it is worthwhile to teach collaborative skills explicitly, which skills would you select to teach to your students, and how would you go about teaching them?

9. Peer feedback on writing is a popular form of peer interaction in L2 instruction. Wee tried to heighten the effectiveness of the feedback by providing guidance specifically tailored to the teaching points she had been emphasizing. What are some points about good writing that you might teach your students? When students supply each other with peer feedback on their writing, how might you provide guidance that jells with teaching points?

8 *Integrating global education and cooperative learning in a university foreign language reading class*

Jane Joritz-Nakagawa

Background

A one-year, two-semester EFL reading course I taught at a private Japanese university was a special learning experience for me. I expected a challenge due to its size (60 students, despite an "official" limit on enrollment of 30) and due to the difficulties I felt I might encounter teaching students in a required, rather than elective, course. I decided to try creating a course based on the following criteria:

- Students would be given opportunities to do stimulating and challenging work related to global issues.
- Students would work fairly independently of me, the teacher.
- Students would be given opportunities to practice oral English in addition to reading / writing skills.
- Students would be given opportunities to work with and exchange opinions with peers.
- Students would be given opportunities to be successful in their course work.

While I believed that a course based on these criteria would succeed, admittedly, I was a little nervous about the outcome. What gave me confidence was that I had taught in this style before. For example, I had never been one to give extended talks in English, if only for the reason that in any large class I could expect to "lose" any number of students if I aimed at the middle (boring the more advanced and frustrating the lower-level students). Also, in previous courses, group activities had been well received.

This chapter describes four components of the course: its beginnings, the first semester project, the second semester project, and course evaluations. The chapter also explains how and why global education was integrated into the course.

EFL in Japan

In the university where I taught this course, students take an entrance test that includes English, as well as a placement test to group them into English classes. Both tests were multiple choice. Despite the sorting achieved by the entrance and placement tests, a range of abilities in a single class is to be expected. The class described herein could be characterized as roughly intermediate in terms of reading skills and roughly lower-intermediate in terms of oral skills. By intermediate reading skills, I mean fairly explicit knowledge of English syntax and a moderately high level of lexical knowledge but without being able to read native-speaker texts. Students at this level may lack the vocabulary necessary even for some simplified native-speaker texts. Japanese students, prior to entering the university, take English courses in which accuracy is often emphasized over fluency due to the exactness required to pass the university entrance exams.

My teaching philosophy and experience with cooperative learning

From the outset of my teaching career, I have been interested in what are called humanistic and student-centered teaching, though initially I was unfamiliar with much of the literature that discusses either term. Student-centered instruction, in fact, became fashionable after I had been at it a while as a teacher. For me, the term means not only attempting to understand and respect students' individual differences, but also using students' ideas and the students themselves, if you will, as the course content, frequently if not chiefly. Humanistic teaching, in my view, assigns great importance to how a student feels in the class, not just whether the student absorbs information.

However, I did not come across the cooperative learning literature until midway into my career. The cooperative learning literature that I had found most personally useful, although adapting the ideas and techniques was very necessary, was that written by Johnson and Johnson (especially Johnson & Johnson 1991, 1997; Johnson, Johnson & Holubec 2002; Johnson, Johnson & Smith 1991) and by Kagan (1994; 1998). Also useful were workshops given by Kagan on cooperative learning and by the University of Minnesota Cooperative Learning Center directed by the Johnsons.

As I began to use cooperative learning more often, I found I was much freer to observe students, since my attention could be focused on them, not on what I was presenting. Observation was key to obtaining the insights necessary to improve my approach. The answers to instructional dilemmas could be discovered by looking at students' faces and by listening to what they had to say. For example, if I took the time to develop rapport with students and had them develop rapport with each other, students would share their thoughts and ideas freely, and these could be used to tailor any course to the enrollees.

To develop rapport between students and myself as well as among students, I found it necessary to foster a class environment that is safe and supportive but encourages some risk-taking and self-expression. Class-building and team-building exercises (many examples can be found in Hadfield 1992, Kagan 1994, and Moskowitz 1978) and being open with students helped set the necessary stage for the collaborative kind of learning I wished to encourage.

I used to use cooperative learning sparingly, but now it is my primary approach. This progression was the result of gaining confidence and experience, as I continued to experiment with adding cooperative learning activities to my courses, encouraged by the positive reactions of students and of colleagues with whom I discussed my courses. My trial-and-error experimentation with cooperative learning has resulted in more orchestrated successes, with fewer lucky accidents and pleasant surprises – though the latter still do occur. This is not to say that I walk into the classroom with a lockstep notion of what to do. These days I walk in with more of a sketch and adapt it to what I see occurring in the classroom. I know now that the best class period I teach is rarely the result of painstaking advance planning, but more likely the result of minimal planning and my being able to adapt on the spot to what I see occurring, whether positive or negative, in the class. The difference now is that I have many trusted cooperative learning tools to pull out of my hat, as needed. These are tools I have used so often that now they are second nature. When new to teaching, I often made detailed lesson plans, writing out each step of my lesson in the order I thought it should best proceed. This is now rarely the case. In other words, I have reached what could be called unconscious competence in cooperative learning.

Global education

My interest in cooperative learning flowed not only from my belief in the efficacy of peer interaction but, at a more fundamental level, in my belief in the concept of positive interdependence (see the Part II Introduction), which I expanded from small groups of students working together for their mutual benefit to all the creatures on our fragile planet linked in an interdependent web of life. Thus, for me, global education is a natural fit with cooperative learning. Global education can be defined as the teaching of global issues.

Global issues, or themes, include world cultures, multiculturalism, world geography, the environment, human rights, sustainable development, peace, and conflict resolution.

Gloria Steinem once mentioned that the personal is political. I also believe that understanding global issues must start with self-understanding and with understanding those around us. For instance, teaching tolerance in the classroom can begin with self-discoveries and learning to get along with and appreciating classmates. This can then be extended to talking about human struggles occurring in various parts of the globe, including trying to understand the viewpoints of the various parties acting and being acted upon.

A professor in the U.S. graduate TESOL program that I attended urged us teachers in training to become advocates for our current or future students. By this he meant that our ESL students in the United States were very often people who as foreigners were disadvantaged. In Japan, most of my students are Japanese. Despite this seeming homogeneity, I have always been concerned about students in my class who may be disadvantaged due to a visible or invisible identity (for example, due to being female or homosexual or due to ancestry). I am also concerned about other out-groups and/or severely stigmatized members of the larger community and whether my students are members of these groups, such as homeless people or foreign manual laborers. Similarly, I am concerned about prejudiced views of Japan held by people outside of Japan. I've had such concerns from an early age, and I feel fortunate to be able to address them as a language teacher through global education.

Many students are receptive to developing intercultural understanding as well as eager to talk about and work on global issues topics. While some critics of global education claim that the use of such themes leads to the forcing of the teacher's views onto students, I have found instead, that since I use global issues in conjunction with cooperative learning, I spend less time airing my own views than I would were I teaching in a teacher-fronted manner. Also, my students typically propose doing more global issues study because they enjoy it and find it meaningful. Indeed, using global issues in second language courses can be a way of making a meaningful course out of what is very often a required course for students who perceive little if any practical need for the language. Studying about something, versus studying just the language, is inherently motivating for many language learners and forms the basics of immersion programs such as those found in Canada. This global issues approach provides a meaningful context for collaboration and supplies subject-matter content that complements the cooperative pedagogy I employ.

Cooperative pedagogy means more than just using some cooperative learning techniques. The next section of the chapter describes how I set out to begin the course in a way that will prepare students with the language skills and the cooperative attitudes and practices needed for successful group activities.

Course beginnings

Overview of English B

English B was a second-year EFL reading course. English courses were required. A full academic year in duration, they met once a week for 90 minutes. The actual number of class meetings per year was about 25. The course enrollment was approximately 60 students. The course emphasized global issues, and readings were accompanied by collaborative tasks involving reading, speaking, listening, and writing in English.

Initial class meetings

UNDERSTANDING THE COURSE

I knew that this course was going to be different from the teacher-fronted mode of instruction to which pupils had been accustomed. To help acclimate them, the initial class meetings were devoted to an overview of the course and icebreaker activities geared toward class and team building, including reading and speaking activities where students talked together about their feelings about reading in English and about learning English in general.

I announced to the students that the course would stress fluency more than accuracy and that a key part of the course would be learning to work together. I assured them that their evaluations would reflect these pedagogical foci on fluency and collaboration. I provided a rationale for my language learning approach, which can be summed up simply: Active learning and collaboration are essential to progress in English in a large class that will emphasize fluency.

BUILDING LEARNING STRATEGIES

In addition to icebreakers, students participated in brief learner strategy training sessions on handling texts in English, for example, skimming and scanning activities and reading without or with scant use of a dictionary. (Japanese students are often heavily dependent on L1 to L2 dictionaries.)

Also, readings that helped students share themselves with others (e.g., auto-biographical texts by people from various cultures) were used as spring-boards for self-disclosure tasks, as were readings that had as their theme learning from a cross-cultural perspective. During the learner strategy train-ing sessions, students typically collaborated on such activities as complet-ing charts and diagrams for readings (e.g., a time line of a chronological narrative, participating in conversations using new vocabulary items, and comparing and discussing the results of a scanning exercise).

A SAMPLE TEAM-BUILDING ACTIVITY

I designed some of the team-building activities and adapted others from such books as Hadfield (1992) and Moskowitz (1978). Many of the activ-ities followed a Jigsaw, or information gap, format (where pairs need to exchange information with each other), and emphasized the sharing of per-sonal information and opinions with classmates. As an example, before reading the poem "Human Family" by Maya Angelou, which invites read-ers to ponder how human beings are different and alike (see Blanton and Lee 1994), students collaborated in groups of two. Each group member made a Venn diagram. In the overlapping portion of their graphic organizer, they wrote similarities between themselves and their partner. On the left (nonoverlapping) side, they wrote their partner's characteristics that rep-resented differences from themselves. On the right (nonoverlapping) side, they wrote traits about themselves that they did not share with the partner. In other words, the left side of the diagram represents the partner, the right side represents the student, and the center created by the overlap represents "us" – the two of them.

After reading the poem, students individually completed a chart listing their thoughts and questions relative to each stanza in the poem. Subse-quently, they compared and discussed their charts with their partner or group. As an individual homework assignment, students wrote in their jour-nals about what all humans, in their view, have in common. These journal writings were shared in groups at the next class meeting, with peers writing comments in classmates' journals.

Student journals formed an important element of the course. Weekly jour-nal assignments were completed individually but were always shared with peers before submitting them to me. The journal assignments required vari-ous forms of responses to readings (composing questions, answering ques-tions, essay or dialog writing, and creating graphs and charts). For example, for homework students made a chart or mindmap listing potential causes and effects, or they made a diagram of arguments posed with accompanying counterarguments. Subsequently, these assignments would be shared in groups, and randomly selected journal writings were sometimes shared with the entire class.

CREATING LEARNER GROUPS AND MONITORING GROUP FUNCTIONING

During the early weeks of the course, membership in groups (with four being the typical group size) was changed almost weekly and sometimes more than once within a class period. This was done in order to give students a chance to get to know and work with as many of their classmates as possible. One way of forming groups at this stage in the course was by students selecting cards from a deck. The card they picked determined their seat assignment, which in turn (based on their physical proximity to others) determined their learning partner or group for that lesson.

I rarely needed to intervene to help poorly functioning groups. When I did, my intervention usually amounted to discussing problems with students, asking students to propose solutions, having them select a solution, and then following up with them to see if the solution was effective. If, for example, a member was not contributing fully, a group would discuss the reasons (it might have been that the student reported feeling tired or unwell) and a solution (the student could leave the group, try harder, or promise to do something extra the next time).

After about a half-dozen weeks of the activities described, the first semester projects were begun. These are explained in the next section.

First-semester group projects

Design and scope of the projects

The composition of groups of approximately four members for these projects was determined by a lottery method in which I selected at ran-dom student name cards prepared by the students. This method of group formation sends the message that students need to be able to work with anyone. After the groups had been formed, each group was then responsi-ble for reporting on a different chapter in the class textbook. (The chapters were also assigned randomly, by having groups draw cards with the chapter numbers on them.)

Each group was asked to prepare an oral summary as well as a writ-ten summary that included an analysis of the chapter they had read. A required length was specified in terms of minutes for the oral report (10 minutes, with each person speaking about 2.5 minutes, assuming a four-member group), and students were told that the written report should be at least the length of a single-spaced page, or about four paragraphs long, roughly half summary and half analysis. In the analysis, students were to share their emotional and critical reactions to what they read and to propose solutions to the problem(s) the readings directly or indirectly posed concerning the global issue(s) covered in their chapter. One report, concerning the global issues in their chapter, was done in class as a model. In addition to a written report, students were required to turn in an oral presentation outline for teacher review at least one week before the presentation day. The outline was gone over during a teacher-group conference intended as an additional editorial step to help students successfully complete their oral presentation.

The textbook readings and the accompanying tasks were considered to be in a difficulty range appropriate to the cooperative learning project groups, (i.e., manageable if the group worked supportively together). I considered the first-semester project worthwhile in itself, but it also served as a practice session for a more difficult second-semester project for which students were able to choose the content themselves. I had decided beforehand that if the first-semester project was successful, we would continue with this more student-determined project in the second semester. I felt that using a textbook for the first project would make it easier for students.

At one point during the semester, I re-formed some project groups at students' requests. The reason for regrouping was the emergence of a few members of different groups who, due to absences and failure to make any amends for their nonappearances, had not contributed to their group's project and, moreover, seemed uninterested in contributing at the level of others. The students in question claimed they had a very heavy course load, many school sports activities, or that English was not their main subject or area of interest. In response to this situation, these students were themselves fashioned into a new, separate group. The new group had to start over, working with a different chapter from the textbook, but with the same deadlines. This group did receive a passing grade for the project assignment, but it was not as high a mark as others had received. However, the students in this one group met their own objective of just getting by in the course.

Promoting equal participation

Each group member's ideas and opinions were to be considered for inclusion in the finished product, and all members were expected to make an equal, visible contribution to the project. Groups were required to discuss what each member's individual, equal role was with the teacher. Most groups chose to split into two pairs, having one pair responsible for creating the summary and one pair responsible for creating the analysis. Another choice was to have each person responsible for a designated quarter of the written report. Subsequently, the group integrated the individual portions into one whole that was reviewed and revised by the entire group.

Evaluation

Fifty percent of the course grade was based on individual participation, with the other 50 percent on the overall project grade, which was to be the average score of two projects, one in the first semester and the other in the second. Each of the two project grades was based equally on the oral report and the written report. The project criteria, as explained to students, considered equality of contributions among group members, comprehensibility of language use, ability to engender interest in the subject matter, and intellectual depth of the end product.

Students got a passing grade for following the basic guidelines of group functioning, a minimum report length, and acceptable comprehensibility and clarity. The requirements for clarity included demonstrating an ability to paraphrase the main points of the reading and expressing group members' opinions in simple language that the whole class could understand, including explaining difficult words if their use was essential. Clarity for the oral reports additionally included the concept of eye contact with the audience and appropriate loudness and rate of speaking. The written reports were assessed by both the writers and the teacher. The oral reports were assessed by the speakers, the classroom audience, and the teacher. A course calendar indicated project workdays, the due dates for outlines and written reports, and class dates for oral presentations. Deadlines were inflexible.

Also, students were told that it was the group's responsibility to see that everyone in their group understood the material. To help ensure comprehension, students were encouraged to solicit the help of other groups or the teacher as necessary. Students were to consult with peers before consulting with the teacher for two main reasons: to strengthen the team and to underscore the notion of students being competent authorities themselves.

I occasionally met with each group during class time to discuss the progress of the project, to encourage and help the students, and to help resolve any difficulties, if needed. Also, I met with each group formally upon completing the project outline and upon completing the written report. Both were submitted prior to the oral report in order to help clear up any difficulties before the students gave their oral reports.

Second-semester projects

Overview and grouping method

The first-semester projects served as a kind of scaffolding for the second-semester projects. These latter projects anticipated a more advanced use of language skills as well as a higher degree of group autonomy. Additionally, the second semester was devoted almost entirely to the second group project. For this project, students were given a list of topics to which they could add others that either represented a global issue or a social issue in Japan. Also, since one of my primary goals for the course was to foster intercultural understanding, groups that chose a social issue in Japan were also required either to include a comparison with another country or to demonstrate the global significance, or universality, of the theme, at least to the extent that it might apply. The list was meant as suggestions only; students were free to choose any appropriate global issues topic, provided there was enough interest to form a group to work on that topic. As homework, students were asked to think about which topics interested them for a group project and to bring a prioritized list of their interests to the next class. Students signed up for a topic for the next class meeting, but I requested that no more than four people sign up for any one topic and that there be a minimum group size of three. The people who signed up for the same topic became a group. All groups ended up being foursomes, although to achieve this, in one instance, two pairs had to be asked to join together and brainstorm a topic that all four would be interested in. This sign up method was used in the hope that students would work best with a topic that truly interested them. I was happy to find that the project groups crossed friendship / clique lines. In other words, students seemed to care more about the topic than about simply working with their pals. The topics chosen included education in Japan contrasted with American education, differing views concerning the decision to drop the atomic bombs in 1945, deforestation, and the rights of the differently-abled. Intergroup collaboration was encouraged.

Differences between the first and second projects

The second-semester project was different from that of the first semester in the following ways:

- Students chose their own topics.
- The reading material did not come from a textbook but from either a portion of a file of newspaper clippings and magazine / book excerpts about

the topic provided by me, or material found by students and approved by me.
- The work was more challenging in terms of the reading level of the material, since it was a requirement that the readings be written for adult native speakers or at that level.
- Students were required to create and conduct a survey of their peers (peers outside of their own cooperative learning group) and to include the results in the written and oral reports; groups wrote questions to other groups about their topics so that they could see what the class was interested in and could use that information in their reports.
- The 2.5-minutes-per-person oral report had to be in the form of questions and answers between the group members, whereas the format of the first-semester oral presentation had been left open; as others had not read the material, students distributed written materials for the audience to help them better follow the presentation (for example, a bilingual vocabulary list or a list of questions they would discuss); students were given more time to work as the project was more involved.

Project criteria

As with the first-semester project, students were given suggestions as to how to divide the work but were free to choose the method they found most effective. Also, students had to discuss their choice of method with me upon deciding. Nearly all groups chose to read four newspaper or magazine articles, with each person in the group responsible for reporting on one of them and everyone checking the final reports. One group chose two very challenging longer articles about Japanese culture, and together brainstormed the content of their summary and analysis. Then they divided the presentation into segments of equal length, assigning one segment to each member.

Students were especially encouraged to use visual aids during the oral presentation as other students had not read the material, making it harder for the listeners to follow groups' oral presentations. Additionally, as previously mentioned, copies of discussion questions and bilingual vocabulary lists containing vocabulary relative to each presentation were copied and distributed prior to the oral presentations to facilitate comprehension.

Individual homework

In the first semester, students had weekly journal homework assignments primarily related to the textbook and other in-class readings. Journal assignments during the second semester were infrequent because students needed more time to work on their more challenging autonomous group projects. A topic of some second-semester journal assignments was student reactions to learning English. The final journal assignment, a reflection upon their learning experiences in English classes during the academic year, was due on the last day of the course. Rather than journal assignments, the bulk of students' individual work during the second semester was constituted by each student working at home on her or his portion of the project.

Encouraging quality projects

To encourage quality group projects, in addition to unambiguous guidelines given both orally and in writing, in my experience, it is also important to furnish examples of the expected work (for example, sample speech outlines and sample written reports). In previous courses, I found students would ask for these if I did not immediately provide them. If examples are not available from previous classes, FL / L2 textbooks that contain samples of student-generated reports such as summaries and analyses, other teachers' student work, or clearly and simply written native-speaker examples can be used. Another option is to have the teacher and class collaborate to create a model in class, with the teacher assuming a role such as scribe, facilitator, and / or editor, and the students proposing the content of the model.

Students were instructed to use outlines or a list of questions to be discussed, but not fully written reports or texts, during oral presentations. The rationale for disallowing the use of complete scripts was to improve the quality of the presentation by encouraging eye contact with the audience, naturalness of speech, and a slow rate of speaking. Practice time was set aside in the class period. Students were given a list of speechmaking hints that we first discussed as a whole class, and then discussed individually among student groups. I noticed many students using this as a checklist when preparing their oral presentations in class. Students were advised to practice in front of their group mates and give each other pointers.

Observing groups

I believe my discreet but attentive role as observer was useful. Throughout the term, I took notes during and after each class meeting in my course diary. These notes contained my observations of the students' academic and social behavior and summaries of any important conversations we had had. Students frequently self-monitored (e.g., one would apologize to the others for creating a distraction), or monitored each other (e.g., by telling a member who was distracting the group from the task to get back on track).

Generally, students appeared content to have their teacher act as observer and guide on the side, with their group being the center of attention. Judging merely from nonverbal behavior, it seemed that most enjoyed working with classmates a great deal. There was a considerable amount of smiling and laughing, with students speaking in excited voices about their projects, as they huddled together like football players discussing strategy prior to the start of the game. Students were later polled formally as to their opinions about the course.

As far as what languages they were using as I observed their interactions, my policy was to allow the L1 during discussion if using the FL was beyond students' current levels of proficiency, and the goal of their L1 use was later to produce something in the FL. I generally heard a mixture of Japanese and English. However, the L1 was disallowed for the actual reports, except for allowing a minimal amount of time for the translation of important vocabulary items for the benefit of the class audience.

Observing students during the projects (especially the more extended second-semester project) was the highlight of the course for me. The atmosphere was exciting and stimulating, I was free to chat with different student groups, and I could help when asked (versus speaking in the front of a room wondering if what I am saying is of use and to how many). Also, I was at maximum liberty to observe students and learn from them through observation. This observation was a key tool in my evaluation of the groups as well as of the course as a whole. The next section of the chapter provides a fuller discussion of the evaluation process.

Evaluation

Teacher Evaluation

During my first review of the written reports for the two projects, I focused on whether the report seemed to follow the guidelines given and on comprehensibility. Regardless of whether a report required revision, there was always a group-teacher conference at this stage, and again later after grading. Comments were directed to the group versus particular individuals, as all group members were, as aforementioned, responsible for the quality of the finished product.

During the oral presentations, I used a checklist containing the grading criteria I had explained to students, and I also wrote notes. After listening to all of the oral presentations, I took all my notes home, reread the written reports, and wrote a narrative summary discussing what I felt were the strong and weak points of both the oral and final written reports. In my comments, I often corroborated what the students themselves (and / or their audience) had said in their peer and self-evaluations (discussed next). Then I printed out one copy of my report for each group member. After each student had had a chance to read my evaluation, I met with each group about their group evaluation and also their individual evaluation. In addition to the project grade, students received an individual grade that reflected attendance, participation, and journal homework for the academic year.

In subsequent courses, I have often graded group projects by assigning a group grade, but I have also given students individual grades for a project as well. I have no blanket rule about this. Rather, I judge each class and assignment as to what seems appropriate in the given teaching situation. My reasons for giving a group grade are to enhance collaboration or to keep evaluation consistent with instruction. (If you ask students to collaborate, but then evaluate them individually, it can seem that you are not serious about having them help each other.) In addition, sometimes it is difficult if not unwise to attempt to differentiate or extricate the individual contributions that make up a single product. For example, for the oral group presentations, I tell students that they are expected to coach each other and practice together so that everyone in the group shares the floor equally and also shines on the presentation day. The goal is a presentation of consistently high quality.

However, I am against penalizing students who worked hard by lowering their grade to take into account the work of slackers or poor performers in the same group. In an EFL composition course I taught, students collaborated on group newsletters, with each group member also writing an individual article to which they signed their names. In the case of one group, students did not pull together, and a few refused to pull their weight or failed to come to class. For this group's newsletter, I graded each person individually. The scores ranged from A to failure for one student who never turned in his article. My comments were directed at the group's need to improve collaborative skills and resolve problems. (Student self-evaluations also acknowledged this need for improvement.) The other groups in this class all produced work of consistently high quality, so I was able to assign a group grade to the other groups.

I felt the teamwork skills in English B were considerable and group functioning was high. Students cooperated to do their fair share throughout the term and during the projects, and the quality of each group's output as a team was consistent within each team. Thus I felt able to assign a group grade. Also, attendance was not a problem, except for the one aforementioned slacker group composed of students who were repeating the course and who had worked out a system of each person playing an equally minimal role that included skipping class sometimes. This one group wished only to receive a passing grade, as they were busy with other course work and not as interested in English. The system they worked out satisfied them and me and did not disrupt the rest of the class (except that we observed a less than stellar presentation from them on the test day). One reason to allow students to self-select their groups is, obviously, that students may not wish to expend an equal amount of effort. Having a student content with merely passing in the same group with other students who want to do their personal best may make for a less than ideal situation. I think the teacher should take into account such factors when deciding how to group and perhaps how to grade.

Peer evaluation

The student audience for the oral presentations completed anonymous evaluations of the group presentations using a form I provided. These evaluations were later made available for student inspection. I did not have groups formally evaluate other groups' written work (mainly due to lack of time in the semester), but this is something I would like to do in the future. However, copies of each group's written report were made available. Also, examples of students' written work (with the authors' names removed) were sometimes circulated for class analysis and discussion.

Self-evaluation

I was impressed by the apparent honesty of students in evaluating themselves as individuals and as a group. For example, rather than merely saying "we deserve an A" (or "we blew it" and hoping the teacher would disagree), many students pointed out weaknesses in their work in what I felt were appropriate, concrete ways. Also, students gave themselves what I felt was deserved praise for things they did well. For example, students referred to specific paragraphs in their report that could benefit from rewriting or commented on their success in expressing a particular opinion in adequate detail during the oral presentation, or they noted that they did not use sufficient eye contact with the class while speaking, or that they succeeded in projecting confidence in front of the class. Quoting what they reported in their self-evaluations in my teacher evaluation enabled me to avoid telling students things of which they, in fact, were already well aware.

Conclusion

Student views

I like to have formal student evaluation of the course, as it shows that I care what the students think, and as with the self-evaluation, I want them to reflect on their experience. Also, it creates an atmosphere of democracy and equality in that I evaluate them and they can evaluate me, which I think is consonant with the power sharing I strive for throughout the course. In relation to the first-semester projects, some students reported that an oral presentation covering something they had already read was very useful for them. At the same time, many students reported that they liked being able to choose their own topics in the second semester. Students were also interested in hearing their classmates speak during both semester projects because they were interested in their classmates' opinions relative to the topics, and a peer model provided a more attainable standard of oral English than a native-speaker model.

Frequent comments concerning the term projects were something along the lines of the following (some of these are paraphrases from the Japanese): "I didn't think we could do it, but we did! I'm so proud!" "We didn't do as well as we should have. However, I'm glad we did it; I learned something from it. I'll try harder next time." One student wrote comparing the course to a traditional reading test, "We learn absolutely nothing from that kind of test; projects are better."

Over the years, based on surveys of students, their course evaluations, their journal entries, and discussions with students, I have found student support for the cooperative learning approach, including projects described in this chapter, to have steadily increased. I believe this is due to the greater experience and expertise I now have in cooperative learning. In other words, as a more experienced and knowledgeable teacher, I have more cooperative learning techniques at my disposal, and I believe I implement these in a more confident, intuitive, and appropriate way. In the course profiled here, support for this type of cooperative learning-based course as opposed to a more teacher-fronted mode was at about 75 percent of the class. (More recently, student support in my courses has consistently been at over 90 percent of every class I teach, I believe due to growth in my cooperative learning teaching abilities gained from experience.) Some students said they enjoyed group activity because it enabled them to study English more actively, and / or enabled them to learn the opinions of their peers about global issues topics, topics that mattered to them. Other comments focused on the enjoyable nature of the activities or the friendships forged in class.

Teacher's viewpoint

My impression of student course work, including the written project reports and the oral presentations in both semesters, was in the main very positive. A relatively weak display of effort led to less satisfying term project results in a few groups that consisted of less motivated members. Other groups produced truly excellent work, the kind of work that makes a teacher feel it has all been worthwhile – masterful and exciting presentations about important topics that showed students' intellectual flexibility and depth, as well as ability to communicate clearly despite difficulties with English. Most reports I would characterize as at least quite good.

The second-semester oral presentations were much better than the first, I believe in part because I brought a microphone to make the presentations easier to hear. In a subsequent course, I had students videotape their practice sessions to help them see what needed to be improved upon before engaging in the final oral presentation (Nakagawa 1999). Another change I have made in some subsequent courses is to have students create visual aids and include gestures. This fits with the idea of providing a rich context for learning.

My own theory as to why the students liked the course is that the global issues-themed content was stimulating and challenging; the activities focused on fluency and communicating with others; the course afforded students opportunities to interact with each other, which they found enjoyable; and they could make many autonomous decisions about the course work themselves. In other words, students could exercise a degree of authority and control over their work.

Discussion points and tasks

1. The author had a class of 60 students. Some teachers worry that cooperative learning is not possible with such a large class. Yet, if students are to have opportunities to speak the L2, large classes make cooperative learning even more important. What is the largest class with which you have ever seen groups or cooperative learning used? Some teachers divide large classes into large groups of 6–10 students each. This reduces the number of groups for teachers to monitor, but it also reduces the speaking opportunities of each group member. Joritz-Nakagawa used groups of about four. Which size would you use? Why? (Chapter 3).

2. Joritz-Nakagawa reports that students used a mixture of L1 and L2 in their groups. Teachers take differing views on the issue, some trying very hard to encourage exclusive use of the L2, others not minding a fair amount of L1 use, for example, if learners use their L1 to help discuss and come to understand aspects of the L2. What do you think about this issue?

3. Joritz-Nakagawa states that one of her criteria in course design is to provide students with stimulating and challenging work. The projects her students did certainly seemed to meet that criterion. What are other stimulating and challenging tasks students can do in cooperative learning groups? What sorts of positive stimulation and complexity do you think cooperative learning tends to add to a task?

4. Joritz-Nakagawa explains that using cooperative learning gave her more chances to observe her students. As a teacher, what would you like to look for when students are working in groups? How would you go about the observation, and how might you share what you find with students and colleagues?

5. Global issues provided a focus for the cooperative learning projects described in this chapter. However, some educators worry that it is inappropriate to bring such potentially controversial issues into the language classroom. What is your view? Have you considered teaching via such issues? Which global issues do you think might appeal to students and to you?

6. The students came to the course somewhat weak in their ability to paraphrase in the L2. Because paraphrasing would be an important skill in the project work, time was spent helping students develop that skill. In this way, Joritz-Nakagawa provided support to the peer interaction. What other language skills do you think would be important to preteach in order to successfully use cooperative learning?

7. Project presentations were done for both projects in the course. Is it necessary for all groups to present to the entire class? How can whole-class presentations be done in a lively way, such that, especially in a large class, students are still paying attention even when the final group is presenting? How can the audience be involved in the presentation? What might be alternatives to whole-class project presentations?

8. For the first project, Joritz-Nakagawa grouped students at random, and for the second project, grouping was done based on interest in a particular topic. Other teachers assign students to groups so as to form heterogeneous groupings. This latter method is the one recommended in many books on cooperative learning. Thus, we have seen three

methods of forming groups: random, student-selected, and teacher-selected. What do you see as the advantages and disadvantages of each?

9. Evaluation of projects is a complex issue and one to which Joritz-Nakagawa has obviously given a good deal of thought. Whether to use group grades is one of the more controversial topics in cooperative learning (Chapter 3). What do you think about this issue?

9 *Teaching, practicing, and celebrating a cooperative learning model*

Kim Hughes Wilhelm

Background

The main focus of this chapter is on my experiences as a classroom teacher with a collaborative learning projects class for high-beginner adult ESL students in an Intensive English Program (IEP). The class was taught in the Center for English as a Second Language at Southern Illinois University, Carbondale, Illinois, where I was also curriculum coordinator of the IEP. I taught the class the first term it was developed, and I also worked with other teachers throughout another two years of course revision and implementation. After an overview of the instructional context, I move into a detailed discussion of how cooperative learning was operationalized in that setting. Throughout that discussion, I reflect upon how teacher, student, and group interactions changed across the eight-week term of the course. To conclude the chapter, I shift perspective from that of teacher and instructional designer to that of curriculum coordinator and administrator. Issues raised and discussed in the concluding section include my perspectives on how to foster and encourage teacher-teacher collaboration and how to better support teachers in their cooperative learning efforts.

Beliefs and values

I think it important to discuss some of my experiences as an educator and how they coincide with my belief in the power and effectiveness of cooperative learning within educational settings. Before becoming an ESL / EFL language teacher and curriculum designer, I worked for several years as a recreation therapist with special populations. A recreation therapist helps clients develop social, occupational, language, motor, and self-help skills through the use of games and recreational activities. A large part of my job was to create and lead small- and large-group activities so as to encourage clients to learn and practice target skills. Throughout, there was an emphasis on positive social interactions based on the philosophy that we "re-create" and replenish ourselves through having fun together. These experiences taught me the power of social interaction and the importance of fun when encouraging people to take risks and practice difficult skills. I also learned to value a multidisciplinary approach and to appreciate professional collaboration while participating as a member of an interdisciplinary team, which included social workers, psychologists, and medical doctors.

As a language educator, my belief in cooperative learning complements my early work as a recreation therapist. Cooperative learning focuses on learning as a social activity and supports the notion that learning should be fun. I particularly like the fact, discussed in the Part I Introduction and Chapters 1 and 2, that cooperative learning draws upon multidisciplinary theoretical foundations and principles, including the work of experiential and constructivist educators, of behavioral, social, and cognitive psychologists, of sociologists, and of language educators and linguists. From a teaching point of view, this approach allows me to function in my preferred roles of instructional developer, learning facilitator, and critical reviewer.

Cooperative learning also meets the special needs and strengths of adult language learners. For example, it encourages learners to draw upon already developed interpersonal and problem-solving skills and to utilize their prior knowledge and experiences. Cooperative learning activities provide meaningful, realistic practice combined with useful developmental feedback. Students are encouraged to view learning as a dynamic process over which they have individual responsibility and group control. The skills developed in using cooperative learning are also important for life-long learning.

In the cooperative learning-oriented language class, the teacher's role is multifaceted and ever changing to complement the developing needs of individual students as they learn what is expected and then begin to take control of group and learning processes. As groups assert greater control of their own learning, the teacher's role increasingly becomes that of language coach, expert reviewer, and evaluator. Some of the more enjoyable teacher roles are those of coparticipant in cooperative learning activities and supportive coach during group *authorship events*. Authorship events are those in which students – individually, in groups, or as a whole class – create something of their own for an audience beyond the teacher and the other class members.

An important element of the successful cooperative learning-oriented class, I feel, is at least one authentic authorship event. The authorship event can be, for example, publication and distribution of a newsletter, performance of a play or poetry readings, putting up a display or an exhibit, or leading an activity for an outside audience. Cooperation and language learning are fostered as students willingly work together to rehearse and improve for performances and displays. Awareness of the authorship event not only helps learners to synthesize content and skills covered but also encourages them to rehearse and go beyond the minimum since they will be dealing with outsiders. The next section provides a brief overview of the instructional setting in which the authorship event took place.

Instructional setting

In the early 1990s, our IEP changed from a skill-separate to a skill-integrated curriculum. One aspect of that change was to begin teaching most classes in longer instructional blocks (2–3 hours) so as to allow time for integrated-skill and communicative group activities within class time. However, the faculty of the IEP felt that students would benefit from even more applied practice through projects and immersion activities, so we developed separate project classes. Depending on level placements, these project courses meet four to eight hours a week. Thematically, the project class described in this chapter followed the theme of "Midwest: Yesterday and Today." ("Midwest" refers to that region of the United States.) Unit topics included The First Americans (Native Americans), Westward Expansion (pioneers), and Seasons in the Midwest (fall harvest and festivals).

I decided to use a *Story Theater* framework. In Story Theater, students read aloud parts from a script. Costumes, sets, and acting are generally kept to a minimum; because students have the scripts in their hands, memorization is not necessary. The scripts used in this course were based on Native American folktales. The class performed their Story Theater for students aged four and five in four preschool classes and also led educational games and activities for these children. The Story Theater preschool presentations thus became the main authorship event and the focus of many of the cooperative learning activities within and outside of class. Students were interested in speaking English and especially motivated to improve their pronunciation. I was also able to locate Native American folktales that would appeal to both the preschoolers and the university students, and that could be easily segmented for dramatic oral reading so that each student had a part in the performance. The Story Theater framework provided cohesion for the course since it incorporated class themes, gave students motivation for language skill improvement, and provided authentic purpose when interacting in cooperative learning group work.

Grouping students

Fourteen students, twelve male and two female, at undergraduate and graduate levels and from a wide variety of countries, were enrolled in the course.

I told students that to start I would put them into groups, and later, after they knew each other better, I would sometimes give them the choice of selecting their own group members. I found, however, that even after they knew each other, they preferred that I put them in groups. Perhaps this was because it was quicker or because of social tension that sometimes develops when classmates select their own group members. Occasionally, I also used random selection of group members for short-term activities.

With particularly difficult materials, I grouped less proficient students with a more proficient partner (if possible, from the same first-language group). In this way, the more proficient student could provide key vocabulary and concepts so as to keep the less proficient learner up with the activity. When multilevel materials (simplified and more challenging versions) were available, I paired learners homogeneously by proficiency level but heterogeneously by language group so that they could work in English with a partner functioning at a similar language level and work pace.

Larger cooperative learning groups were formed when I wanted students to take more control over decision-making and when, in terms of teacher attention and instructional support, it made sense for the class to divide into only two or three groups. For example, large cooperative learning groups were formed during bulletin board activities and story reading (Story Theater) rehearsals. I typically assigned students to large groups so as to form groups that were similar in terms of age and topic interest, but were diverse in terms of home language and culture, paying special attention to the perceived status of particular individuals in the group and seeking to utilize natural leaders effectively. I also considered where students lived, to make it easier for groups to meet outside of class, and I took under consideration what I had observed about whom they liked to spend free time with.

Since I work in an American university setting in which students are expected to mix freely without regard to gender, I usually do not worry about gender when assigning groups except in the following circumstances: 1) it is early in the class and one gender is in the extreme minority (in which case I try to put them in a group with at least one person from the same gender for moral support); 2) when dealing with a gender-related topic and same-gender or mixed-gender groupings will ease discussion; or 3) when gender differences infringe on students' ability to function well together (e.g., too much flirting, or cultural-based discomfort in mixed-gender groups).

Instructional sequence

In retrospect, I realize that the instructional sequence of this course proceeded according to three phases during which participant roles and cooperative learning activities changed fairly drastically. During the first phase, instruction was for the most part teacher-directed and reflected my major goals of building a cooperative classroom culture, teaching the students what was expected, and helping students develop the knowledge and skills to participate fully in this educational model, including language skill-building and theme development. This phase also incorporated participation in our first field trip. I think of this phase, which lasted the first three weeks of the course, as the Teaching the Model phase.

The second phase began the end of week three and continued through week six. My role during this phase changed from a more traditional one to that of learning facilitator, guide, and advisor, as students began to take charge of their own learning. Students became involved in individual and group projects, met in and out of class to rehearse for Story Theater presentations, and developed informal cooperative learning groups on their own. I think of this as the Practicing the Model phase of the course. Students, having in the first three weeks become aware of what was expected of them, practiced skills and used concepts introduced during Phase 1, and began to take more control of individual and group work. In the final phase, weeks seven and eight, my role evolved to that of friendly critic, expert reviewer, coparticipant, and cheerleader. I think of this third phase as Celebrating the Model, which culminated in public displays and presentations. This was the phase during which the class celebrated its successes and reflected upon its learning interactions. Each phase is discussed separately in the sections of the chapter that follow.

Phase 1: Teaching the cooperative learning model

In my experience, it helps students if I explain my teaching philosophy and expectations, both at the start of a class and also when introducing each major activity. When teaching using a cooperative learning model, we are expecting students to accept and adapt to student and teacher roles that may be very different from those to which they are accustomed. I therefore combine cooperative learning with Teaching the Model activities at the outset. I also look for opportunities to build social relationships and a cohesive classroom culture.

Developing a class constitution

I began by using Write-Pair-Square (Kagan 1994). Students seated in groups of four considered what their goals were when taking the class, jotted down at least one idea (the Write step), and shared that with the person sitting to their right (the Pair step). Partners then shared with the pair to their left (the Square step), reading their goals aloud to each other. Next, we used Numbered Heads Together (Kagan 1994). Students in each group of four numbered off and discussed three goals that they thought most important, and prepared to share their discussion with the rest of the class. I then called a number from one to four, and the student with that number shared with the whole class. I summarized by saying that regardless of the exact answer given, most people in class wanted to become fluent and confident users of English. Students then stayed in the same groups, and I asked them to list in 10 minutes as many ideas as they could about how as a class they could achieve the overall goal of becoming fluent and confident users of English. When the time was up, each group wrote their answers on the chalkboard. Groups decided who would write on the board – some groups sent one person to the board and others ended up with all four members at the board. I also used this as a language editing activity, telling students how many errors there were after they finished their list and asking the group to fix their list (misspelled words were also used to construct their first spelling quiz list).

After the whole class read through each group's corrected list, I asked the students to confer in groups again and decide which of the collective ideas listed on the board they could all agree to as rules in the class constitution. I suggested that if even one person could not live with an idea, the class could not select it for the constitution. The students debriefed as a whole class again, with me erasing ideas from the board that the groups found that they could not all live with. Using this technique, the students came up with the following list: 1) be on time and have your homework ready, 2) try to use English whenever possible, 3) have fun and encourage each other.

As the course progressed, I found that I very seldom had to remind students to be on time, and they would often come to class early and look over homework together in preparation for the class. Even during class breaks, I found students would remind each other to "Try to speak in English." I noticed that the Korean students (the largest language group in the course) would physically remove themselves from the class break area if they wanted to use Korean rather than English. On field trips, students would even call out "Remember the rule – use English" if someone tried to converse in his or her native language. It helped, of course, that there was such a diversity of L1s represented, but most students really did try to follow the class rules on their own throughout the term.

Learning as a social activity

As another part of the process of orienting students to the course, after we had agreed on a class constitution, I listed and explained in simple language the major instructional goals I had in mind for the course. I asked that students write them down and as homework look over these basic goals and come to class ready to decide if any should be added or deleted. (They had no changes to make, but I felt this exercise helped them to better understand what I wanted from them in the class.) I also used this occasion to explain that I would often ask them to work together cooperatively in groups, just as they had when coming up with the class constitution.

Since a large part of learning a language is having opportunities to practice it, I explained that they would be asked to share ideas, discuss, and make decisions together. I encouraged them to actively participate, taking advantage of opportunities to speak in English within a supportive group. I emphasized class constitution rule number 3, that they have fun and encourage each other (so that they felt OK taking risks with the language). I then invited everyone to a class social at my home the first weekend of class. At that event, students met my family, saw my home, and were able to gain insights into my personal life and interests. The social also established that I wanted to be around them as people.

When planning the social, we talked about who lived close to each other, and I encouraged the students to meet in small groups to come together to the event. This gave them more language contact and gave me a reason to organize and distribute contact information for all the members of the class. I encouraged them to bring to the party scrapbooks or pictures to share, games, musical instruments, special dishes, special friends (e.g., roommate or significant other), and cameras. I found that the party was very important in terms of class building in that it enabled them to meet quickly those who lived nearby, helped to establish friendly small groups with similar interests (music, sports, families), and gave them the opportunity to find quickly other members of class with whom they enjoyed interacting. I took note of these connections among class members. This greatly aided me in deciding cooperative groups during week two, when otherwise I would have had to rely only on observations during class.

Cooperative learning linked with class and team building

SHARING PHOTOS

Other class-building cooperative learning activities conducted the first few weeks of the term introduced unit topics while also orienting students to their roles and responsibilities during group work. For example, an early homework assignment (day 2 of class) was to bring at least two photos to class. I asked that the photos show some place the students had traveled in the Midwest. If there were newcomers with no Midwest photos, I asked that the photos show their home region or some special event or person in their lives. Then we used Inside-Outside Circle (Kagan 1994). Students numbered off (1, 2), and number ones formed an inside circle facing outward and number twos an outside circle facing inward toward the ones. Students shared, discussed, and asked questions about the person in the other circle whom they were facing until time was called, at which point the outside circle moved clockwise so that everyone had a new partner. It helped that we had reviewed close-ended versus open-ended questions and the form of *Wh*-questions just before Inside-Outside Circle began. As part of this review, I wrote on the chalkboard several sample questions to help students get started such as: Where are you? Who is this person? When did you go there? What is this? What did you like about this place?

FIELD TRIP

Collaborative learning and theme-based instruction were integrated during field trip activities, as well. The first field trip was to a log cabin museum and pioneer festival of arts and crafts. For this event, students drew numbers and worked with the student who drew the same number to investigate a pioneer art or craft. Each team received a short (2–3 paragraphs) reading about their craft written at about the fourth-grade level (e.g., quilt making, candle making, leather carving, soap making, wool dyeing, making linen, rug making). They were also shown how to use video and still cameras that I took along on the field trip. I told them their assignment while on the trip was to film someone talking about and demonstrating their topic. I asked them to also be ready to explain, in class after the field trip, the craft processes and steps involved.

I found that there were several problems with this cooperative learning pair activity. First, it would have been better if I had assigned particular students to pairs rather than pairing them randomly. Some pairs shared the same first language and reverted to it during the field trip. One pair had two low-proficient students who struggled through the reading and assigned tasks. In this latter case, I should have helped all pairs understand the basic vocabulary and ideas related to their topic (maybe give each team a quiz over their reading).

During the follow-up activity in class on Monday in which pairs were to tell about their craft, I quickly found that this task was much too difficult for them and not worth the learner stress involved. Two pairs attempted the activity before I apologized and abandoned it. We instead decided to create a bulletin board display based on what the students had learned and the still photos we had taken. Pairs willingly worked together outside and inside class to organize their bulletin board display (which were put up during the next class period), grateful to be "off the hook" about doing a class presentation.

Introducing the Story Theater project

By this point in the course, students were becoming increasingly comfortable working in groups. They quickly and willingly moved into groups when asked and seemed to expect frequent group work. Also, I had a pretty good sense of learners who worked well together, those who were least and most proficient, and those who were natural leaders. It was time to get them interested in the Story Theater project. I first asked the students to read a Native American short story that was lacking an ending. As a weekend homework assignment, each of us – myself included – wrote an ending.

As students arrived in class on Monday, we all traded papers, reading as many story endings as possible before I called time. The students then worked in three large groups of four or five members each, and I gave each group endings written by other students. Each group had to negotiate together and decide, on a scale of 1 to 5, or ratings for each ending based on which they found most interesting and enjoyable to read. (I likened the scale to that used to rate hotels.) I then collected the endings and scored them myself according to effort, language use, and creativity, with that grade going in the grade book. Regardless of the grade I gave, those endings receiving a three-star rating or above from classmates were published in the all-program newsletter and posted on the bulletin board. The author had the choice of anonymous publication and posting, with only one writer choosing that option. The students seemed to enjoy sharing their story endings with classmates (rather than just having the teacher read and mark them) and responded enthusiastically to seeing them in print and on display.

This activity helped to prepare the class for a more difficult activity in which I kept them in the same work groups but now asked that each group read a different set of four Native American folktales, some of which would be selected for Story Theater performances. Reading the stories took place over the course of two or three days so that group members could trade stories until everyone had read the entire set. I then asked that they negotiate and rank the stories 1–4, with 1 and 2 those they liked the most. From this set of six tales (two from each of the three groups in the class) I selected four that I then began to arrange into Story Theater parts.

Although focusing on reading, a goal of starting work on the Story Theater project so early was to encourage students to become invested in it. I think it helped to ask the students to rate the various stories rather than simply choosing the stories myself. The students started to become curious about how I would organize their stories into parts. Learners were also familiar with at least one of the four stories chosen. They helped each other understand content and unfamiliar vocabulary, using English effectively while discussing and negotiating story rankings. Students also had time to get used to the idea of performing the stories and expressed interest in learning their assigned stories and parts.

Teacher's role during Phase 1

As you can probably tell from my discussion of this Teaching the Model phase of the class, I functioned very much as instructional leader, activity director, and social organizer. I also tried to teach students their roles and my expectations by giving group and individual feedback. As instructional leader, I worked to identify readiness-to-learn moments. For example, I identified needed vocabulary and wrote them on the chalkboard, or I conducted a quick role-play activity to focus attention on the correct words or phrases to use. I conducted ongoing needs analysis so as to effectively prepare for whole-class and more individualized instruction. As activity director, I was busy during cooperative work, clarifying and repeating instructions, establishing the pacing for activities, and monitoring or assisting groups. I also spent a little time working on language associated with collaboration. During immersion events (e.g., the class social and the field trip), I functioned as social organizer and group member. When there were uneven numbers in class-based cooperative learning work, I would often step out of my teacher role and interact as a cooperative group member as well. Another aspect of my role as teacher was to give feedback so that students would better understand my expectations of them as group and class members.

Providing feedback

I wanted to diminish progressively my role as instructional director and lead students to make a transition to more learner-initiated negotiation, decision-making, and collaboration. One method I used was to take an hourly active participation grade for each student. Students who were actively involved with the groups' collective goals, prepared, and helped self and others to learn, earned the maximum 2 points possible. Those who were present but inactive, tardy, or unprepared received 1 point for the hour. Any who were absent but notified me in advance received a 0, and those who were absent without prior notice received a negative score of −1. I informed students of their active participation score midway through week 2 and again midway through week 3, and reminded them that it was considered as a major portion (15%) of their class grade.

Another way I encouraged students to be active was that when closing cooperative learning activities during this phase of the class, I often provided positive feedback to individuals and groups, focusing on what I saw members and groups as a whole doing right. This feedback was, in part, based on notes I had taken about individual learners and group functioning during early group work (who took the lead, which groups effectively asked questions or clarified information, who stayed on task, who tried to lead the group to closure, and which groups seemed to have fun together).

The first few times the class had a cooperative activity, I attempted more in-depth follow-up discussion and evaluation to encourage learner reflection regarding how well groups worked together. For example, two or three times during the first two weeks after a group activity students rated themselves as active group members. However, I quickly found that students were uncomfortable with this self-assessment, thinking that it was a bit silly and took time away from what they perceived of as more important learning activities. The students in this particular class were, in general, sophisticated and effective group members. My attempts to ask them to evaluate group interactions made it appear that I did not notice how well they were doing as group members.

When a group had difficulties, I attempted to give solid and specific feedback based on my observations and documentation. I also met individually with members to help focus attention on what they might do to improve group performance.

Establishing appropriate pacing

Some students and teachers worry that the use of group activities does not constitute the most efficient use of class time. To address this concern, during the first phase of the course, I worked hard to establish appropriate pacing for activities. This makes the point that class time is precious and students should always be actively engaged. I joked that it was "against the law" to have nothing to do. Upon arrival at class, I often listed the day's agenda in a corner of the chalkboard before class began, helping students to have materials ready and also giving them an idea of everything I wished to accomplish during our time together. I erased each activity as it was completed and, at the end of class, asked students to recall what had been accomplished. I found this to be an easy and effective way to encourage them to reflect upon what they had accomplished and what they had learned or practiced that day. This was especially important in establishing that the projects course was contributing to their language learning and that I, as teacher, had specific objectives in mind for each class period (e.g., listen / read and differentiate main ideas versus details, recognize and use punctuation cues when reading orally, or correctly pronounce *th* when speaking phrases and sentences). I was concerned that if the links between the project and the learning objectives were not made clear, students might feel that doing the projects was just playing games, and they might not take the class as seriously as another class taught more traditionally. This concern is an important one when cooperative learning is used.

Another time issue I recognized is that not all groups work at the same pace. Thus, I prepared follow-up extension activities – also known as sponge activities because they soak up extra time – that I could implement as each group finished. Awareness that there would be follow-up activities encouraged efficient use of group time along with an awareness of the need to reach closure. Midway through a cooperative learning activity, I would take around handouts required for the extension activity and place them on a nearby desk. Alternatively, I wrote next-step directions on the chalkboard. If there was a slow-moving group that was motivated to continue, I would sometimes allow the completed groups to take a quick break as the others continued (this tended to motivate the slow group to finish, as well). Students quickly learned, when wrapping up their group work, to check for handouts or directions and then move immediately into the follow-up activity.

Extension activities consisted of language awareness activities such as reinforcing grammar or vocabulary or discussing one aspect or another of the classroom assignment they had just completed (in pairs or small groups); sometimes, especially during written work, I would move around the room, going from one student to the next, answering his or her questions about something I had circled on an assignment I had just handed back. On the whole, students responded well to these activities.

Balancing group and individualized instruction

During this first phase of the course and continuing into the other two phases, I worked individually with learners in tutorials and through individual conferences. It is important to balance student-student cooperative learning activities with teacher-student individualized learning so that students feel

I am addressing their unique problems and working with them on their individual strengths and needs. For example, immersion events (such as the social and the field trip) allowed for some individualized interaction, and I also asked students to hand in (for scoring) taped readings of words and poems, which I assessed for group and individual problem utterances. Following group instruction, I conducted individual sessions in which I went through each learner's problem sounds and utterances before asking the learner to repeat the assignment so as to evaluate improvement on the second tape.

Phase 2: Practicing the cooperative learning model

At this point in the course, students were ready to practice what they had learned and to proceed with preparation for the Story Theater presentations for preschoolers. Students knew what to expect in regard to class activities, cooperative work, and immersion events. They were also ready to begin more independent work on their projects. They were accustomed to theme-based reading and listening activities and were beginning to understand how project work and field trips related to content covered in class. We began this phase of the course with a visit to the public library, which, compared to the university library, was more easily managed by the ESL students, has more diverse materials of an appropriate nature, and gives the students a chance to encounter life in the larger community. At the library, students met individually with me and also found and checked out at least three useful resources for their individual research project. The next day, they brought the library resources they had collected to class, and we all browsed each other's books to find materials useful for each person's topic. This served to orient students to each other's topics, and they continued, in the next few weeks, to share resources they found that could be of use to another person. To further encourage cooperative work, I assigned students to pairs and trios to work cooperatively on a bulletin board display that focused on various aspects of Native American and pioneer life.

Grouping

I based cooperative learning group makeup on how closely related the topics of individual research were to each other. This cooperative learning activity provided another way for students to become familiar with each other's resources and gave them some practice in talking about their topic with others. It also helped me to easily see which students needed extra help in locating materials. Although I planned that students would only work in these groups to do the bulletin board display, I found that longer-term cooperative learning groups emerged naturally as the students went on to plan for the preschool presentation. The person who selected face painting, for example, ended up working quite often with the one who was teaching hand signs for various animals since they both wanted to use the same texts. The extent to which they wanted to interact and cooperate on individual topics was left up to the students themselves. About a third of the class worked closely together in a group of 4–6 people, even meeting and constructing their posters at someone's house. Another third worked in pairs, and the remaining third chose to work alone (but with occasional peer and teacher help and feedback).

To decide Story Theater groups (i.e., who would work together on which story), I considered social group preferences, home locations, English proficiency, L1s, and leadership. By this time, several groups were meeting informally outside of class for lunch, project work, and other social activities, and I kept those social group preferences in mind when assigning stories. I tried to arrange group members heterogeneously in terms of individual learner fluency and intelligibility. Finally, I made sure that at least one class leader was in each story group. I organized and distributed story parts based on the number of "voices" required for each story and, in the case of the major role, gave that part to a more outgoing student who would be understood fairly easily. However, I told students they could trade parts with another person if they so desired, and in one case this did occur. I also found it necessary to later arrange backup readers for each story in the case of an absent reader. The backup readers had to be familiar enough with the story to step in and take the place of the missing reader. This provided a nice challenge opportunity for the more proficient learners. I did not intend, originally, for the students to act out the stories, but during rehearsals in class, listeners started to dramatize the story on their own, so we decided to incorporate props and actions to complement each reading. As it turned out, each story had a group of 4–6 assigned readers and a smaller group of 3–4 actors.

Teacher's role

This was a very interesting phase in the course for me since I was reminded almost daily of the need to give up control and to adjust to the various learning and work styles of students in the class. Some students were very organized and detailed; they had all their materials prepared and shown to me well in advance of the presentation day. Others were confident but (from my point of view) disorganized and OK with just pulling it all together at the last minute. I had to remind myself that these were *their* projects and that I could not interfere or take charge too much.

My role during this phase of the class changed to that of learning facilitator, guide, and advisor as I helped students to polish their performances, to plan project displays / activities, and to improve in both language and content areas of instruction. I continued a balance of individualized and whole-class instruction as I reacted to group work. In the individualized instruction, I found it important to let students know that I did not expect them to all progress and produce at the same pace and in the same areas. I explained that I viewed each of them from the position of their unique strengths and needs in English and that, as long as they were trying to improve, actively participating, and contributing to their group, I was happy with their performance as learners. For me as a teacher, this was a very exciting phase of the class as I was able to watch students transition from learning the model to actually practicing and taking the lead in cooperative learning-oriented activities.

Evaluation

GRADING

About midterm time in a typical course, students begin to worry a little about what their grades will be. In this particular course, I wondered how worried students would be about their grades since we were using such a nontraditional format. I found that although they were interested, grades were much less an issue to this class than other classes. This may be because I met with each student individually at midterm and also gave regular feedback as to active participation and other scores, so they felt they were doing OK in the course. I am more inclined to think, however, that the students seemed unconcerned about their grades, except for the peer assessment component (to be explained later), because they were focused on class activities and performance events and were more concerned about pleasing an outside audience (the preschool children) than with a grade. In fact, a great deal of class time during this phase of the course was spent in rehearsal and preparation for the Story Theater event.

ERRANT GROUP MEMBERS

I believe that the class-building activities during Phase 1 and a smooth, comfortable transition from teacher-directed to learner-directed activities between Phase 1 and Phase 2 helped to foster cooperative learning success, as did learner control and choice. Don't get the impression that everything went perfectly, however. For example, there was a problem with some students who had celebrated an important cultural holiday too late into the night and did not show up for class. The rest of the class was quite upset with them since they could not rehearse for the performance. The class members present asked me to telephone the missing students and ask where they were. They arrived an hour later and I left the room while they sorted out what to do. The class rehearsed in the remaining time available but also decided to meet extra outside of class (without me) to rehearse. The absent students were very apologetic and were among the most active during the actual school performance. I think this was a turning point in some ways because those students appeared to take ownership of the project rather than working on it only because I required it or they thought it might please me. I also think it helped that I left the room so that they could sort out the problem by themselves.

PEER AND TEACHER EVALUATION

Each group handed in a tape of their coordinated practice readings, after which I asked that they assess all the members in terms of contribution to the group. I instructed them to write each group member's name on a slip of paper and then score each other's contribution to the group by distributing $100 (as opposed to points, for example, just to add an element of fun) among the group members. For example, a group member who did not show up for practices or was not well prepared, I suggested, should get less "pay" than one who took the lead to arrange rehearsals, was always prepared, and made an effort to improve. One grade for group work was therefore based solely on the pay allocated to each member of the group by the group members themselves. I also evaluated the taped readings with each group able to receive up to 20 points for pronunciation, pacing, fluency, intonation and stress, and acting (reading dramatically). I gave each group their grade for the first tape (all group members receiving the same grade), and they then worked to improve and handed in a second tape of group story readings a week or so later. We again conducted individual assessment by cooperative learning group as described above for the second group reading, and I again evaluated the tape recordings, giving each group mate the same grade within a group.

I found that, in general, the students were more critical in their assessment of each other for the second group tape. When asked to pay each other the first time, most tended to simply assign equal points to each group member. The second time they were asked to assess, however, they gave somewhat higher pay to those who took responsibility (those who informally led or otherwise helped the group) and much less pay to members who were late for rehearsals or did not work to prepare their parts.

Final preparations for Story Theater event

At this point in the course, students were working regularly outside of class in informal cooperative learning groups on learning station activities and complementary research topic poster displays. These learning station activities were done with the preschool children along with the Story Theater. The students spent about half an hour one day in class with each student showing the whole class his or her poster and then explaining the hands-on activity each would conduct for the preschool children. This encouraged students to get their posters done and handed in to me a week before the event. It also helped them to identify key words to use, and to think in detail about language, verbal directions, and demonstration techniques to use when interacting with the children. As each class member presented, I made a list of materials required for the hands-on activity with the children (e.g., tape, scissors, construction paper, finger paint, crayons) so that I could learn what the school could provide and what we would have to bring ourselves. We also talked as a whole class about the schedule and created a sequenced list of main events and time schedule.

Phase 3: Celebrating the cooperative learning model

To my joy as a teacher, this was the phase of the class during which I was able to contribute mostly as a friendly critic, expert reviewer, coparticipant, and cheerleader who supported and praised students for their accomplishments. I participated as a class member myself during field trip and display events. In follow-up activities, I encouraged students to reflect upon their learning experiences and to consider their reactions during language contact activities so as to be encouraged to continue risk-taking in English. I gave feedback by sharing my perceptions of their progress and continuing needs in English while communicating the ways that I felt they had contributed to successful group and class experiences. Finally, I helped them to collect photos and other artifacts of our time together so as to preserve their memories of the class and our cooperative learning interactions.

Four major celebration events took place the final two weeks of the eight-week course. Each had a different flavor in terms of the kind of group interactions that evolved. The first event of this phase was our second (and final) field trip. We all felt a bit nostalgic and sad, I think, with an element of memory building entailed since we would part ways soon. The second event, our Story Theater performance and learning station work with the preschool children, was filled with nervousness at first, followed by relief when the students actually pulled it off. The third event was our final class social, an enjoyable celebration of friendship mixed with recognition of the class culture we had developed together. The final celebration was public display of our work for an outside audience, more formal in nature yet also intimate since pairs and individuals had time to talk together during the event. Each is described in more detail below.

Final field trip

The first event of the celebration phase of the course was the second and final field trip, during which we visited an ancient Native American cultural site and saw firsthand examples of traditional Native American culture. Usually during a field trip I feel a lot of pressure to interact with students so that they get language practice, and I try to see that everyone has a good time. At this point in this course, however, I was able to simply drive the van, assist as requested with language or logistical concerns, and participate in the event. This was the most relaxing field trip I had ever been on because the learners were quite content and comfortable interacting with each other and with outsiders in English. I never had to remind anyone to use English, and I was by no means the central focus of the group. The class knew by now that I encouraged them to explore, ask questions, take pictures, and have fun on their own. I can't help but think that a great deal of the success of this event was due to the true friendships and enjoyment the class shared with each other by this point in the course. We all knew that this was our final field trip together, and there was an aspect of memory building that I feel contributed much to our enjoyment of the event.

Story Theater

The second celebration event was the preschool Story Theater presentation day held during week 7 of the term. The students performed twice – once for the morning session children and again for the afternoon session. The students did their Story Theater presentations (two short stories for each of the two preschool classes). After Story Theater, each ESL student was in charge of a learning station for small groups of children. The ESL students explained their individual research topics, using the posters they had constructed as visual aids. They then helped the children get involved with complementary hands-on activities (puzzles, games, crafts, dances, face painting, and so on). The children were free to move from learning station to learning station as they wanted, so the ESL students had a chance to present their information and lead their activities several times for different children. The preschool children had a good time, as did their new friends from the university.

Before the second Story Theater presentation, for the afternoon preschool program, we shared lunch while reflecting upon and discussing how the morning session went and what could be improved. Based on this discussion, we rehearsed the Story Theater so as to improve the afternoon session. Again, the reaction from the children was very positive. After we left, the preschool teachers asked the children what they had liked most about the day, wrote their children's answers, and sent drawings and thank-you letters from the children to our ESL students. We responded by giving the school a copy of the photos we had taken, as well as a copy of the videotape. Some students also decided to donate their individual research topic poster to the school.

Final class social (Evidence of a class culture)

There was a great deal of relief once the Story Theater presentations were over, and the class was definitely in the mood to celebrate at a final social gathering and dinner at my house the following weekend. The earlier social meant students came prepared to enjoy themselves. Quite a number of them brought guests, and they also thought to bring and share photos from the final field trip and school presentations. Several brought special dishes to share, and some brought games.

I have already discussed the importance of building a classroom culture early on when teaching and learning cooperatively. At the final party, it was obvious that a classroom culture had developed as students told inside jokes that referred to funny events in class or class member personalities. They stayed fairly late, singing songs. The most popular ones were the pioneer songs students learned when preparing for the preschool presentations. Students even taught party guests the same dance they had taught the preschoolers.

Open house exhibit (Closure)

As the final celebration and synthesis event, the class participated in an all-IEP open house End-of-Term (EOT) exhibit in which the class showed videos (the preschool presentations and field trips), displayed individual research topic posters, and gave verbal explanations to visitors. Students also constructed and presented a bulletin board of class events from throughout the term (e.g., photos taken on field trips, brochures collected, letters from the preschool children saying what they liked best about the presentation, and reflective statements from the students about what they learned and enjoyed from the ESL class). The students also contributed to a newsletter publication constructed by another class and distributed to visitors at the EOT exhibit.

As a whole, my IEP colleagues and I have found that the End-Of-Term exhibit is very important as a cumulative term event for our program. It provides authorship or performance opportunities as well as a realistic and authentic opportunity for communicative interaction. It is also a means for visitors and other participants to provide feedback through conversation that is useful for both teachers and learners, and it allows for authentic assessment of students as they present project and other class work. For my class in particular, the exhibit allowed them an opportunity to discuss their projects, presentations, and field trips with outsiders. I think many students were amazed to see the physical evidence of their experiences and accomplishments during the eight-week term. This was also the first time that students had seen the videotapes of their field trips and the school presentations (as did visitors to the exhibit). Students enjoyed seeing the children's and their own reactions on video. The videos provided a wonderful way to help the students see progress made during the term, since they could easily compare their fluency, confidence, and comfort interacting in English during the first versus the final field trip. Students signed up to staff the display every half hour, and I was at the display the entire time. The open house thus allowed some time for us to chat quietly together between visitors. It was really nice to have this quiet time with students individually or in pairs at the end of the course.

Learning as a social activity

My belief in the efficacy of social interaction as a cornerstone of enjoyable and effective learning was reinforced as I observed the strong friendships that developed among these learners. At least two groups continued long-term in what could be described as self-selected *base groups*. (See Chapter 1.) Even two years after the class had ended and after they had entered full-time academic work, these base groups continued to meet together for lunch and socials once a month. Even students who returned to their home countries stayed in e-mail contact with members of their groups. A number of the students still call and visit me regularly – often to invite me to special events their group has organized (to meet visiting family members, to attend a birthday celebration, thesis defense party, or even a baby shower). Whenever I see them, they mention the projects course as a favorite language learning experience, also catching me up with what is happening with various members of the class.

Teacher collaboration

At this point, I would like to step out of my teacher role and talk from the point of view of a curriculum coordinator and administrator to discuss how I attempted to promote and encourage teacher collaboration and cooperative learning-oriented instruction. An important aspect of our projects courses has been teacher collaboration, both within the IEP and between the IEP and teachers in other settings.

Teachers as instructional designers

In the IEP, teachers work closely with *area supervisors*, teachers who are assigned a specific area such as grammar, projects, writing, or level, and who take the lead to document revisions to the instructional plan for courses so as to recycle and improve courses for the next term. Teachers receive and add to a course notebook and an electronic record, which is submitted to the area supervisor at the end of the term for review before passing it to the next teacher of that course. Constant attention to updating class notebooks and weeksheets (profiles of course events during a week) involves teachers as instructional designers while also encouraging reflection and improvement of learning guides, assessment tools, class calendars, and other instructional matters.

Mentoring novice teachers and sharing stories

The experienced teachers in the IEP work with a number of graduate students who are teaching assistants in our program. These mentor teachers frequently observe and give feedback, much of which includes providing coaching in strategies for group formation and functioning. We also conduct weekly seminars for teaching assistants, with group work and collaborative techniques included as topics. We make books, videos, and other resources about cooperative learning available to teachers through purchasing them for our teacher resource room and our language media center and through the teacher resource pages of our IEP Web site.[1]

I believe we could do even more, however, and I am interested in asking teachers to demonstrate model cooperative learning lessons and / or videotape cooperative activities already under way in their classrooms. One avenue for dissemination is a language teaching miniconference that I initiated in cooperation with the linguistics, curriculum and instruction, reading education, and foreign language education departments on our campus. At this four-hour conference, teachers and graduate students presented a variety of cooperative techniques and model lessons. We also set up a room to display new and / or popular textbooks and materials, some on cooperative learning.

Giving teachers time to collaborate

An essential, but often overlooked, element in teacher-teacher collaboration involves teachers being able to find time to work together. Here the role of administrators is key. Since my early experiences working in interdisciplinary teams, I have always believed in making sure time is allocated to teacher discussion and planning together. Teachers should not have to carve out time to talk together from their already busy teaching and meeting schedules. In our IEP, regular classes are held four days a week with Wednesdays allocated to teacher meetings, learner-teacher conferences, and special events or special classes (e.g., field trips, school visits, and special topic courses). This schedule ensures that all teachers working with the same group of students have time to meet weekly or bimonthly to target skills and to discuss problems, successes, and upcoming themes. We also organize informal monthly teacher lunches to which administrators, departmental professors, and clerical staff are usually invited. This allows socializing and interacting together informally and, I feel, aids in more effective communication between members of the department while establishing us as part of the same professional team. All the ideas described in this section are designed to ensure that teachers are staying in touch and sharing their stories with each other.

Conclusion

In this chapter, I have related a specific example of cooperative learning as operationalized within a low-proficient, adult ESL language learning

---

[1] www.siu.edu/~ces1/teacher.html

context. I thought it important that you know a bit about my beliefs and values as a language educator and how those have led to the integration of collaborative learning within my teaching. After describing generally the instructional setting and ways in which cooperative learning is included in our IEP's curriculum, I described a particular course and how cooperative learning was implemented in an effective, enjoyable way for all participants. Integrated within this case description were a number of suggestions for those wishing to use cooperative learning in similar contexts (Wilhelm 1999). For example, I recommended that teachers design instruction so that cooperative learning activities lead to authentic performance or display events with outside audiences. It is equally important to focus on having fun together so that learning is viewed as an enjoyable, social interaction with friendships and group celebrations as natural outcomes of an effective educational experience. Finally, I think it necessary that we overtly teach the cooperative learning model so that participants can become aware of their roles and responsibilities in nontraditional classroom contexts.

As the final segment in this chapter, I shared ideas and techniques to foster teacher collaboration and administrative support of cooperative learning in educational settings, discussing both techniques used in our program and ideas sparked through the process of writing my chapter in this book on cooperative learning in L2 instruction.

Discussion questions and tasks

1. Wilhelm was teaching at the same time as acting in a supervisory role with colleagues. What special opportunities does a person in that position have to facilitate the implementation of innovations such as cooperative learning?
2. Wilhelm describes how she provided her students with opportunities to take part in authentic authorship events. What does this term mean to you? How might students take part in such events?
3. A key audience for Wilhelm's university students' cooperative learning projects was classes of primary school learners. This type of cross-age tutoring has advantages for both parties. The older L2 learners have a willing audience that presents an appropriate level of challenge, and the younger students have the chance to interact with people with whom they may not often come into contact. How might you arrange cross-age or other forms of tutoring for students?
4. Wilhelm explains how her students sometimes worked alone before working in pairs and eventually working in foursomes. Indeed, in

many cooperative learning techniques, students first work alone and / or work with one partner before forming larger groups. What do you see as advantages and disadvantages of these arrangements?

5. Wilhelm used out-of-class experiences, such as social gatherings at her home, to generate a cooperative environment in the class. To what extent can out-of-class nonacademic collaboration promote successful academic collaboration? In addition to the class socials that Wilhelm describes, what other forms could out-of-class nonacademic collaboration take?

6. One activity that Wilhelm tried – the one during the first field trip – turned out to be too challenging for students, so she abandoned the activity. This raises the issue of finding tasks that are challenging, yet achievable through cooperative means. Usually, students working collaboratively can accomplish more difficult tasks than students working alone. How can you monitor group interaction to see if tasks are too difficult? What would you do if some groups seemed to be doing OK at a task while other groups seemed to be failing?

7. When some groups were progressing faster than others, Wilhelm offered the faster groups sponge activities to do. Sponge activities "soak up" extra time in useful ways. Think of some tasks that your students do or might do in groups. What are some sponge activities that you could propose to groups that finish ahead of others? How might you get students to develop their own?

8. Educators strive to replace grades as students' primary motivation. Wilhelm reports some success toward this goal in that her students seemed more interested in the success of their projects than in the grade they obtained. How might the group aspect of the projects also have contributed to her students' relatively lower emphasis on grades? How can cooperative learning alter the motivation picture?

9. Wilhelm used an innovative approach to peer assessment in groups by having students "pay" each other. Do you agree with such an approach? Why or why not? What other means could you use to involve students in assessing each other's contributions?

Conclusion

Ana Christina DaSilva Iddings

Throughout the book we (the authors) have focused on some of the key aspects of cooperative learning, such as the concepts of interdependence, individual accountability, and equitable participation. In the first part of the book, we delved into the supportive work on cooperative learning in psychology and examined the educational relevance of this approach to what we know about second language learning. In the narrative chapters, we illustrated how cooperative learning has been instituted in second language classrooms around the world and across grade levels. In this conclusion, we wish to make salient some of the significant contributions of the volume. It is important to point out that the contributions accented here are representative of the teachers' and students' lived experiences as, together, they created versatile structures for cooperative learning, promoted second language learning, and fostered authentic classroom interactions.

Versatile structures for cooperative learning

One of the major offerings of the book is the description of an array of structures for the use of cooperative learning within a variety of classroom environments. That is, as the narrative chapters illustrate, the teachers did not simply implement a mechanical model of a single set of cooperative learning rules. Instead, cooperative learning took different forms, taking into account the particulars of each context, including students' cultural backgrounds, ages, interests, and needs, as well as their ability to work together to create collective goals. For example, in Chapter 4, McCafferty and DaSilva Iddings described cooperative learning activities as they took shape in a multilingual kindergarten classroom in the American Southwest, where students were entering school for the first time. In that setting, cooperative learning was loosely structured – emphasis was placed on developing students' collaborative dispositions and creating a social-emotional environment conducive to cooperation. This is clearly a different scenario than the one described in Chapter 6, where Jones and Taylor focused on high school students enrolled in French classes in Toronto, Canada, students engaging in multiple, highly structured activities created and / or adapted by the instructors to emphasize the content of instruction while at the same time aiming to build classroom community.

Second language learning and teaching

The narrative chapters often illustrate how language learners provided a *scaffold* (Chapter 1) for one another for promoting language learning. One aspect of this process focused on the development of sociolinguistic competence through students engaging in the use of language that conveys collaborative dispositions as a part of participating in cooperative activities. In Chapter 7, for example, Wee and Jacobs discussed students' involvement in process writing activities that focused on the development of reading, writing, listening, and speaking. Through their participation in these activities, students learned appropriate language (e.g., praise vocabulary) to be able to listen to, discuss, and critique each other's work in collaborative and nurturing ways. Likewise, Wilhelm (Chapter 9) described the affordances of cooperative learning in fostering language learning as students worked together rehearsing and providing each other with constructive feedback to help create and improve performance events such as Story Theater, poetry readings, and presentations of posters and displays.

It is noteworthy that although we believe that the development of fitting language for collaborative work is a natural by-product of cooperative learning, we in no way mean to suggest that complacency and harmony are always necessary for cooperation to occur. Instead, we realize that tensions, conflicts, and disagreements are bound to happen during group activities. Moreover, we argue that such discord is important to second language development – students need to become able to hedge, defend their ideas, and effectively resolve disputes, for instance. The examples provided in the narrative chapters concerning how teachers and students helped to resolve difficulties in a productive way are useful not only in relation to cooperative learning but to teaching as a whole.

Also, with regard to L2 learning, cooperative approaches provide opportunities for *authentic* activities to occur within a classroom setting. According to Moll and Greenberg (1990), authentic activity in a school setting must have the characteristics of real activity for real purposes as stemming from the concerns of the people involved. Cooperative learning as found in the narrative chapters produced authentic circumstances for interaction, for example, when students worked together to decide what to do in order to accomplish a task. Such student-centered conditions permit student choice, promote unpredictability, and allow for the possibility of an equitable distribution of duties and talk as a natural outcome of cooperative interaction. These are all features that are thought to have a positive impact on language learning.

Moreover, when realized, authentic activity gives rise to classroom practices that move pedagogy away from transmission models (delivery of information) and towards transformation. In Chapter 5, for example, Ghaith and Kawtharani wrote that cooperative learning techniques offered them an alternative to teacher-centered instruction as they provided opportunities for highly communicative and meaningful classroom interactions in a low-risk, stress-reduced environment. Likewise, Joritz-Nakagawa (Chapter 8) described the affordances of cooperative learning in creating greater authenticity in classroom activities as the students, in groups, based on their collective interests, created their own set of reading materials for the class by using newspaper clippings and excerpts from articles, thus no longer having to rely on standardized textbooks.

Some final considerations

Although the benefits of cooperative approaches to L2 teaching and learning are many, teachers sometimes shy away from using cooperative learning activities as they are perceived to be too time-consuming in lesson preparation. Furthermore, teachers may experience a sense of having lost control of what students learn during their interactions. We hope we were able to counter these perceptions through the narratives we presented by highlighting the fact that once the necessary infrastructures for cooperative practices are in place within a classroom community, it is relatively simple to implement lessons. We also gave examples of how to account for individual students' work as they participate in joint activity. Certainly, assessment issues are of major importance to curricular concerns, and cooperative learning recognizes this in both how it is conceptualized and how it is implemented.

We would also like to mention the role of professional development found in the narrative chapters because it is, of course, an important means of supporting teachers' efforts to become proficient users of cooperative learning. Both Wee (Chapter 7) and Wilhelm (Chapter 9) promoted cooperative learning at their respective schools as administrators, providing teachers with the opportunity to try it out in their own classrooms, to get help from others more familiar with the practice, and to collaborate with their fellow teachers through observing each other's classrooms or collectively reflecting on the approach and its activities. The narrative chapter authors also consider their own growth as they became more skilled with using cooperative learning. On this level, we want to stress that the careful examination of what takes place within a classroom – action research – is a crucial part of coming to effectively utilize any pedagogical approach.

Finally, although we recognize that there are aspects of the book that deserve further discussion, and moreover, that there are elements of cooperative learning itself that deserve further attention, we hope that the ideas contained in this book will inspire prospective and in-service teachers to become adept in the use of collaborative practices in the teaching of another language. We also hope that this book offers support, validation, and a sense of renewal for those who are already disposed toward using cooperative learning in their classrooms.

Appendix:
Cooperative learning
techniques and activities

George M. Jacobs

This appendix provides a glossary of sorts for the cooperative learning techniques and activities mentioned in this book. The key purpose of the glossary is to provide a handy, all-in-one-place, alphabetically-ordered reference that makes it easier for educators to remember and use the techniques and activities in their own teaching.

Three points need to be made before we begin. First, by *technique* we mean a generic procedure into which content from any subject area or area of language learning can be fitted. An *activity* is the procedure plus the content. For instance, we can take the cooperative learning technique Numbered Heads Together, described in Chapter 5 and elsewhere, and combine it with working on a set of algebra problems or reading comprehension questions in order to create a mathematics activity or a reading activity. Techniques are generalizable to any subject area and age level, whereas activities are not.

The second point is that all techniques and activities can and should be modified to fit particular teaching and learning contexts. Thus, there is no one correct way to do any of the techniques and activities described hereafter. That said, when making modifications, educators should bear in mind principles of good teaching generally and of cooperative learning in particular, as outlined in Part I of this book.

The third point concerns to whom to give credit for the techniques and activities and how to name the techniques and activities. As Kearney (1993) found, crediting specific cooperative learning techniques to particular authors can be "like trying to catch the first drop of rain." Also, the same technique may appear under more than one name, while at the same time the same name may be used for two somewhat different techniques. In this book, the general approach has been to give a technique the name which in our (the editors and authors of the various chapters) experience is used most frequently and to attribute a technique to author(s) based on what appears in the books on our bookshelves or those of our favorite libraries.

We have also discovered when explaining cooperative learning techniques to educators that they sometimes had developed similar techniques on their own. Note: The chapter references are to this book.

Chalkboard Share (Kagan 1992) [Chapter 8]

This technique can be used with others, such as Numbered Heads Together, to enable groups to quickly share their ideas with the class.

1. While groups are working together on a task or after they have finished, one member of each group goes to the board to write the group's response to the task. Or, responses can be written on individual-sized whiteboards, which can be held up for other groups to see.
2. Members of other groups can respond with suggestions or praise. They may also wish to revise what their group has done based on what is learned from other groups.

Circle and Square (Jones & Taylor, Chapter 6, this book)

This activity is designed to build group solidarity as students share information about themselves and become aware of the similarities among group members.

1. Students are in groups of four. This is a square, as a square has four sides.
2. Each group member writes in a circle one thing about themselves that other members do not know. Groups discuss this information.
3. Groups make a list of commonalities among group members.
4. They use these commonalities to create a team name and logo.

Concept Attainment (Bruner, Goodnow & Austin 1967) [Chapter 6]

This activity gives students practice in understanding categories.

1. Students are in pairs.
2. A number of statements are presented to the class. Each statement is one of two colors, red or blue.
3. Group members work alone to identify what the statements of each color have in common, exchange views with their partner, and share with the class.
4. The process repeats, except this time statements without any color are presented, and pairs work in the same way to determine to which color the statements may belong.

Concept Formation (Taba 1992) [Chapter 6]

As in Concept Attainment, students put data into categories.

1. Students are given a set of words, and groups collaborate to be sure all group members understand the words.
2. Each group member works alone to put the words into categories according to their meaning and then shares their system with group mates.
3. Groups agree on one category system and create a visual to display their system.
4. One group member stays behind to explain, as groups tour the classroom to view the category systems of the other groups.
5. As in Concept Attainment, this activity can be used for categorization of any type.

Co-op Co-op (Kagan 1992) [Chapter 8]

As in Group Investigation, students work together on projects.

1. The teacher leads whole-class discussion of the topic the class will be investigating.
2. Students form groups based either on achieving heterogeneity among group members or on interest in the same subtopic. Groups then do team-building activities to promote knowing and trusting their group mates.
3. Groups select subtopics and divide their subtopic among the group members, who individually prepare and then present what they learned to group mates.
4. Group mates work together on a presentation to the entire class.
5. Students along with the teacher take part in evaluating the work of their group mates and other groups.

Cooperative Integrated Reading and Composition (CIRC) (Slavin 1995) [Chapters 1, 5]

This technique is an adaptation of STAD (further description follows) specifically designed for teaching reading and writing.

1. Teacher provides instruction on whatever teaching point(s) is the focus of the lesson.
2. In groups that are mixed as to past achievement, students practice the points taught by the teacher in preparation for a quiz. Students do

not take a quiz until their teammates have determined that they are ready.

3. Groups receive nongrade rewards based on group members' performances on the quiz and other assessments. These performances are measured via improvement scoring (i.e., based on an individual's performance relative not to others' performances but to the individual's own past performance).

The Five Friends (Jones & Taylor, Chapter 6, this book)

In this activity, students collaborate to read for clues that will enable them to answer questions.

1. Students in groups of four collaborate to understand clues about five fictional characters and use the clues to complete a chart about the characters.
2. They use the chart to answers questions about the characters.
3. Groups create a mindmap based on their information.
4. Group members are called on at random to present their mindmaps to the class or other groups.

Flip It! (Jones & Taylor, Chapter 6, this book)

This is a picture description technique that can be generalized to any type of discussion. The key is that everyone has an equal amount of time to contribute to the discussion.

1. Each pair has a picture of one or more people.
2. One partner begins a description of the picture, including going beyond what can be seen to hypothesize about the people in the picture.
3. The teacher says "Flip It!" and the other partner continues the description.
4. This procedure repeats several times.
5. Students are randomly selected to share their pair's description with the class.

Gallery Tour (Kagan 1992) [Chapter 6]

In this technique, groups view and give feedback on the work of other groups.

1. Groups work on a task. The task can be assigned by the teacher or chosen by the groups.
2. They display their work. This can be done on the walls of the class-room, where the groups are seated, on flip charts or easels, and so on.
3. Groups circulate around the room to view, learn from, and give feed-back on the work of other groups. One group member may stay behind to explain the group's work.

Graffiti (Gibbs 1987) [Chapter 6]

In this technique, groups work together to share ideas with the entire class.

1. The class has a common theme, and each group is given or writes a statement or question on the theme. This is written at the top of a large sheet of poster/chart paper.
2. Group members write words, phrases, or short sentences in response to the statement or question and then pass their paper to another group, or they post it on a wall.
3. Groups take turns adding responses to other groups' statements and questions.
4. Groups review the responses they have received from other groups.

Group Dialoging (DaSilva Iddings & McCafferty, Chapter 4, this book)

In this whole-class activity, students learn about taking turns.

1. The class sits in a circle.
2. Students take turns sharing experiences or talking about any topic. Possession of a wand indicates who has the floor.
3. The class selects one of the students' personal oral narratives to jointly construct as a written text.

Group Investigation (Sharan & Sharan 1992) [Chapter 3]

In this technique, students work together on projects.

1. The whole class works on one overall theme, with each group inves-tigating one aspect of the theme.
2. Students work either in teacher-assigned heterogeneous groups or in groups based on interest in the same subtopic.

3. Each group decides how it will conduct its investigation and assigns tasks to the members.
4. Groups plan and carry out presentations of their findings to the whole class.
5. Evaluation is done by each student of themselves, their group mates, the other groups, and the teachers.

Inside-Outside Circles (Kagan 1992) [Chapters 6, 9]

In this technique, as in Mixer Review, students work briefly with a range of classmates.

1. The class forms two facing circles, one inside the other. Each circle has the same number of members. Students in the inner circle face outward; students in the outer circle face inward.
2. Each student has a partner in the other circle. Partners discuss a topic, ask each other questions, or share experiences.
3. Members of one circle rotate one place, so that everyone now has a new partner in the other circle.
4. The process repeats.

Jigsaw (Aronson, Blaney, Stephan, Sikes & Snapp 1978) [Chapters 1, 5, 8]

In this technique, group mates share information with each other.

1. Students begin in their home team. Each home team member is given or researches information on one part of an overall topic.
2. Students form expert teams with a small number of classmates (normally four or less) to study their part of the topic and prepare to teach it to their home teammates.
3. Students return to their home teams and teach their group mates.
4. Students take a quiz or work together on a task that involves all the different parts of the topic.

Jigsaw II (Slavin 1995) [Chapter 5]

The same as Jigsaw, except that all students receive all the information, rather than only the information relevant to their part of the topic. The expert teams function as before, but home team members are less dependent on each other because they have the information that their group mates are teaching them.

Magic Box (Jones & Taylor, Chapter 6, this book)

In this class-building activity, students give classmates magic boxes.

1. Each student imagines something.
2. Students move around the room taking turns to tell what they have imagined to individual classmates. They ask each other questions and prepare to share what they have heard with others.

Magic Sentences (Jones & Taylor, Chapter 6, this book)

In this activity, pairs collaborate to construct sentences.

1. Each pair is given a table containing words and phrases.
2. The goal is to earn points for one's pair by making sentences using adjoining words from the table.

Mixer Review (Winn-Bell Olsen 1982) [Chapter 5]

In this technique, students mix with a variety of classmates to review material.

1. Students form two facing lines with each student facing a classmate. Each line has the same number of students. Each student has the same set of questions.
2. Partners discuss the first question with the person from the other line facing them. If the pair cannot agree or has trouble with the question, the pair uses notes or asks another pair.
3. At a signal from the teacher, one line moves down one step so that everyone is now facing a new partner. This means that one student from the line that moved has to go to the other end of his or her own line. New partners respond to the next question, using the same procedure they followed in answering question 1.
4. The same procedure, moving down one step, is repeated for each new question, until the question sheet is completed.

MURDER (Hythecker, Dansereau & Rocklin 1988) [Chapter 1]

This is an acronym for a reading technique in which pairs examine the ideas in a text.

1. Mood – A pair of students sets a relaxed yet purposeful mood before beginning their work. They make sure they are clear on the procedure to follow and engage in a little chit-chat.

2. Understand – A reading passage (or section from a textbook) has been divided into sections. (The teacher can do this or students can use natural breaks in the passage, such as chapter sections.) Each student reads the first section silently.

3. Recall – Without looking at the text, one member of the pair acts as a recaller who summarizes the key ideas of the section.

4. Detect – The other partner looks at the text, detects any errors, omissions, or unnecessary information in the summary and discusses these with the recaller. The roles of recaller and detector rotate for the next section.

5. Elaborate – Both students elaborate on the ideas in the section. Types of elaborations include:
   * connections with other things the students have studied
   * links between the section and students' lives
   * additions of relevant information not included in the section
   * agreements or disagreements with the views or ideas expressed in the section
   * reactions to the section such as surprise, gladness, or anger
   * applications of the ideas and information
   * questions, either about things not understood or questions sparked by the section

   Groups repeat the Understand, Recall, Detect, and Elaborate steps for all the sections of the text.

6. Review – When the entire text has been completed, the pair combines their thoughts to summarize the entire text.

MURDER may seem a rather hostile acronym. A sunnier alternative with exactly the same steps is SUMMER: Set the mood, Understand by reading silently, Mention the main ideas, Monitor the summary, Elaborate on the main ideas, and Review.

My Imaginary Friend (Jones & Taylor, Chapter 6, this book)

In this class-building activity, students use their imaginations and retell descriptions of people created by classmates.

1. Each student creates an imaginary friend, giving the person (or animal) a name and other details (e.g., physical description and favorite activities).

2. Students describe their imaginary friend to a classmate. Students form new pairs and tell each other about their former partner's imaginary friend.

3. This continues as students recount the description of the imaginary friend that they had last heard described.
4. The teacher calls on students to tell the class the name of the imaginary friend they created. The last person who heard that friend described retells the description they heard.
5. The creators recount their original descriptions, and the two descriptions are compared.

Numbered Heads Together (Kagan 1992) [Chapters 5, 7, 8, 9]

In this technique, students work together and check that all group members can explain what their group has done.

1. Each group member has a number (e.g., 1, 2, 3, 4).
2. Students work alone to do a task assigned by the teacher.
3. Each student shares his or her answer, and students put their heads together to try to agree on an answer.
4. A number is chosen. Students with that number report and explain their group's work.

Paper Bag Share (DaSilva Iddings & McCafferty, Chapter 4, this book)

This is an information gap activity that links with drawing and sharing of possessions.

1. Students bring an object from home in a paper bag.
2. Partners use the sense of touch to try to figure out what is in the bag and draw what they think it is.
3. The objects are taken out of the bags and shown to partners.

Paraphrase Passport (Kagan 1992) [Chapters 3, 7]

In this technique, students focus on active listening.

1. One member of a pair speaks.
2. The partner attempts to paraphrase what the first person said.
3. The first person checks the paraphrase for accuracy.
4. When the paraphrase has been approved, the second person responds to what the first person has said.
5. The cycle repeats after each partner has spoken.

People Hunt (also known as Find Someone Who) (Kagan & Kagan 1998) [Chapter 5]

In this technique, students mix with and get to know a bit about a large number of classmates.

1. Students begin in pairs. Each person has a Find Someone Who table (e.g., if there are 30 students in the class, a 6 × 5 grid composed of 30 boxes). The number of boxes should be no more than the number of people in the class. In each box is a question (e.g., *Do you like oranges?* or *Can you play badminton?*)
2. Partners take turns to read the rules. The first in the pair reads the first rule. The second person paraphrases (or repeats) the rule.
   Rules:
   - Walk up to a classmate and ask a question from the sheet. If the person doesn't answer yes to that question, keep asking the questions until they answer yes to a question.
   - Have the person sign in the appropriate box. Ask the person a follow-up question and write his or her answer in the box.
   - Then move on to another person. Each classmates name should be in only one box.
   - Try to fill in all the boxes.
3. After about 10 minutes, students rejoin their partners and check their partner's Find Someone Who table to see if the boxes are properly filled in and to offer suggestions about where to find people to fill in the empty boxes. Students do not copy from each other's tables.
4. When a couple of students have completed the table, the partners again check each other's tables.
5. The teacher goes through the table calling on students to name a person for each box. Students use their partner's sheet to respond, including their partner's follow-up question.

RoundRobin (Kagan 1992) [Chapter 3]

In this speaking technique, each group member has a designated turn to participate.

1. The group has a speaking prompt, task, or question.
2. Each person takes a turn to speak. The speaker may wish to stand while speaking.
3. The turn to speak passes around the group for as many rounds as possible.

4. One group member may be asked to share with the class what their group mates have said.

RoundTable (Kagan 1992) [Chapters 3, 5, 7]

In this writing technique, each group member has a designated turn to participate.

1. The group has a writing prompt, task, or question.
2. Each person writes a response or a portion of a response.
3. After writing their response, they pass the paper to their left.
4. RoundTable can be done with one piece of paper per group (Sequential RoundTable) or with one piece of paper per group member (Simultaneous RoundTable).
5. One group member may be asked to share with the class what their group has written.

Sam's Diary (DaSilva Iddings & McCafferty, Chapter 4, this book)

This activity enables students to tell classmates about themselves and to share a common experience.

1. Each student in the class takes a turn to take home a teddy bear named Sam.
2. With help from parents or other caregivers, students write diary entries about what they did with Sam.
3. Students read their diary entries to the class.

Same Game (Jacobs, Power & Loh 2002) [Chapter 8]

This activity is used for building a feeling of trust among group mates. The activity is based on the cooperative learning technique Reverse Snowball (Kearney 1993).

1. Each person in a foursome lists a total of 12 likes or dislikes.
2. The members of each of the two pairs in the foursome explain their lists to each other and then make a list of eight common likes or dislikes. Pairs can add ones that were not on either person's list.
3. The two pairs come together and repeat the same process, trying to come up with a list of four common likes or dislikes.

Sequential RoundTable (Kagan 1992) [Chapter 5]

See RoundTable

Shared Story Box (DaSilva Iddings & McCafferty, Chapter 4, this book)

In this activity, groups use objects to help them retell a story told to them by the teacher.

1. The teacher tells the class a story.
2. Groups retell the story, with each group member taking turns to retell a part or to add to what others have recalled.
3. As they do so, students use objects representing humans, animals, fantasy creatures, and things in the story, placing the objects in a box in the order in which they appear in the story.

Silent Celebration (Jones & Taylor, Chapter 6, this book)

In this technique, each group builds team spirit and quietly rewards themselves for a job well done.

1. Each group invents a special group handshake, cheer, dance, and so on. Anything is OK, but it must be silent.
2. Groups work on a task.
3. When a group feels they have completed a good effort, members do their silent celebration.

Simultaneous RoundTable (Kagan 1992) [Chapter 7]

See RoundTable

Spot the Difference (Morgan Bowen 1982) [Chapter 1]

In this technique, group mates share information in order to complete a task.

1. Each group member has a picture or text that is similar but not the same.
2. Group mates exchange information in order to identify the differences in their pictures or texts.

STAD (Student Teams-Achievement Divisions) (Slavin 1995) [Chapters 1, 5]

In this technique, recognition serves as a tool to motivate students to help one another learn content taught by the teacher.

1. The teacher provides instruction on a particular topic.
2. Students study the topic further in their groups in preparation for a quiz.
3. Students take the quiz independently of their group mates.
4. The teacher (or students) scores the quiz. Students' scores are compared to their past averages. Students earn points for their group based on how well they did relative to their previous quizzes.
5. Groups earn recognition based on the average number of points earned by their members.

Stay-Stray (Kagan 1992) [Chapter 7]

In this technique, groups share with other groups rather than with the entire class.

1. Groups complete a task.
2. Two or three group members leave the group and stray individually to other groups.
3. The remaining group member(s), the stayers, explain what their group has done to the visiting strayers, who ask questions and provide feedback.
4. Strayers return to their home group and report what they learned, while stayers report on the feedback they received.
5. Groups can revise their work, and another round of Stay-Stray can take place with new stayers.

Story Theater (also known as Reader's Theater) (Barchers 1994) [Chapter 9]

In this technique, students work in groups to do performances.

1. Each group member has a part to read and act out in a play or skit.
2. Students work alone to prepare.
3. Groups rehearse.
4. Preparation is shorter, easier, and less expensive than for a play because:
   • No full memorization. Scripts are held during performance.
   • No full costume. If used at all, costumes are partial, or neutral and uniform.
   • No full stage sets. If used at all, sets are simple and suggestive.
5. Groups perform the play or skit.

Strip Stories (Gibson 1975) [Chapter 1]

In this technique, group mates must exchange information in order to complete a task.

1. Each student has one or more strips of paper on which are written sentences from a text.
2. Students read but do not show their strips to group mates.
3. The group uses their knowledge of language and content to put the strips into a correct order.

Teams Games Tournament (TGT) (Slavin 1995) [Chapter 5]

As in STAD, recognition serves as a tool to motivate students to help one another learn content taught by the teacher.

1. The teacher provides instruction on a particular topic.
2. Students study the topic further in their groups.
3. Students leave their groups and go to tournament tables with students from other groups. The students at these tables are homogeneous in terms of past achievement.
4. Students take turns to attempt to answer questions on the content studied.
5. Students earn points for their groups based on how many questions they answer correctly.
6. Groups earn recognition based on the average number of points accumulated by their members.

Think-Pair-Share (Lyman 1992) [Chapters 6, 7]

This can be seen as a family of three-step techniques (many of which have been given labels by Kagan 1992). In Step 1, students work individually. In Step 2, with a partner, students take turns to talk. In Step 3, they share with others what was discussed.

Step 1 – Students think, write, draw, visualize.
Step 2 – Students take turns to tell or describe.
Step 3 – Students report to the class (Share), combine pairs to discuss in a foursome (Square), or change partners and discuss (Switch). Students can either talk only about what their original partner said or did, or they can report on the discussion that took place in their pair.

Of course, steps can be repeated with various combinations resulting (e.g., Write-Pair-Switch-Square).

Timed-Pair-Share (Kagan 1992) [Chapter 3]

In this technique, a specific length of time is assigned to each partner's speaking turn.

1. Each member of a pair has a designated amount of time (e.g., 45 seconds) to speak. While a person is speaking, the partner only listens, except to ask questions or offer other types of prompts if the person has not used all of the allotted time.
2. One partner may be asked to share with the rest of the class what the other said.

Universal Stories Activity (DaSilva Iddings & McCafferty, Chapter 4, this book)

In this activity, students compare different versions of a well-known story and then create their own.

1. The teacher tells two versions of a well-known story.
2. Groups use Venn diagrams to identify similarities and differences in the elements of the two versions.
3. Groups create their own versions of the story.

Write-Pair-Share (Kagan 1992) [Chapter 7]

See Think-Pair-Share

Write-Pair-Square (Kagan 1992) [Chapters 4, 9]

See Think-Pair-Share

Write-Pair-Switch (Jacobs, Power & Loh 2002) [Chapter 3]

See Think-Pair-Share

You Be the Judge! (Jones & Taylor, Chapter 6, this book)

This activity is based on the Jigsaw technique. Students delve into the characters in a story and try to agree on an issue arising from the story.

1. Students are in home groups of four. Each member is to specialize in one character from a story.
2. Students form expert groups with classmates specializing in the same character. The expert groups answer questions about their character.
3. Experts return to their home groups and share their answers to the questions.
4. Home groups debate an issue arising from the story and try to reach consensus.
5. Students are called on at random to share either their group's consensus or the differing views of their group mates.

References

Abraham, K. (1998). *Cause to communicate: Global issues in language learning.* London: Anti-Slavery International.

Alfassi, M. (1998). Reading for meaning: The efficacy of reciprocal teaching in fostering reading comprehension in high school students in remedial reading classes. *American Educational Research Journal, 35(2)*, 309–332.

Allan, S. D. (1991). Ability-grouping research reviews: What do they say about grouping and the gifted? *Educational Leadership, 48*, 60–65.

Alport, G. W. (1954). *The nature of prejudice.* Cambridge, MA: Addison Wesley.

Amores, M. J. (1997). A new perspective on peer-editing. *Foreign Language Annals, 30*, 513–522.

Aronson, E., Blaney, N., Stephan, C., Sikes, J., & Snapp, M. (1978). *The jigsaw classroom,* Beverly Hills, CA: Sage.

Aronson, E., & Goode, E. (1980). Training teachers to implement jigsaw learning: A manual for teachers. In S. Sharan, P. Hare, C. Webb, and R. Hertz-Lazarowitz (Eds.), *Cooperation in education* (pp. 47–81). Provo, UT: Brigham Young University Press.

Bailey, K. M., Dale, T., & Squire, B. (1992). Some reflections on collaborative language teaching. In D. Nunan (Ed.), *Collaborative language learning and teaching* (pp. 162–178). Cambridge: Cambridge University Press.

Barnes, D. (1973). *Language in the classroom.* Bletchley, England: Open University Press.

Bassano, S., & Christison, M. A. (1992). *Drawing out.* Englewood Cliffs, NJ: Prentice Hall.

Beauvois, M. H. (1998). Conversations in slow motion: Computer-mediated communication in the foreign language classroom. *Canadian Modern Language Review, 54*, 198–217.

Bennett, B., Rolheiser-Bennett, C., & Stevahn, L. (1991). *Cooperative learning: Where heart meets mind.* Toronto: Educational Connections.

Bejarano, Y., Levine, T., Olshtain, E., & Steiner, J. (1997). The skilled use of interaction strategies: Creating a framework for improved small-group communicative interaction in the language classroom. *System, 25*, 203–214.

Bergstrom, K. (1987). *The world citizen curriculum*. Denver, CO: Center for Teaching International Relations.

Blanton, L., & Lee, L. (1994). *The multicultural workshop: A reading and writing program* (Book 2). Pacific Grove, NJ: Heinle & Heinle.

Brandt, R. (1987). On cooperation in schools: A conversation with David and Roger Johnson. *Educational Leadership, 45*, 14–19.

Brookes, A., & Grundy, P. (1990). *Writing for study purposes*. Cambridge: Cambridge University Press.

Brown, K., & Butterworth, A. (1998). *Air quality today*. Surry Hills, NSW: New South Wales Adult Migrant English Service.

Brown, A., & Palincsar, A. (1985). Reciprocal teaching of comprehension strategies: A natural history of one program for enhancing learning. Urbana: University of Illinois Center for the Study of Reading. *Technical Report No. 334.*

Bruffee, K. A. (1993). *Collaborative learning: higher education, interdependence and the authority of knowledge*. Baltimore, MD: Johns Hopkins University.

Bruner, J. S., Goodnow, J. J., & Austin, G. A. (1967). *A study of thinking*. New Brunswick, NJ: Transaction Books.

Bruton, A., & Samuda, V. (1980). Learner and teacher roles in the treatment of oral error in group work. *RELC Journal, 11(2)*, 49–63.

Buzan, T. (1983). *Use both sides of your brain* (Revised ed.). New York: E. P. Dutton.

Calderon, M., Hertz-Lazarowitz, R., Ivory, G., & Slavin, R. E. (1997). *Effects of bilingual Cooperative Integrated Reading and Composition on students transitioning from Spanish to English reading. Report No. 10.* Center for Research on the Education of Students Placed at Risk, Johns Hopkins University & Howard University.

Canale, M., & Swain, M. (1980). Theoretical bases of communicative approaches to second language teaching and testing. *Applied Linguistics, 1(1)*, 1–47.

Carle, E. (1969). *The very hungry caterpillar*. New York: Philomel.

Carson, J., & Nelson, G. (1994). Writing Groups: Cross-cultural issues. *Journal of Second Language Writing, 3*, 17–30.

Cates, K. (1990). Teaching for a better world: Global issues in language education. *The Language Teacher, 14*, 3–5.

Chamot, A. U., & O'Malley, J. M. (1994). *The CALLA handbook: Implementing the cognitive academic language learning approach.* Reading, MA: Addison-Wesley.

Cheng, W., & Warren, M. (1996). Hong Kong students' attitudes toward peer assessment in English language courses. *Asian Journal of English Language Teaching, 6*, 61–75.

Christison, M. A. (1995). Multiple intelligences and second language learners. *Journal of the Imagination in Language Learning, 3*, 8–13.

Chung, J. (1991). Collaborative learning strategies: The design of instructional environments for the emerging new school. *Educational Technology, 31(12)*, 15–22.

Clay, M. (1985). *The early detection of reading difficulties* (3rd ed.). Portsmouth, NH: Heinemann.

Coelho, E. (1994). *Learning together in the multicultural classroom.* Scarborough, ON: Pippin.

Coelho, E., Winer, L., & Winn-Bell Olsen, J. (1989). *All sides of the issue: Activities for cooperative jigsaw groups.* Englewood Cliffs, NJ: Prentice Hall.

Cohen, E. G. (1994). Restructuring the classroom: Conditions for productive small groups. *Review of Educational Research, 64*, 1–35.

Cohen, E. G., & Lotan, R. A. (Eds.) (1997). *Working for equity in heterogeneous classrooms.* New York: Teachers College Press.

Connor, U., & Asenavage, K. (1994). Peer response groups in ESL writing class. *Journal of Second Language Writing, 3*, 257–276.

Cooper, C., & Boyd, J. (1994). *Collaborative approaches to professional learning and reflection.* Launceston, Tasmania: Global Learning Communities.

Cotterall, S. (1995). Readiness for autonomy: Investigating learner beliefs. *System, 23(2)*, 195–206.

Coughlan, P., & Duff, P. A. (1994). Same task, different activities: Analysis of a SLA task from an activity theory perspective. In J. P. Lantolf & G. Appel (Eds.), *Vygotskian Approaches to Second Language Research* (pp. 173–194). Norwood, NJ: Ablex.

Crago, M. (1992). Communicative interaction and second language acquisition: An Inuit example. *TESOL Quarterly, 26*, 487–505.

Craik, F. I. M., & Lockhart, R. S. (1972). Levels of processing: A framework for memory research. *Journal of Verbal Learning and Verbal Behavior, 11*, 671–684.

Crandall, J. (Ed.) (1987). *ESL through content-based instruction.* Englewood Cliffs, NJ: Prentice Hall.

Crookall, D., & Oxford, R. L. (Eds.) (1990). *Simulations, gaming, and language learning*. New York: Newbury House.

Crookes, G., & Schmidt, R. W. (1991). Motivation: Reopening the research agenda. *Language Learning, 41*, 469–512.

Csikszentmihalyi, M. (1990). *Flow: The psychology of optimal experience*. New York: Harper & Row.

Cuban, L. (1987). Cultures of teaching: A puzzle. *Educational Administrative Quarterly, 23(4)*, 25–35.

Daniels, H. (1994). *Literature circles: Voice and choice in the student-centered classroom*. York, ME: Stenhouse Publishers.

DaSilva Iddings, A. C. (2005). Linguistic access and participation: English language learners in an English-dominant community of practice. *Bilingual Research Journal, 29(1)*, 165–183.

Davidson, N., & Worsham, T. (Eds.) (1992). *Enhancing thinking through cooperative learning*. New York: Teachers College Press.

Davis, R. L. (1997). Group work in NOT busy work: Maximizing success of group work in the L2 classroom. *Foreign Language Annals, 30*, 265–279.

Deen, J. Y. (1991). Comparing interaction in a cooperative learning and teacher-centered foreign language classroom. *I.T.L. Review of Applied Linguistics*, 153–181.

Delgado-Gaitan, C. (1994). Sociocultural change through literacy: Toward the empowerment of families. In B. Ferdman, R. Weber, & A. Ramirez (Eds.), *Literacy across languages and cultures* (pp. 143–170). Albany, NY: State University of New York Press.

Derewianka, B. (1990). *Exploring how texts work*. Rozelle, NSW: Primary English Teaching Association.

Deutsch, M. (1949). A theory of cooperation and competition. *Human Relations, 2*, 129–152.

Deutsch, M. (1962). Cooperation and trust: Some theoretical notes. In M. R. Jones (Ed.), *Nebraska symposium on motivation* (pp. 275–319). Lincoln, NE: University of Nebraska Press.

Dewey, J. (1966). *Democracy and Education*. New York: Free Press. *53(4)*, 609–633.

DiCamilla, F., & Anton, M. (2004). Private speech: A study of language for thought in the collaborative interaction of language learners. *International Journal of Applied Linguistics, 14*, 36–69.

Dishon, D., & O'Leary, P. W. (1993). *A Guidebook for Cooperative Learning* (Revised ed.). Holmes Beach, FL: Learning Publications.

Doise, W., & Mugny, G. (1984). *The social development of intellect*. New York: Pergamon.

Donato, R. (1994). Collective scaffolding in second language learning. In J. P. Lantolf & G. Appel (Eds.), *Vygotskian Approaches to Second Language Research* (pp. 33–56). Norwood, NJ: Ablex.

Dornyei, Z. (1997). Psychological processes in cooperative language learning: Group dynamics and motivation. *Modern Language Journal, 81*, 482–493.

Doughty, C., & Pica, T. (1986). Information gap tasks: Do they facilitate second language acquisition? *TESOL Quarterly, 20(2)*, 305–326.

Dunn, W., & Lantolf, J. P. (1998). Vygotsky's Zone of Proximal Development and Krashen's *I + 1*: Incommensurable Constructs; Incommensurable Theories. *Language Learning, 48*, 411–442.

Echevarria, J., & Graves, A. (1997). *Sheltered content instruction: Teaching English-language learners with diverse abilities*. Boston: Allyn & Bacon.

Edge, J. (1992). *Cooperative development: Professional self-development through collaboration with colleagues*. London: Longman.

Edge, J. (1993). *Essentials of English language teaching*. Harlow, Essex: Longman.

Engestrom, Y., Miettien, R., & Raija-Leena, P. (1999). *Perspectives on activity theory*. Cambridge: Cambridge University Press.

Fitz-Gibbon, C. I., & Reay, D. G. (1982). Peer-tutoring: Brightening up FL teaching in an urban comprehensive school. *British Journal of Language Teaching, 20(1)*, 39–44.

Flowerdew, L. (1998). A cultural perspective on group work. *ELT Journal, 52*, 323–329.

Foster, P. (1998). A classroom perspective on the negotiation of meaning. *Applied Linguistics, 19(1)*, 1–23.

Fountain, S. (1995). *Education for development: A teacher's resource guide for global learning*. Portsmouth, NH: Heinemann.

Frawley, W., & Lantolf, J. P. (1985). Second language discourse: A Vygotskian perspective. *Applied Linguistics, 6*, 19–44.

Freeman, D. E., & Freeman, Y. S. (1994). *Between worlds: Access to second language acquisition*. Portsmouth, NH: Heinemann.

Freire, P. (1970). *Pedagogy of the oppressed*. New York: Seabury.

Fullan, M. (1998). *Change forces: The sequel (Educational Change and Development Series)*. London: Falmer.

Fullan, M. G., Bennett, B., & Rolheiser-Bennett, C. (1990). Linking classroom and school improvement. *Educational Leadership, 47(8)*, 13–19.

Gallese, V., & Goldman, A. (1998). Mirror neurons and the simulation theory of mind-reading. *Trends in Cognitive Sciences, 2*, 493–501.

Gambrell, L. B., & Almasi, J. F. (1993). Fostering comprehension through discussion. In L. M. Morrow, J. K. Smith, & L. C. Wilkinson (Eds.), *Integrated language arts: Controversy to consensus* (pp.71–90). Boston, MA: Allyn & Bacon.

Gardner, H. (1983). *Frames of mind: The theory of multiple intelligences.* New York: Basic Books.

Geddes, M. (1981). The four skills in communicative language teaching: Listening. In K. Johnson and K. Morrow (Eds.), *Communication in the classroom.* London: Longman.

Gerow, S. (1997). Posting to Cooperative Learning discussion list, February 5.

Ghaith, G. M., & Shaaban, K. A. (1995a). Peace education in the ESL / EFL classroom: A framework for curriculum and instruction. *TESL Reporter, 27(2)*, 55–62.

Ghaith, G. M., & Shaaban, K. A. (1995b). Cooperative learning and inservice teacher training: A suggested approach. *TESL Reporter, 28(1)*, 25–31.

Gibbs, J. (1994). *Tribes: A new way of learning together* (4th ed.). Santa Rosa, CA: Center Source Publications.

Gibbs, J., & Bennett, S. (1994). *Tribes: A new way of learning together* (4th ed.). Santa Rosa, CA: Center Source Publications.

Gibson, R. E. (1975). The strip story: A catalyst for communication. *TESOL Quarterly, 9(2)*, 149–154.

Gomasatitd, W. (1997). *An investigation of the use of cooperative learning with Thai university undergraduates.* Unpublished masteral dissertation. Bangkok: Ramkhamhaeng University.

Guerrero, M. C. M. de, & Villamil, O. S. (1994). Social-cognitive dimensions of interaction in L2 peer revision. *Modern Language Journal, 78*, 484–496.

Hadfield, J. (1992). *Classroom dynamics.* Oxford: Oxford University Press.

Halliday, M. A. K. (1970). Language structure and language function. In J. Lyons (Ed.), *New horizons in linguistics* (pp. 140–165). Harmondsworth: Penguin.

Harley, B., Allen, P., Cummins, J., & Swain, M. (Eds.) (1990). *The development of second language proficiency.* Cambridge: Cambridge University Press.

Harmer, J. (1998). *How to teach English.* Harlow, Essex: Addison Wesley Longman.

Hatch, E. (1978). Acquisition of syntax in a second language. In J. C. Richards (Ed.), *Understanding second and foreign language learning* (pp. 34–70). Rowley, MA: Newbury House.

Hatch, E., Flashner, V., & Hunt, L. (1986). The experience model and language teaching. In R. R. Day (Ed.), *Talking to learn: Conversation in second language acquisition* (pp. 5–22). Rowley, MA: Newbury House.

Hawkins, J. D., & Weiss, J. G. (1983). The social development model: An integrated approach to delinquency prevention. In R. J. Rubel (Ed.), *Juvenile delinquency prevention: Emerging perspectives of the 1980's*. San Marcos, TX: Institute of Criminal Justice Studies, Southwest Texas State University.

Heath, S. (1986). Sociocultural contexts of language development. In California State Department of Education, *Beyond language: Social and cultural factors in schooling language minority students* (pp.143–186). Los Angeles: Evaluation, Dissemination and Assessment Center, California State University.

Hertz-Lazarowitz, R., Lernor, M., Schaedel, B., Walk, A., & Sarid, M. (1992). Story-related writing: An evaluation of CIRC in Israel. *Journal of Linguistic Education*.

High, J. (1993). *Second language learning through cooperative learning*. San Clemente, CA: Kagan Cooperative Learning.

Hilt, P. (1992). The world-of-work connection. In N. Davidson & T. Worsham (Eds.), *Enhancing thinking through cooperative learning*. New York: Teachers College Press.

Hofstede, G. (1980). *Culture's consequences*. Beverly Hills, CA: Sage.

Horwitz, E., Horwitz, M., & Cope, J. (1991). Foreign language classroom anxiety. In E. Horwitz & D. Young (Eds.), *Language anxiety – from theory to research to classroom implications* (pp. 27–36). Englewood Cliffs, NJ: Prentice Hall.

Huckin, T. N., & Olsen, L. A. (1991). *Technical writing and professional communication for non-native speakers of English* (2nd ed.). New York: McGraw-Hill.

Hughes Wilhelm, K. (1997). Sometimes kicking and screaming: Language teachers-in-training react to a collaborative learning model. *Modern Language Journal, 81*, 527–543.

Hymes, D. (1972). On communicative competence. In J. B. Pride & J. Holmes (Eds.), *Sociolinguistics* (pp. 269–293). Harmondsworth: Penguin.

Hythecker, V. I., Dansereau, D. F., & Rocklin, T. R. (1988). An analysis of the processes influencing the structured dyadic learning environment. *Educational Psychologist, 23*, 23–37.

Jacobs, G. M. (1987). First experiences with peer feedback on compositions: Students and teacher reaction. *System, 15*, 325–333.

Jacobs, G. M. (1989). Miscorrection in peer feedback in writing class. *RELC Journal, 20(1)*, 68–76.

Jacobs, G. M. (1994). The changing nature of workplace literacy as a rationale for the use of groups in ESP. *ESP Malaysia, 2(2)*, 106–117.

Jacobs, G. M. (1997). Cooperative learning or just grouping students: The difference makes a difference. In W. A. Renandya & G. M. Jacobs (Eds.), *Learners and language learning* (pp. 172–193). Singapore: SEAMEO Regional Language Centre.

Jacobs, G. M., Crookall, D., & Thiyaragarajali, R. (1997). The evolution of group activities in ELT coursebooks. *Folio, 4(2)*, 21–24.

Jacobs, G. M., & Goatly, A. (2000). The treatment of ecological issues in ELT coursebooks. *ELT Journal, 54*, 256–264.

Jacobs, G. M., & Kline-Liu, K. (1996). Integrating language functions and collaborative skills in the second language classroom. *TESL Reporter, 29*, 1: 21–33.

Jacobs, G. M., & Ratmanida. (1996). The appropriacy of group activities: Views from some Southeast Asian second language educators. *RELC Journal, 27*, 103–120.

Johnson, D. W. (1997). *Cooperative learning: Past and present.* Keynote address, International Conference on Cooperative Learning and Constructivism, Penang, Malaysia.

Johnson, D. W., & Johnson, F. P. (1997). *Joining together: Group theory and group skills* (6th ed.). Boston: Allyn & Bacon.

Johnson, D. W., & Johnson, R. T. (1991). *Teaching students to be peacemakers* (video). Edina, MN: Interaction Book Company.

Johnson, D. W., & Johnson, R. T. (1989). *Cooperation and competition: Theory and research.* Edina, MN: Interaction Book Company.

Johnson, D. W., & Johnson, R. T. (1994a). *Leading the cooperative school* (2nd ed.). Edina, MN: Interaction Book Company.

Johnson, D. W., & Johnson, R. T. (1994b). *Learning together and alone* (4th ed.). Needham Heights, MA: Allyn & Bacon.

Johnson, D. W., & Johnson, R. T. (1994c). Professional development in CL: Short-term popularity vs. long-term effectiveness. *Cooperative Learning, 14*, 52–54.

Johnson, D. W., & Johnson, R. T. (1995). Cooperative learning and nonacademic outcomes of schooling. In J. E. Pedersen & A. D. Digby (Eds.), *Secondary school and cooperative learning* (pp. 81–150). New York: Garland.

Johnson, D. W., & Johnson, R. T. (1999). *Learning together and alone: Cooperative, competitive, and individualistic learning* (5th ed.). Boston: Allyn & Bacon.

Johnson, D. W., Johnson, R. T., & Holubec, E. J. (2002). *Circles of learning* (5th ed.). Edina, MN: Interaction Book Company.

Johnson, D. W., Johnson, R. T., & Smith, K. (1998). *Active learning: Cooperation in the college classroom* (Revised ed.). Edina, MN: Interaction Book Company.

Johnson, D. W., Johnson, R. T., & Stanne, M. B. (2000). *Cooperative learning methods: A meta-analysis*. Retrieved May 23, 2003, from www.clcrc.com/pages/cl-methods.html.

Johnson, K. (1981). Writing. In K. Johnson & K. Morrow (Eds.), *Communication in the classroom* (pp. 93–107). Harlow, Essex: Longman.

Johnson, K. E. (1995). *Understanding communication in second language classrooms*. Cambridge: Cambridge University Press.

John-Steiner, V. P. (1985). The road to competence in an alien land: A Vygotskian perspective on bilingualism. In J. V. Wertsch (Ed.), *Culture, Communication, and Cognition: Vygotskian Perspectives* (pp. 348–371). Cambridge: Cambridge University Press.

Kagan, S. (1992). *Cooperative Learning*. San Clemente, CA: Kagan Cooperative Learning.

Kagan, S. (1995). Group grades miss the mark. *Educational Leadership, 52(8)*, 68–71.

Kagan, S. (1998). New cooperative learning, multiple intelligences, and inclusion. In J. W. Putnam (Ed.), *Cooperative learning and strategies for inclusion: Celebrating diversity in the classroom* (2nd ed.) (pp. 105–138). Baltimore, MD: Paul H. Brookes.

Kagan, S., & Kagan, M. (1994). The structural approach: New tools for teachers. *The Language Teacher, 18*, 10, 12–17.

Kagan, S., & Kagan, M. (1998). *Multiple intelligences: The complete MI handbook*. San Clemente, CA: Kagan Cooperative Learning.

Kagan, S., & McGroarty, M. (1993). Principles of cooperative learning for language and content gains. In D. D. Holt (Ed.), *Cooperative learning: A response to linguistic and cultural diversity* (pp. 47–66). McHenry, IL and Washington, DC: Delta Systems and the Center for Applied Linguistics.

Kearney, P. (1993). *Cooperative learning techniques*. Hobart, Tasmania: Artemis Publishing.

Kinginger, C. (2002). Defining the zone of proximal development in U.S. foreign language education. *Applied Linguistics, 23(2)*, 240–261.

Kinsella, K. (1996). Designing group work that supports and enhances diverse classroom work styles. *TESOL Journal, 6(1)*, 25–30.

Kleiner-Brandwein, Y. (1995). Pair and small group work is dead and living in Ramat Aviv. *English Teachers' Journal (Israel), 48*, 143–147.

Kluge, D., McGuire, S., Johnson, D. W., & Johnson, R. T. (Eds.) (1999). *Cooperative learning*. Tokyo: Japan Association for Language Teaching.

Knapp, C. E. (1988). *Creating human climates outdoors: A people skills primer*. Charleston, WV: Appalachia Educational Laboratory.

Kohn, A. (1992). *No contest: The case against competition*. Boston: Houghton Mifflin.

Koschmann, T. (Ed.) (1996). *CSCL: Theory and practice of an emerging paradigm*. Mahwah, NJ: Lawrence Erlbaum.

Kowal, M., & Swain, M. (1994). Using collaborative language production tasks to promote students' language awareness. *Language Awareness, 3(2)*, 73–93.

Kowal, M., & Swain, M. (1997). From semantic to syntactic processing: How can we promote metalinguistic awareness in the French immersion classroom? In R. K. Johnson & M. Swain (Eds.), *Immersion education: International perspectives* (pp. 284–309). Cambridge: Cambridge University Press.

Kramsch, C. J. (1981). *Discourse analysis and second language teaching*. Washington, DC: Center for Applied Linguistics.

Krashen, S. D. (1985). *The input hypothesis: Issues and implications*. New York: Longman.

Krashen, S. D., & Terrell, T. D. (1983). *The natural approach*. Oxford: Pergamon.

Ladousse, G. P. (1987). *Role Play*. New York: Oxford University Press.

Lantolf, J. P. (Ed.) (2000). *Sociocultural theory and second language learning*. Oxford: Oxford Applied Linguistics.

Lantolf, J. P. & Appel, G. (1994). Theoretical framework: An introduction to Vygotskian perspectives on second language research. In J. P. Lantolf & G. Appel (Eds.), *Vygotskian approaches to second language research* (pp. 1–32). Norwood, NJ: Ablex.

Lave J., & Wenger, E. (1991). *Situated learning: Legitimate peripheral participation*. Cambridge: Cambridge University Press.

Leki, I. (1990). Potential problems with peer responding in ESL writing classes. *CATESOL Journal, 3(1)*, 5–19.

Lewis, M. (1988). *Adult literacy students: Perceptions of reading held by English and Spanish speakers*. Paper presented at the Modern Language Association Right to Literacy Conference, Columbus, OH.

Little, D. (1990). Autonomy in language learning. In I. Gathercole (Ed.), *Autonomy in language learning* (pp. 7–15). London: Centre for Information on Language Teaching.

Littlejohn, A. P. (1982). *Teacherless language learning groups: An experiment*. Manuscript, University of Lancaster.

Long, M. H. (1983). Native-speaker / non-native speaker conversations and the negotiation of comprehensible input. *Applied Linguistics, 4*, 126–141.

Long, M. H. (1996). The role of the linguistic environment in second language acquisition. In W. C. Ritchie & T. K. Bhatia (Eds.), *Handbook of second language acquisition* (pp. 413–468). San Diego: Academic Press.

Long, M. H., Adams, L., McClean, M., & Castanos, F. (1976). Doing things with words – verbal interaction in lockstep and small group classroom situations. In J. F. Fanselow and R. H. Crymes (Eds.), *On TESOL '76* (pp. 137–153). Washington, DC: TESOL.

Long, M. H., & Porter, P. A. (1985). Group work, interlanguage talk, and second language acquisition. *TESOL Quarterly, 19*, 207–228.

Lyman, F. T. (1992). Think-Pair-Share, Thinktrix, Thinklinks, and Weird Facts, and interactive system for cooperative thinking. In D. Davidson & T. Worsham (Eds.), *Enhancing thinking through cooperative learning* (pp. 169–181). New York: Teachers College Press.

Maag, J. W. (1990). Social skills training in school. *Special Services in the School, 6(1–2)*, 1–19.

Macaro, E. (1997). *Target language, collaborative learning and autonomy*. Clevedon, Avon: Multilingual Matters.

Magee, V. Y. G., & Jacobs, G. M. (2001). Comparing second language student participation under tree teaching modes. *Journal of the Chinese Language Teachers Association, 36(1)*, 61–80.

Mangelsdorf, K., & Schlumberger, A. (1992). ESL student response stances in a peer-review task. *Journal of Second Language Writing, 1*, 235–254.

Maslow, A. H. (1968). *Toward a psychology of being* (2nd ed.). New York: Van Nostrand.

Matthews, R. S., Cooper, J. L., Davidson, N., & Hawkes, P. (retrieved 1999). *Building bridges between cooperative and collaborative learning*. http://eminfo.emc.maricopa.edu/innovation/ccl/index.html

Mawer, G. (1991). *Language audits and industry restructuring*. Sydney: National Centre for English Language Teaching and Research, Macquarie University.

McCafferty, S. G. (1992). The use of private speech by adult second language learners: A cross-cultural study. *Modern Language Journal, (76)*, 179–189.

McCafferty, S. G. (1998). Nonverbal expression and L2 private speech. *Applied Linguistics, 19(1)1*, 73–96.

McCafferty, S. G. (2002). Gesture and creating zones pf proximal development for second language learning. *The Modern Language Journal 86(2)*, 192–203.

McCafferty, S. G., Roebuck, R., & Wayland, R. (2001). Activity theory and the incidental learning of second language vocabulary. *Language Awareness, 10(4)*, 289–294.

McGrath, H. (1998). *What works best? A comparison of three classroom social skills programs.* Paper presented at the annual conference of the American Educational Research Association, San Diego.

McGroarty, M. (1992). Cooperative learning: The benefits for content-area teaching. In P. A. Richard-Amato & M. A. Snow (Eds.), *The multicultural classroom: Readings for content-area teachers* (pp. 58–69). White Plains, NY: Longman.

Mesch, D., Lew, M., Johnson, D. W., & Johnson, R. T. (1986). Positive interdependence, academic and collaborative skills, group contingencies and isolated students. *American Educational Research Journal, 23(3)*, 476–488.

Mitchell, R., & Myles, F. (1998). *Second language learning theories.* Oxford: Oxford University Press.

Moffett, J. (1968). *Teaching the universe of discourse.* Boston: Houghton Mifflin.

Moll, L., & Greenberg, J. B. (1990). Creating zones of possibilities: Combining social contexts for instruction. In L. C. Moll (Ed.), *Vygotsky and education: Instructional implications and applications of sociohistorical psychology* (pp. 319–338). Cambridge: Cambridge University Press.

Morgan Bowen, B. (1982). *Look here! Visual aids in language teaching.* London: Macmillan.

Moskowitz, G. (1978). *Caring and sharing in the foreign language class: A sourcebook on humanistic techniques.* Rowley, MA: Newbury House.

Murphey, T. (1992). *Music & song.* Oxford: Oxford University Press.

Murray, D. (1968). *A writer teaches writing.* Boston: Houghton Mifflin.

Murray, F. B. (1982). Teaching through social conflict. *Contemporary Educational Psychology, 7*, 257–271.

Nabei, T. (1996). Dictogloss: Is it an effective language learning task? *Working Papers in Educational Linguistics, 12(1)*, 59–74.

Nakagawa, J. J. (1999). A cooperative performance test for Japanese university conversation classes. In D. Kluge et al. (Eds), *Cooperative Learning* (pp.179–187). Tokyo: Japan Association for Language Teaching.

Newman, F., & Holtzman, L. (1993). *Lev Vygotsky, revolutionary scientist.* New York: Routledge.

Nolasco, R., & Arthur, L. (1988). *Large classes.* London: Macmillan.

Nor, A. A. (1997). Open classrooms: Peer observation for professional development. *The English Teacher, 26,* 82–99.

Nunan, D. (1992). *Research methods in language learning.* Cambridge: Cambridge University Press.

Oliver, R. (1998). Negotiation of meaning in child interactions. *Modern Language Journal, 82,* 372–386.

Olsen, R. E. W-B. (1992). Cooperative learning and social studies. In C. Kessler (Ed.), *Cooperative language learning: A teacher's resource book* (pp. 85–116). Englewood Cliffs, NJ: Prentice Hall.

Omaggio, A. C. (1982). Using games and interaction activities for the development of functional proficiency in a second language. *Canadian Modern Language Review, 38,* 517–546.

Oxford, R. L. (1990). *Language learning strategies: What every teacher should know.* New York: Newbury House.

Palincsar, A. S., & Brown, A. L. (1984). Reciprocal teaching of comprehension-fostering and comprehension-monitoring activities. *Cognition and Instruction, 1(2),* 117–175.

Palincsar, A. S., Brown, A. L., & Martin, S. M. (1987). Peer interaction in reading comprehension instruction. *Educational Psychologist, 22,* 231–253.

Pica, T. (1987). Interlanguage adjustments as an outcome of NS-NNS negotiation interaction. *Language Learning, 38,* 45–73.

Pica, T. (1996). Do second language learners need negotiation? *International Review of Applied Linguistics in Language Teaching, 34,* 1–21.

Pica, T., & Doughty, C. (1985). Input and interaction in the communicative language classroom: A comparison of teacher-fronted and group activities. In S. M. Gass & C. Madden (Eds.), *Input and second language acquisition* (pp. 115–132). Rowley, MA: Newbury House.

Pica, T., Holliday, L., Lewis, N., & Morgenthaler, L. (1989). Comprehensible output as an outcome of linguistic demands on the learner. *Studies in Second Language Acquisition, 11,* 63–90.

Pica, T., Kanagy, R., & Falodun, J. (1993). Choosing and using communication tasks for second language instruction and research. In G. Crookes & S. Gass (Eds.), *Tasks and language learning* (pp. 9–33). Clevedon, Avon: Multilingual Matters.

Pike, G., & Selby, D. (1988). *Global teacher, global learner.* London: Hodder and Stoughton.

Platt, E., & Brooks, F. B. (1994). The "acquisition-rich environment" revisited. *Modern Language Journal, 78*, 497–511.

Porter, P. A. (1983). *Variations in the conversations of adult learners of English as a function of the proficiency level of the participants.* Ph.D. dissertation, Stanford University.

Prapphal, K. (1991). Cooperative learning in a humanistic English class. *Cross Currents, 18*, 37–40.

Puchta, H., & Schratz, M. (1993). *Teaching teenagers: Model activity sequences for humanistic language learning.* Harlow, Essex: Longman.

Rankin, W. (1997). Increasing the communicative competence of foreign language students through the FL Chatroom. *Foreign Language Annals, 30*, 542–546.

Reardon, B. (1988). *Educating for social responsibility.* New York: Teachers College Press.

Reid, J. M. (1987). The learning style preferences of ESL students. *TESOL Quarterly, 21(1)*, 87–111.

Reid, J. M. (1993). *Teaching ESL Writing.* Englewood Cliffs, NJ: Regents / Prentice Hall.

Rich, Y. (1990). Ideological impediments to instructional innovation: The case of cooperative learning. *Teaching & Teacher Education, 6*, 81–91.

Richards, J. C., & Lockhart, C. (1994). *Reflective teaching in second language classrooms.* Cambridge: Cambridge University Press.

Richards, J. C., & Rodgers, T. S. (2001). *Approaches and methods in language teaching* (2nd ed.). Cambridge: Cambridge University Press.

Roebuck, R., & Wagner, L. C. (2004). Teaching repetition as a communicative and cognitive tool: Evidence from a Spanish conversation class. *International Journal of Applied Linguistics, 14*, 70–89.

Rogers, C. (1979). *Freedom to learn: A view of what education might become.* (Revised ed.). Columbus, OH: Merrill.

Rogers, J. (1978). *Group activities for language learning.* Singapore: SEAMEO Regional Language Centre.

Romney, J. C. (1997). Collaborative learning in a translation course. *Canadian Modern Language Review, 54*, 48–67.

Ruddock, J. (1978). *Learning through small group discussion.* Guilford, Surrey: Society for Research into Higher Education, University of Surrey.

Rulon, K. A., & McCreary, J. (1986). Negotiation of content: Teacher-fronted and small-group interaction. In R. R. Day (Ed.), *Talking to learning: Conversation in second language acquisition.* Rowley, MA: Newbury House.

Samway, V., Whang, G., & Pippitt, M. (1995). *Buddy reading: Cross-age tutoring in a multicultural school*. Portsmouth, NH: Heinemann.

Sapon-Shevin, M., & Schniedewind, N. (1991). Cooperative learning as empowering pedagogy. In C. E. Sleeter (Ed.), *Empowerment through multicultural education* (pp. 159–178). Albany, NY: State University of New York Press.

Scarcella, R. C., & Oxford, R. L. (1992). *The tapestry of language learning: The individual in the communicative classroom*. Boston: Heinle & Heinle.

Scardamalia, M., & Bereiter, C. (1996). Computer support for knowledge-building communities. In T. Koschmann (Ed.), *CSCL: Theory and practice of an emerging paradigm* (pp. 249–268). Mahwah, NJ: Lawrence Erlbaum.

Schinke-Llano, L., & Vicars, R. (1993). The affective filter and negotiated interaction: Do our language activities provide for both? *Modern Language Journal, 77*, 325–329.

Schneider, P. (1993). Developing fluency with pair taping. *JALT Journal, 15*, 55–62.

Scovel, T. (1978). The effect of affect on foreign language learning: A review of the anxiety research. *Language Learning, 28*, 129–142.

Shannon, N. B., & Meath-Lang, B. (1992). Collaborative language teaching: A co-investigation. In D. Nunan (Ed.), *Collaborative language learning and teaching* (pp. 120–140). Cambridge: Cambridge University Press.

Sharan, S. (1980). Cooperative learning in small groups: Recent methods and effects on achievement, attitudes and ethnic relations. *Review of Educational Research, 50*, 241–271.

Sharan, Y., & Sharan, S. (1992). *Expanding cooperative learning through group investigation*. Colchester, VT: Teachers College Press.

Shiman, D. (1993). *Teaching human rights*. Denver, CO: Center for Teaching International Relations.

Slavin, R. E. (1987). Cooperative learning: Where behavioral and humanistic approaches to classroom motivation meet. *Elementary School Journal, 88*, 29–37.

Slavin, R. E. (1991). Are cooperative learning and "untracking" harmful to the gifted? *Educational Leadership, 48*, 68–71.

Slavin, R. E. (1995). *Cooperative learning: Theory, research, and practice* (2nd ed.). Boston, MA: Allyn & Bacon.

Slavin, R. E., & Yampolski, R. (1991, April). *Success for all and the language minority student*. Paper presented at the annual convention of the American Educational Research Association, Chicago.

[Cambodians learning English in the U.S. CL positive effects on L2 proficiency.]

Snow, M. A., & Brinton, D. M. (Eds.) (1997). *The content-based classroom: Perspectives on integrating language and content.* Boston: Addison-Wesley.

Soh, B. L., & Soon, Y. P. (1991). English by e-mail: Creating a global classroom via the medium of computer technology. *ELT Journal, 45,* 287.

Sproull, L., & Kiesler, S. (1991). *Connections: New ways of working in the networked organization.* Cambridge, MA: MIT Press.

Sullivan, P. N. (2000). Playfulness as mediation in communicative language teaching in a Vietnamese classroom. In J. P. Lantolf (Ed.), *Sociocultural theory and second language learning* (pp. 115–132). Oxford: Oxford Applied Linguistics.

Swain, M. (1985). Communicative competence: Some roles of comprehensible input and comprehensible output in its development. In S. Gass & C. Madden (Eds.), *Input in second language acquisition* (pp. 235–253). Rowley, MA: Newbury House.

Swain, M. (1991). French immersion and its offshoots: Getting two for one. In B. F. Freed (Ed.), *Foreign language acquisition research and the classroom* (pp. 91–103). Lexington, MA: D. C. Heath.

Swain, M., (1993). The output hypothesis: Just speaking and writing aren't enough. *The Canadian Modern Language Review, 50,* 158–164.

Swain, M., & Lapkin, S. (1995). Problems in output and the cognitive processes they generated: A step towards second language learning. *Applied Linguistics, 16,* 371–391.

Swain, M., and Lapkin, S. (1998). Interaction and second language learning: Two adolescent French immersion students working together. *The Modern Language Journal, 82,* 320–337.

Taba, H. (1962). *Curriculum development: Theory and practice.* New York: Harcourt, Brace & World.

Takahashi, E. (1998). Language development in social interaction: A longitudinal study of a Japanese FLES program from a Vygotskyan approach. *Foreign Language Annals, 31,* 392–406.

Tang, C. (1996). Collaborative learning: The latent dimension in Chinese students' learning. In D. Watkins & J. Biggs (Eds.), *The Chinese learner: Cultural, psychological, and contextual influences* (pp. 183–204). Hong Kong: Comparative Education Research Centre and the Australian Council for Educational Research.

Thorne, S. L. (2000). Second language acquisition theory and the truth(s) about relativity. In J. P. Lantolf (Ed.), *Sociocultural theory and second language learning* (pp. 219–244). Oxford: Oxford University Press.

Tjosvold, D., & Tjosvold, M. M. (1991). *Leading the team organization: How to create an enduring competitive advantage.* New York: Macmillan.

Tsui, A. B. M. (1996). Reticence and anxiety in second language learning. In K. Bailey & D. Nunan (Eds.), *Voices from the language classroom* (pp. 145–164). Cambridge: Cambridge University Press.

UNESCO. (1987). *Consultation on content and methods that could contribute in the teaching of foreign languages and literature to international understanding and peace (Linguapax).* Paris: UNESCO.

van Lier, L. (1991). Inside the classroom: Learning processes and teaching procedures. *Applied Language Learning, 2(1),* 29–68.

van Lier, L. (1996). *Interaction in the language curriculum: Awareness, autonomy & authenticity.* London: Longman.

Varonis, E. M. & Gass, S. (1985). Non-native / non-native conversations: A model for negotiation of meaning. *Applied Linguistics, 6,* 71–90.

Vygotsky, L. S. (1978). *Mind in society.* M. Cole, V. John-Steiner, S. Scribner, and E. Souberman (Eds.). Cambridge, MA: Harvard University Press.

Vygotsky, L. S. (1981). The genesis of higher mental functions. In J. V. Wertsch (Ed.), *The concept of activity in Soviet psychology.* Armonk, NY: M. E. Sharpe.

Vygotsky, L. S. 1986. *Thought and language.* Cambridge: MIT Press.

Wajnryb, R. (1990). *Grammar dictation.* Oxford: Oxford University Press.

Warschauer, M. (1996). *Computer-mediated collaborative learning: Theory and practice (Research Note No. 17).* Honolulu, HI: University of Hawai'i, Second Language Teaching and Curriculum Center.

Warschauer, M. (1997). Computer-mediated collaborative learning: Theory and practice. *The Modern Language Journal, 81(4),* 470–481.

Watcyn-Jones, P. (1984). *Pair work.* London: Penguin.

Webb, N. M. (1989). Peer interaction and learning in small groups. *International Journal of Educational Research, 13,* 21–39.

Webb, N. M., & Farivar, S. (1994). Promoting helping behavior in cooperative small groups in middle school mathematics. *American Education Research Journal, 31,* 369–395.

Wegerif, R., & Scrimshaw, P. (Eds.) (1997). *Computers and talk in the primary classroom.* Clevedon, England: Multilingual Matters.

Wells, G. (1999). *Dialogic inquiry: Toward a sociocultural practice and theory of education.* Cambridge: Cambridge University Press.

Wenden, A. (1991). *Learner strategies for learner autonomy.* London: Prentice-Hall International.

Wenden, A. (1997). Designing learner training: The curricular questions. In G. M. Jacobs (Ed.), *Language classrooms of tomorrow: Issues and responses* (pp. 238–262). Singapore: SEAMEO Regional Language Centre.

Wilhelm, K. H. (1999). Collaborative "dos and don'ts." *TESOL Journal 8(2)*, 14–19.

Williams, M., & Burdon, R. L. (1997). *Psychology for language teachers: A social constructivist approach.* Cambridge: Cambridge University Press.

Winn-Bell Olsen, J. (1992). Cooperative inservice education. In C. Kessler (Ed.), *Cooperative learning: A teacher resource book.* Englewood Cliffs, NJ: Prentice Hall.

Wittrock, M. C. (1974). Learning as a generative process. *Educational Psychologist, 11*, 87–95.

Wood, D., Bruner, J., & Ross, G. (1976). The role of tutoring in problem solving. *Journal of Child Psychology and Psychiatry, 17*, 89–100.

Yoshihara, K. (1993). Keys to effective peer response. *CATESOL Journal, 6(1)*, 17–37.

Index